To Jimmie D - unfailing
supporter of all things pork,
excessive, a [illegible]
Thanks

7/18/03

Domain Errors!
Cyberfeminist Practices

Domain Errors!
Cyberfeminist Practices

A subRosa project
Edited by Maria Fernandez, Faith Wilding,
and Michelle M. Wright

Project collective:
Steffi Domike, Christina Hung, Laleh Mehran,
Lucia Sommer, Hyla Willis, Faith Wilding.

AUTONOMEDIA

ACKNOWLEDGEMENTS

subRosa's thanks and roses to participants in initial subRosa meetings, discussions, and projects: Maureen Clarke, Krista Connerly, Emily de Araujo, Camilla Griggers, Carolina Loyola, Elizabeth Monoian, Ann Rosenthal, Suzie Silver, Rebecca Vaughan.

And special thanks to our collaborators and helpers: Molly B.Froelick, Christopher Coleman, Hope Kurtz, Shaila Christofferson, Sean Bidic, Jimmie D, Elizabeth Hess, and Terri Kapsalis. We also wish to acknowledge the indispensable love and support of our lovers, families, friends, and co-workers who are too numerous to list individually.

For help and support of many kinds, we also thank: James Duesing, Robert Bingham, Bryan Rogers, Margaret Meyers and the STUDIO for Creative Inquiry at Carnegie Mellon. We also thank Louise May and St. Norbert Arts Center, Winnipeg for support of Knowing Bodies; the Institute for Studies in the Arts at Arizona State University, Tempe, for support of the Sex and Gender in the Biotech Century project; Art Happens! Mainz, Germany, for commissioning Expo EmmaGenics.

Heartfelt thanks and roses also to our fellow travelers and co-conspirators in becoming autonomous: Critical Art Ensemble, and our Singapore friends: Irina Aristarkhova, Margaret Tan, Adeline Kueh, Gunalan Nardarajan.

And finally we thank Jim Fleming and the Autonomedia Collective for their ongoing support and belief in our project. Partial funding for the production of this book has been provided by grants from the Pennsylvania Council on the Arts, the Creative Capital Foundation and the New York State Council on the Arts. Thanks also go to EDGE studio for supporting the design and production of this book.

This book was designed and composed by Hyla Willis at EDGE studio <http://www.edge-studio.com> in Pittsburgh, Pennsylvania, U.S.A. on a Macintosh G4 using QuarkXpress.

Text is 9 pt "Nimrod" by Agfa Monotype
Folios are "Dead History" by Emigre

Cover by Laleh Mehran, Faith Wilding, and Hyla Willis at EDGE studio.
Satellite photo and wrecked home courtesy National Oceanic and Atmospheric Administration archives. Front cover: Image of the bicornate uterus, 1522.

Contents

Table of Contents

III. Research! Action! Embodiment! Conviviality!

Appendices:

Introduction:
Practicing Cyberfeminisms

subRosa and the Editors

> It is also true that every new movement, when it first elaborates its
> theory and policy, begins by finding support in the preceding move-
> ment, though it may be in direct contradiction with the latter. It
> begins by suiting itself to the forms found at hand and by speaking
> the language spoken hereto. In time...the new movement finds its
> forms and its own language. —ROSA LUXEMBURG, 1900

Domain Errors! Cyberfeminist Practices* was born and developed in
several subRosa meetings following an intensive summer reading group
on the intersections of discourses of race, technology, and cyberfeminism. In
October 1999, subRosa began work on a publication project intended to initiate
a feminist and postcolonial critique of embodiment, difference, and racial prejudice within cyberspace, biotechnologies and cyberfeminism—topics that had
barely begun to be addressed at the time. We wanted the contents of the project
to go beyond general critiques of cyberfeminism and gender, which have already
been addressed in other publications, to include areas repressed in previous
cyberfeminist discourse and criticism. These included: The intersections of
discourses of race and technology; the embodiment of racial prejudice; the
transformations of sex and gender through biotech and new medical technologies; the reification of notions of heterosexism, eugenics, and compulsory
motherhood in Assisted Reproductive Technologies (ART) and the difficulties
of connecting activism in cyberspace and conditions in Real Life. subRosa was
also committed to seeking out contributions by women whose voices had not
been heard in the cyberfeminist context.

Working almost exclusively through cyber communications, and distributed geographically over many countries, the subRosa collective, three editors, and sixteen contributors took much longer to shape and finish the manuscript than originally planned. Thus some of the topics addressed here have now also begun to be discussed in publications, conferences, and lists (such as Undercurrents)—which is very welcome. We hope the contents of this book will contribute to, and deepen, these emerging discussions. As Caroline Bassett said in a paper read at the "Technics of Cyberfeminism" lab in Bremen in December 2001, "Cyberfeminism is a project with work to do." We offer *Domain Errors!* as our contribution to the ongoing project of formulating a critical politics and practice of cyberfeminisms, and as a way of disseminating these in more accessible forms to a wider, more diverse audience.

The book's final content closely reflects subRosa's initial desires and concerns. Furthermore, it manifests subRosa's social relations of collaboration and conviviality, its practice of welcoming productive differences and misunderstandings, and its commitment to solidarity with women from different backgrounds. subRosa's social politics of welcoming, invitation, and inclusion have led to fortunate meetings, collaborations, and connections with dynamic feminists from many parts of the world who have enriched the offerings of this book and are beginning to develop a growing cyberfeminist gift economy.

As the feminization of the information society, and of work, become ubiquitous globally, women (and men) around the world are enmeshed in daily encounters with the incursions of cyber and bio technologies in their lives and communities—and many of them are struggling with ways to both resist and negotiate the power and authority of these technologies. Be it as artists, students, cultural workers, mothers, theorists, academics, technology workers, data maintenance workers, activists, organizers—or combinations of these— the contributors to this book speak and act from various economic, sexual, age, and racial positions. Our collective strengths have been enriched by this collaboration.

The relevance of issues of difference to electronic culture is often questioned as the belief in the singularity, disembodiment and anonymity of electronic communication still prevails. As in the material world, in digital realms social and political power relations are deeply structured by sexist and racist ideologies of domination. Feminists, minoritarian groups, net activists, artists, among others, have begun to mount effective critiques of these structures and ideologies, as well as contesting imaginatively to maintain and expand autonomous territories on the Internet and in digital domains. A cyberfeminist politics must foster and welcome embodied differences and initiate desiring social relations, while refusing to disappear into the myths of virtuality. How autonomy and solidarity are struggled for and practiced matters profoundly. Doubts about the effectiveness of various contestational strategies on the Internet and in digital domains must be met with the willingness to experiment with a variety of tactics—even at the risk of failure. A cyberfeminist critique of the social relations of women—as they are affected by science and digital technologies—needs to be launched inside and outside of cyberspace simultaneously to include the many that do not have digital access. Each contribution to this book—whether text, image, performative project, manifesto or rant—suggests strategies for critical and tactical cyberfeminisms. *Domain Errors!* invites readers to jump-start new projects, theories, conversations, connections, actions, and becomings.

Domain Errors! is divided into three sections that combine theory, practices, critique, and artist projects. Section One, "Racism and Cyberfeminism in the Integrated Circuit," discusses lived aspects of the intersections of race, gender, and technology in the situations of women in different countries and cultures of technology. An introductory discussion of "Situated Cyberfeminisms" contextualizes the contents of the book within a critical history of previous cyberfeminist discourses and practices—including critiques of the cyborg—while it also suggests the outlines of a politically engaged cyberfeminism. The section also contains a proposal for a striking new approach towards identifying and combating racism in everyday life; a historical and critical analysis of why blacks are deemed to be less "technologically advanced"; an eloquent meditation on the "fortress" mentality that fostered ancient and modern methods of exclusion and xenophobia in Moscow; an analysis of race in "The Matrix"; a discussion and examples of regressive Finnish gender ideologies manifested on commercial Web-sites addressing women; and an e-dialog about the politics of designing a cyberfeminist e-commerce for traditional hand-weavers in India.

Section Two, "The Female Flesh Commodities Lab," offers searching discussions of the molecular invasion and colonization of the female body by Assisted Reproductive Technologies (ART), recombinant genetics, and new medical and surgical flesh technologies such as aesthetic vulvar surgery. The mapping of formerly invisible bodily territories—like the clitoris and its subcutaneous tissues, and the interior of the womb—promises new understanding of possibilities for female sexual pleasure while simultaneously posing the dangers of commodification and medical invasion of the female body. Other essays tackle the appropriation of the feminist rhetoric of "choice" by ART marketeers, and the increasing application of vision technologies developed for military purposes in the surveillance and control of female (and male) bodies. The complex personal and political issues of infertility, and the increasing use of repro-genetic technologies to 'solve' fertility problems, are contrasted with a consideration of the potentially liberating possibilities of queer cyborg parenthood. A social/emotional anatomy of the "cyborg mommy," figured in digital artist pages, reveals the conditions of posthuman motherhood. The section also contains a sobering summary history of eugenics in the U.S., and ends with a photo-illustrated time-line and commentary about the commodification of children.

Section Three, "Research! Action! Embodiment! Conviviality!" takes a hands-on approach to theoretical and embodied cyberfeminist practices. It offers a mix of activist and artist pages and projects, along with a photo-illustrated essay about the connections between the American Girl doll and eugenic reproduction. There's also an illuminating look at collaborations between feminist artists in Singapore; an interview with a feminist Reiki master; temp(t)ing job descriptions for disposable, feminized technology workers; and a rant for menopausal cyborgs.

Domain Errors! ends with a manifesto, "Refugia! Becoming Autonomous Zones," that is a call for new activist concepts and projects of "becoming autonomous." Autonomy is not a fixed, essential state or quality. Like gender, autonomy is created through its performance, by doing/becoming; it is a political practice. To become autonomous is to refuse authoritarian and compulsory cultures of separation and hierarchy through embodied practices of welcoming difference. It is a powerful antidote to domination, exclusive expertise, and ruthless competition. Becoming autonomous is a political position for it thwarts the exclusions of proprietary knowledge and jealous hoarding of resources, and replaces the social and economic hierarchies on which these depend with a politics of skills exchange, welcome, and collaboration. Freely sharing these with others creates a common wealth of knowledge and power that subverts the domination and hegemony of the master's rule. subRosa hopes that our call to becoming autonomous will inspire tactics and actions as yet unimagined.

> Arise for the struggle! Arise for action! The time for empty manifestos, platonic resolutions, and high-sounding words is gone! The hour of action has struck!
>
> —ROSA LUXEMBURG, DECEMBER 25, 1918

Racism and Cyberfeminism in the Integrated Circuit

Situating Cyberfeminisms

Maria Fernandez and Faith Wilding

During the 1980s, in the U.S., the second wave women's liberation movement which had swept the country in the late '60s and throughout the '70s became fragmented, de-centered, and beset by dissention and various forms of cultural and political backlash. While more nomadic and de-territorialized feminisms allowed many new voices and tactics to flourish often in regard to local concerns, it became harder to organize coalitions and concerted action regarding issues which affect large groups of women globally. Currently, there is no longer a vocal, visible, public feminist movement in the U.S.—though there are many local pockets of feminist practice—but there is pressing need for a renewed vision and engagement in local and global feminist action. Much of this need is created by the dramatic effects of digital media on multiple areas of communications, knowledge and lived experience. The scientific understanding of what constitutes a human being, the ways in which we're conceived and born into the world, our education, socialization, work, health, illness, and death are mediated by digital technology (as a presence or a lack). This is an important moment for the re-examination of historical feminist issues and their relation to the condition of women in "the integrated circuit"—a term coined by Rachel Grossman to "name the situation of women in a world [so] intimately restructured through the social relations of science and technology."[1]

CYBERFEMINISM AND FEMINISM

Historically, waves of feminism have often accompanied technological expansion, and feminists have both embraced and contested technological developments. At the beginning of the twenty-first century the advancing global hegemony of U.S. information and communication technologies (ICT)—that make the overwhelming success of pan-capitalism possible—presents radically new challenges for feminist theory and practice.

An early response to these conditions has been the emergence of the eclectic formation of cyberfeminism. In the last ten years, cyberfeminism has become a significant field in contemporary cultural practice. Cyberfeminist web sites and electronic publications have increased from a handful in the early nineties to nearly two thousand in 2002. Yet at present, cyberfeminism functions more as a label to grant currency to a panoply of positions than as a political movement. The importunate question of feminism in cyberfeminism still haunts virtually every discussion of cyberfeminism.[2]

Heir to both postfeminism and poststructuralism, cyberfeminism has neither welcomed a definition nor a clear political positioning within feminisms. For example, in discussions at the First Cyberfeminist International at Documenta X, in Kassel in 1997, definition of cyberfeminism was declined in favor of the declaration that cyberfeminism was a practice which embraced a gamut of attitudes towards art, culture, theory, politics, communications and techno-logy—the terrain of the Internet. This was a tactic presumed to attract women from diverse backgrounds and orientations, particularly young women un-willing to call themselves feminists. Instead of a definition, the participants (including Wilding) devised the 100 anti-theses—definitions of what cyber-feminism is not:

    4. *cyberfeminism is not ideology*

  10. *cyberfeminism ist keine praxis*

  18. *cyberfeminism is not an ism*

  19. *cyberfeminism is not anti-male*

  24. *cyberfeminism nije apolitican*, etc.

The anti-theses included the statement "Cyberfeminism is not a-political" but the politics remained unspecified. The creation of a label or identity as a signature for various kinds of tactical political interventions and cultural productions has been used as an activist strategy. For instance, "Luther Blissett" lends its name to anyone who wants to use it. This has resulted in a prolific and diverse production attributed to the fictional character Luther Blissett. While this strategy allows activists and artists to remain anonymous and intervene in ways that would otherwise be met with brutal retribution by disciplinary agencies and institutions, the issue of anonymity does not seem to play a part in the pluralistic tendencies of cyberfeminism. To the contrary, as competence in theoretical and technological discourses have become professional requirements in the arts and in academia, women artists and academics are increasingly eager to be identified as cyberfeminists. Clearly, it is necessary to negotiate between tactics that might attract support from a wide variety of people, and devising radical political strategies to challenge and disturb the patriarchal status quo.

The question of how to negotiate the crucial link of cyberfeminism to feminism is at the heart of the often-contradictory contemporary positions of women working with the new technologies. It has been the subject of heated debates both on and off-line as many women like the name "cyberfeminist" but do not want to be identified with feminist politics. As one contributor to an all-women mailing list put it, "I like the 'cyber' it's sexy, but I do not like to be called a feminist. It gives people a bad impression."

In the introduction to the *First Cyberfeminist Reader* Cornelia Sollfrank writes, "The 'feminism' in Cyberfeminism is obvious, it cannot be overlooked. And that's as it should be. Feminism's heritage is our life-blood, but its institutionalization in public life and in the academies makes it inaccessible to most women today. In addition, the mass women's movement of former years has been fragmented into a bewildering variety of feminismS. Identifying oneself as a woman is no longer enough to serve as a productive connecting link. We have to find new strategies for political action."[3] Sollfrank implies that the Internet (cyberspace) can make feminism more accessible to an entirely new audience of diverse women immersed in technology. But the strategies of how to do this are still to be invented and tested. The ambivalence many wired women still have to what they perceive as a monumental past feminist history, theory, and practice must first be negotiated. Sadly, some manifestations of this ambivalence stem from ignorance of even very recent feminist histories and the falsification and disregard of the great differences within feminisms' theory and practice and their relevance to contemporary conditions.

Our experience teaching in various institutions of higher education in the United States suggests that many young college women (ages 18–23) of various classes and backgrounds know little of the history of feminist thought and action. They talk incessantly about the tyranny of the fashion world and mass media, the pressure to be thin, pretty, nice, and to get a boyfriend, as well as the high incidence of eating disorders and sexual violence experienced by themselves and their friends. When asked for a definition of feminism they most often say that it means equal rights for women, and they are quite sure that in the United States we have these. When they encounter the radical demands of early feminists, for example, the abolition of the State, the Church, and the Family, many of them are shocked and affronted. They have grown up with a vague belief that as women in the United States they can do anything they want to do. They are invariably surprised to learn that the Equal Rights Amendment has never been ratified by enough states to become constitutional; that despite narrowing gaps in higher education very few women reach the upper levels of education, science, and business; and that in most of the developed world women still earn less than men. It is evident that these women don't identify feminism as a strategy or philosophy that they could use to help deal with the obvious sexism and gender discrimination that they still encounter in their own lives. Ignorance of feminism is by no means limited to the U.S. Many younger cyberfeminists world-wide are alienated from a feminist past they perceive as irrelevant to their own situations.

SHARED TERRITORIES

Despite its ambivalence toward historical feminism, cyberfeminism shares multiple aspects with second wave feminism. Cyberfeminist practice has already adopted many of the strategies of avant-garde feminist movements, including strategic separatism (women-only lists, self-help groups, chat groups, networks, and woman-to-woman technological training), feminist cultural, social, and language theory and analysis, creation of new images of women to counter rampant sexist stereotyping (feminist avatars, cyborgs, trans- or non-gendered figures), feminist net critique, strategic essentialism, and the like. Cyberfeminism began with strong techno-utopian expectations that the new electronic technologies would offer women a fresh start to create new languages, programs, platforms, images, fluid identities and multi-subject definitions in cyberspace; that in fact women could recode, redesign, and reprogram information technology to help change the feminine condition. This is reminiscent of many of the goals of the 1970s feminist art movement and cultural feminism which worked to create new images, identities, and subjectivities for women within the art world and mass media as well as the real world. In much the same way as '70s feminist artists appropriated non-traditional media, technologies, and techniques (such as performance, installation, video, and media interventions) to present a new content in art, wired women are now beginning to appropriate digital technologies that do not yet have an established aesthetic history. This is an exciting and promising moment.

Still, there are many problems and pitfalls and it is precisely a knowledge of past feminist history and its mistakes and omissions which can be instructive here. For example, although cyberfeminism presents itself as inclusive, cyberfeminist writings assume an educated, white, upper middle-class, English speaking, culturally sophisticated readership. Ironically, this attitude replicates the damaging universalism of "old-style feminism." There is little mention of the crucially different conditions—be they economic, cultural, racial or ethnic, geographic, or environmental—under which women worldwide experience sexuality and pleasure, aging, menopause, motherhood, child rearing, ecology and the environment; or of alternative ways of living and working that may preclude ICT. These subjects, central to postcolonial feminist work in theory, literature and the arts, remain peripheral to the core of cyberfeminist writing.[4]

The marginalization of postcolonial studies within cyberfeminism is due to various factors including the inconspicuousness of postcolonial theory in most of Europe, and inherited, often unquestioned attitudes towards ethnic and racial difference. As is common in new fields, cyberfeminists adopted aspects of a previously established body of theoretical work in electronic media. Despite the theoretical eclecticism evident in this field, during the last twenty years, the impact of postcolonial studies on electronic media practice, theory, and criticism has been negligible.[5]

In cyberfeminism, the difference most celebrated and discussed (apart from sexual orientation) is the often-narcissistic construction of the self as Other by adopting the cyborg and the monster as figures of liberation and self-represen-tation. To be sure, the transformation to "cyborgs" of bodies previously cast as "unfit" has been uplifting and enabling for numerous individuals. Yet, a cyborg identity is primarily claimed by those categorized as the norm in previous colo-nial and eugenic taxonomies: If you are white, educated and affluent, the cyborg is your ticket to difference.[6]

OLD AND NEW CYBERFEMINISM

Distinctions can be made between two overlapping waves of cyberfeminism: An initial wave that celebrated the innate affinities of women and machines, and a second, more critical, wave. The first current is best articulated by British cultural theorist Sadie Plant and the Australian artist collective VNS Matrix, both indebted to Donna Haraway's influential article, "A Manifesto for Cyborgs." Sadie Plant's position on cyberfeminism has been identified as "an absolutely posthuman insurrection—the revolt of an emergent system which includes women and computers, against the world view and material reality of a patriarchy which still seeks to subdue them."[7] A humorous and self-ironizing illustration of this can be found in VNS Matrix's "Cyberfeminist Manifesto for the 21st Century" which declares: "We are the virus of the new world disorder/ rupturing the symbolic from within/saboteurs of big daddy mainframe/the cli-toris is a direct line to the matrix..."[8] Julianne Pierce of VNS Matrix describes the first wave of cyberfeminism, "Cyberfeminism was about ideas, irony, appropriation and hands-on skilling up in the data terrain. It combined a utopic vision of corrupting patriarchy with an unbounded enthusiasm for the new tools of technology. It embraced gender and identity politics, allowing fluid and non-gendered identities to flourish through the digital medium. The post-corporeal female would be an online frontier woman, creating our own virtual worlds and colonising the amorphous world of cyberspace." Pierce then describes how cyberfeminism has changed, "somehow 'feminism' is the problem, some of the old guard see it as a vacuous fashion statement...and the young guard don't need feminism any more." By contrast, Pierce describes the "new" cyberfeminism as being "about confronting the top-down with the bottom-up, creating a culture where the info heavy cyber babe can create her own space within a clever info society. It's about creating foundations to build upon, so that in the next millennium we can carve our own paths, create our own corporations...in the words of VNS Matrix—'unbounded, unleashed, unforgiving, we are the future cunt.'" This statement certainly has sobered up from the *jouissance* of the first manifesto (perhaps sadly so for we sorely need utopia and *jouissance*). Yet in the compressed statement "confronting the top-down with the bottom-up" we have what amounts to a radical political strategy for cyberfeminism, one that is reminiscent of classic Marxism/socialism.

More critical orientations to cyberfeminism and ICT were also evident in various presentations at the Second Cyberfeminist International in Rotterdam in March 1999, and in recent work by Caroline Bassett, Susanna Paasonen, Renate Klein and Susan Hawthorne among others.[9] These cyberfeminists have critiqued the a-political stance of previous theorists and advocate the development of an embodied and politically engaged cyberfeminism. Current debates among "new" cyberfeminists are only now beginning to emphasize the importance of feminist difference and colonial and postcolonial discourses to an engaged feminist net theory, politics and practice.

AREAS FOR INTERVENTION

Although recently cyberfeminists have critiqued fundamental predicates of earlier cyberfeminism including the desirability of a cyborg future and the presupposition of women's universal access to computers, some celebrate the impending development of a "universal sisterhood" forged though electronic communication. The utopian promises so often associated with the new technologies demand our sharpest critical attention, for it is foolish to believe that major social, economic, and political issues can be addressed by throwing technology at them. As radical net critics have repeatedly pointed out, cyberspace is not an arena inherently free of the old feminist struggle against a patriarchal capitalist system. The new media are embedded in a framework of pan-capitalist social relations and economic, political, and cultural environments that are still deeply sexist and racist. Pan-capitalism is predicated on imperialism and domination. Historically, the goal of economic expansionism has brought about the exploitation and destitution of natural resources and third world populations—the majority of whom are women. In this context, a crucial question to be posed by cyberfeminists is whether non-specificity of purpose and politics are viable strategies for survival, resistance, and for a more just distribution of resources and power which is one of the central goals of feminism. subRosa proposes that it is time a politically radical, activist cyberfeminism take the lead in critiquing Net-culture and politics, and challenging Net-practices through tactical texts, artworks, and contestational projects.

Far from being obsolete, feminist political philosophy and analysis can be fruitfully brought to bear on the new conditions that ICT has created for women. For example, we need much more research on the specific impact of ICT on different populations of women whose lives are being profoundly altered by the new technologies, often in ways that lead to extreme physical and mental health problems. This is as true for highly educated professional women in academia, the sciences, medical, and computer industries, as it is for clerical and factory workers in the just-in-time telecommunications and home-work industry, as well as rural and urban women working in chips factories and assembly sweat-shops.

Since most women are already doing a "double shift" (production and reproduction) the demands and pressures of the high-speed, just-in-time economy affect them differently than it does most men. The high levels of Chronic Fatigue Syndrome, depression, and stress disorders even among professional women (the most documented group) attest to the high human costs of our economic and cultural systems of productivity. In order to strategize action we must examine the impact of the new technologies on women's sexuality and subjectivities; the conditions of production and reproduction—always already linked for women; gender roles, social relations, and public and private space; and we need to contest the naturalized value placed on speed and efficiency when they take no heed of the limits and needs of the organic body.

Pan-capitalism has blurred the distinctions between developed/underdeveloped, first world/third world as these conditions coexist in almost all geographical locations. In the aftermath of colonialism, there are more migrants, refugees and exiles than ever before and many of these migrants are women. These people have tremendous impact on the urban environment, the home, the careers, the language, culture, diet, and, ultimately, the subjectivity of people from the traditional imperial centers. As women from developing countries increasingly become the home-service and child-care labor employed by wealthier families—as well as the world's electronic parts manufacturers, assemblers, and data maintenance workers—the lives of white women and women of color are mutually reliant. This interdependence stresses the relevance of postcolonial studies for critical cyberfeminisms. Far from being subjects irrelevant to electronic media and cyberfeminism, migrants often result from devastations caused by the interventions of empire. We must begin de-colonization in our own networks and embodied relations.

Developments in biogenetic technologies that will profoundly affect environmental and human futures must be a major focus of cyberfeminist concern, particularly since much cutting edge medical technology is being developed and tested by the military, with the proviso that there be lucrative civilian applications. Some of these military technologies are already having far reaching effects on women, as for example in ultrasound pregnancy monitoring, telesurgery, robotic medical monitoring and care, and invasive imaging techniques. Organic bodies and bodily processes—particularly those of women and fetuses—are being invaded at the molecular level and re-engineered to meet the cyborgian and eugenic needs of the global market place. Cyberfeminist scientists and technicians—as well as artists—working with these technologies are well positioned to expose and subvert the ideologies and practices of the new flesh, reproductive, and genetic technologies, and assess their particular political, economic, social and eugenic impact on different groups of women globally. In the '70s the Feminist Women's Health Movement challenged the medical establishment in the U.S. by establishing its own clinics, new abortion procedures, alternative healing practices, and feminist sexual counseling. These tactics subverted patriarchal medical authority and eventually forced women's health care providers in the U.S. to change some of their standard gynecological and obstetric practices. Similarly, cyberfeminists could spearhead activism and education about Assisted Reproductive Technologies and new eugenics to expose how profoundly traditional conceptions of women's bodies and gender roles are implicated in the deployment of these technologies.

A contestational cyberfeminism must also address the circumstances of young women now entering the technocratic class. As Wilding and CAE have written in a previous essay: "We do not support a reductive equality feminism, i.e. support the existing system, but believe there should be equal gender representation in all its territories. We do not support pan-capitalism. It is a predatory, pernicious, and sexist system that will not change even if there was equal representation of gender in the policy-making classes. Our argument is that women need access to empowering knowledge and tools that are now dominated by a despicable "virtual class" (Kroker). We do not mean to suggest that women become part of this class. To break the "glass ceiling" and become an active part of the exploiting class that benefits from gender hierarchy is not a feminist goal, nor anything to be proud of."[10] In this context, bell hooks' definition of feminism proposed almost two decades ago, remains relevant to cyberfeminists: In her words, feminism "is not simply a struggle to end male chauvinism or a movement to ensure that women will have equal rights with men; it is a commitment to eradicating the ideology of domination that permeates Western culture on various levels—sex, race, and class to name a few—and a commitment to reorganizing U.S. society so that the self-development of people can take precedence over imperialism, economic expansion, and material desires."[11]

DOMAIN ERRORS, CYBERFEMINIST PRACTICES

Cyberfeminists have begun to open the contested territory of the Internet for interrogation, play, and pleasure—as well as for new feminist political campaigns, education, critique, tactical interventions, activist alliances, and all manner of collaborations both local and international. New cyberfeminism has just begun to scrutinize, publicize, and contest the complex effects of technology on many aspects of women's lives; and to fashion a politics of presence and embodiment that insists on full engagement with the discourses of technology and power. The foregoing delineates a terrain for a politically active contestational cyberfeminism. This anthology can but touch on a few of the issues raised here for there is much work to be done. Our purpose is to go beyond general critiques of cyberfeminism and to open areas heretofore repressed in cyberfeminist discourses, criticism, and practice. We conceive of each piece in this book as an intervention, both textual and performative, and as an invitation to future performativity and elaboration. ★

---

1 Donna Haraway, "A Cyborg Manifesto," *Simians, Cyborgs, and Women* (New York: Routledge, 1991), p. 165.

2 Faith Wilding, "Where is the Feminism in Cyberfeminism?" *n.paradoxa* 2 (1998): 6–12.

3 Cornelia Sollfrank, "Introduction," *First Cyberfeminist International Reader* (Hamburg: Germany, 1998), p. 1.

4 A notable exception here is the group Les Penelopes which has addressed many of these issues in their work. Yet, Les Penelopes neither identify themselves as cyberfeminists nor do they figure prominently in electronic media culture. Les Penelopes' web site <http://www.penelopes.org> features a section on cyberfeminism among other subjects.

5 For a more detailed analysis on the intersection of postcolonial studies and electronic media theory see Maria Fernandez, "Postcolonial Electronic Media Theory," *Third Text* (Summer 1999) and expanded version in *Art Journal* (Fall 1999).

6 Susan Hawthorne, "Cyborgs, Virtual Bodies and Organic Bodies: Theoretical Feminist Responses," in *Cyberfeminism,* eds. Susan Hawthorne and Renate Klein (Melbourne: Spinifex, 1999).

7 Caroline Bassett, "With a Little Help from Our (New) Friends?" *mute* (August 1997): 46–49.

8 All quotes in this paragraph from Julianne Pierce, *First Cyberfeminist International Reader*, p. 10.

9 Caroline Bassett, "A Manifesto Against Manifestos," and Maria Fernandez & Faith Wilding, "Feminism, Difference, and Global Capital," *Next Cyberfeminist International Reader* (Hamburg: Old Boys Network, 1999); Hawthorne, "Cyborgs," and Susanna Paasonen, "Digital, Human, Animal, PLANT: The politics of Cyberfeminism," *n.paradoxa* 2 (1998).

10 Faith Wilding and CAE, "Notes on the Political Condition of Cyberfeminism." *First Cyberfeminist International Reader*, p. 23.

11 bell hooks, *Ain't I a Woman: Black Women and Feminism* (Boston: South End Press, 1981), p. 194–195.

Cyberfeminism, Racism, Embodiment

Maria Fernandez

> The permanence of domination cannot succeed without the complicity of the whole group: the work of denial, which is the source of social alchemy, is, like magic, a collective undertaking. —PIERRE BOURDIEU

> I'm clear now...that there's a whole range of important responses to racism that are not at the level of argument and at the level of the intellectual...and it seems to me that if I wanted to identify another line of approach to racism, along with the intellectual one, it would be one that said, 'Look, in the end, people find it easiest to be comfortable with and nice to people with whom they have done things.' And I would say I would put a lot of faith in children growing up together, not because we're lecturing them all the time about being nice to each other but because they just grow up together and they form friendships. —ANTHONY APPIAH

Among feminists it is often assumed that no feminist can be racist because of her awareness of gender oppression. Yet, still today, racist attitudes prevent women from establishing politically and personally enriching connections. Among cyberfeminists, belief in the myth of "equality" in the equally mythical realm of cyberspace is widespread. Electronic media theorists and commercial entities alike maintain that "differences" of gender, race and class are nonexistent in the Internet due to the disembodied nature of electronic communication.[1]

Because the hierarchies of RL (Real Life) are believed to be inapplicable to cyberspace, discussions of race have only recently been initiated in electronic media theory and criticism. In an influential 1999 publication, Beth Kolko, Lisa Nakamura, and Gilbert B. Rodman observe that in academic electronic mailing lists participants studiously avoid and actively silence discussions of race.[2]

Kolko et al. argue that "outing race" would render more accurately the diversity of cyberspace but they do not specify how making race visible might change existing power relations. In their words: "Cyberspace has been construed as something that exists in binary opposition to 'the real world,' but when it comes to questions of power, politics and structural relations, cyberspace is as real as it gets."[3]

Despite the increasing interest of academics in issues of race and cyberspace (evident in conferences and presentations during the preceding year), the relation of racist attitudes and behavior to electronic communication remains largely unexamined. One explanation for this might be that racist behavior "in the flesh" is still little understood.

In what follows, I will discuss racism in relation to feminism/cyberfeminism and theories of embodiment. Like many other scholars I believe that racism is a multifaceted system of oppression involving ideological, psychological and practical aspects. Here, I concentrate on embodied dimensions of racism because I believe that racism is, in large part, a complex of embodied practices sometimes quite separate from ideological positions.

It may seem pointless to discuss racism at a time in which the biological concept of race has been proven bankrupt by new genetic technologies. Recent genetic research strongly supports the hypothesis of the African origin of humankind, and challenges traditional concepts of humanity by rendering bodies and organisms progressively malleable. While there is potential in these new conditions, this does not mean that racism has ended. Practices based on previous understandings and valorizations of race still dictate social, political and economic agendas. This discussion of racism and embodiment is only the beginning of a larger project. Increased understanding of racist attitudes in the fleshed world is necessary to combat racism and may shed light on manifestations of racism in electronic communications.

DIFFERENCES

The history of feminism suggests that the interpretation of differences in culture, class, race, sexual orientation, religion, and politics segregate women.

Some cyberfeminists believe that it is useless to talk about differences because they can never be resolved.[4] While I believe that the erasure of difference is neither desirable nor even possible, I like to imagine the possibility that differences could be read as something other than alienating or threatening qualities. One of the most contentious differences among women has been race. I use the term "race" not because I believe in its validity as a scientific category but because regardless of how differences are explained i.e. "ethnicity," "culture," perceptions of "difference" are still largely based on epidermal schemas.

Racial differences were divisive in second wave feminism. During the late seventies and eighties multiple women theorists of color challenged the universalist assumptions of previous feminisms. Simultaneously, the postmodern/posthumanist stress on difference, anti-essentialism and the politics of multiculturalism redefined equality from "the right to be the same to the right to be different," de-emphasizing intergroup affiliations and coalitions.[5]

In the nineties, communications between feminists of color and other streams of feminism improved little. Various theorists including bell hooks and Chela Sandoval ultimately proposed "an ethics of love" as the solution for women's fragmentation.[6] Indisputably, this is the ideal solution. Yet, to love through difference, to forget misunderstandings and resentments accumulated for centuries is easier wished for than achieved. "Love" is the message that multiple religions have disseminated for millennia with very limited results. Part of the problem is that "love" is not only an ethical decision but also a set of incorporated practices, habitual ways of doing things *with one's body*—doing things with other people, "growing up together" as in Appiah's statement quoted above. During the last decade, fissures along the lines of "difference" continued to be evident in various strains of "bad girl-ism" and in cyberfeminism.[7]

Donna Haraway's foundational text, "A Manifesto for Cyborgs," was created in the aftermath of painful fractures in the feminist movement. Haraway attempted to mediate antagonisms by invoking a politics of "coalition—affinity not identity" and by basing the cyborg on a model of *mestizaje*, the racial mixing which took place after the Spanish Conquest of the New World. In her view, the cyborg could not be subject to identity politics because it was a hybrid of animal, machine and human.

In Haraway's ironic fiction, the cyborg is the illegitimate offspring of military technologies, socialism, and patriarchal capitalism. The cyborg's origins are inspired by Mexican American versions of the life of Malinche, Hernán Cortéz's Aztec mistress popularly identified as mother of the *mestizo* "bastard race" of the New World. Haraway's designation of Malinche as "mother" to women of color remains unexplained.

More troublesome than any semblance of historical accuracy is Haraway's theorization of women of color as quintessential cyborgs. In her view, "women of color" might be understood as "a cyborg identity, a potent subjectivity synthesized from fusions of outsider identities..." As in the work of Chela Sandoval, Haraway's cyborgs include impoverished women of color working in sweatshops and electronic assembly lines. She posits that "Ironically, it might be the unnatural cyborg women making chips in Asia and spiral dancing in Santa Rita whose constructed unities will guide effective oppositional strategies."[8] The promise of the cyborg as a sign of emancipation obscures the fact that the union of human and machine that such women exemplify results from sheer necessity. These women work long hours under exploitative conditions at tedious repetitive tasks, which are often physically damaging.

Inspired by Haraway's text, cyberfeminism developed in various parts of the world. Cyberfeminists championed the union of women and machines discarding Haraway's socialist-feminist and anti-racist politics. The work of the Australian cyberfeminist pioneers VNS Matrix was practically unknown in the United States until after the group disbanded in 1997. These artists created sensual, feminized and humorous representations of the data world that opposed the sanitized, masculinist imagery prevalent at the time. VNS Matrix's *Cyberfeminist Manifesto* (1991) was universalist in character implying that all differences among women were subsumed in the Matrix.

In Sadie Plant's polemical book, *Zeros + Ones*, women of color form part of a universal conspiracy between women and machines that will ultimately undermine patriarchy. In her view, this quiet revolution has already dramatically advanced the economic status of women throughout the world, especially in Asia.[9] Although Plant tells us that the vast majority of electronic assembly jobs are held by women, and that these jobs have "always been low status, poor-

VNS Matrix, Cyberfeminist Manifesto, 1991.

ly paid, sometimes dangerous," the fact that the work of these "virtual aliens" forms part of a long history of women's involvement with technology is sufficient to close the argument for Plant. In Plant's own words, "If she hasn't had a hand in anything, her fingerprints are everywhere."[10] Plant seems oblivious of the applicability of this observation to other kinds of invisible female labor including that of domestic servants, sweatshop and agricultural workers. By repeatedly referring to "the cultures of the old white world" Plant also alludes to the undoing of white supremacy, but does not elaborate this idea.

The recent anthology *Cyberfeminism* edited by Susan Hawthorne and Renate Klein includes articles by women of color but does not discuss directly the subject of race. In sum, race and racism have been more or less ignored in cyberfeminism. To discuss these issues might help cyberfeminists to develop and sustain diverse strategic and pleasurable alliances. To date, the most prominent cyberfeminist groups in Europe and the United States are predominantly white, despite various attempts to make the groups inclusive.[11]

I AM NOT RACIST, BUT...

Racism is a painful and often taboo topic in most social contexts. In the West, most people accept the existence of racism as an abstract entity but frequently fail to identify its manifestations in specific individuals.

In Western academic theory, racism, both overt and covert, is discussed predominantly as an ideology. Some scholars also investigate psychological aspects of racism, primarily its relation to desire and the imaginary.[12] Regardless of orientation, most theorists recognize that racism is a multifaceted system of oppression that legitimates the privileges of a specific group.[13] As a tool of validation for an established social order, racism forms part of our historical, social and cultural legacy. For centuries, diverse media from story telling to scientific literature, from photography to the World Wide Web, have reinforced stereotypes of specific groups. As various studies demonstrate, the stereotypes of people of color (and of groups construed as such) are often negative and at best, contradictory.[14]

Because racism is founded on the construction of racial hierarchies some theorists propose to eradicate it by undermining the concept of race. Multiple postcolonial theorists uphold hybridity as the ultimate form of resistance as hybrids presumably elude classification. Noel Ignatiev and his collaborators in the periodical *Race Traitor* encourage white people to become "race traitors" by refusing identification based on traditional racial categories.

The abolition of the concept of race is essential for the development of a nonracist world. Yet, neither hybridity nor the renunciation of existing racial categories is in itself sufficient to end racism. History demonstrates that cultures may exhibit transnational and multicultural elements and simultaneously maintain racial hierarchies.[15] The examples of colonial Mexico, Brazil and various Caribbean countries demonstrate that hybridity can accommodate intricate classifications based on skin color. In eighteenth-century Mexico, for instance, there were more than twenty terms to designate racial mixtures.[16] Ignatiev himself admits that the propositions of *Race Traitor* are extremely difficult ones. In order to become "race traitors" people must be willing to give up the privileges of belonging to a dominant group and this rarely occurs.

Multiple theorists recognize that racism entails ideas as well as actions, yet the relation of the psychological and ideological aspects of racism to practices of the body has received little attention.[17] If racism is manifested in actions, then I propose that at least part of our investigations should focus on performance.

To illustrate one example among many, in the United States women of color often report being made "invisible" by their white counterparts.[18] I suggest that the enforcement of invisibility is achieved by means of specific bodily cues and behavior. Consider the following examples:

1. Lila has moved from Guatemala to a small U.S. city in the Northeast. She tells a Chinese-American college friend living in Texas that people in her new circle seem to feel uncomfortable around her: "They do not seem to know what to speak to me about, most of the time they simply pretend I'm not there, they do not talk to me, they do not look at me, they interrupt me when I speak and sometimes they do not respond to me at all. Even people whom I like, nervously cross and uncross their arms and legs and fidget with their fingers whenever they find themselves alone with me. "It's funny," the friend says, "I've had similar experiences here."

2. Lupe, a Mexican-American homemaker, begins a small catering business from her home. Her neighbor, Jane, asks to join and Lupe accepts. Within two weeks, Jane has contracted with new clients and invited several of her friends to become partners without consulting Lupe. Within a month, Lupe's original business plans are transformed beyond her recognition. Lupe quits the partnership and Jane and her friends run her original business. Lupe confronts Jane about not having been consulted in her schemes. Jane admits no wrongdoing and accuses Lupe of "having a chip on her shoulder."

3. Tina, an artist of Afro-Cuban origin is invited to participate in a prestigious international art festival. On arrival, she is introduced to Ann, an American artist of European descent. At the end of the week, a dinner is organized for the festival's guests. Tina and Ann are assigned seats facing each other. Tina says "Hi" to Ann. Ann nods slightly but says nothing. At dinner she converses with other people at the table consistently ignoring Tina. Thinking that perhaps Ann

does not recognize her, Tina volunteers "We were introduced at..." "I know," Ann interrupts and continues to ignore Tina for the rest of the evening.

4. Some years ago, bell hooks visited the University of Florida at Gainesville. At the beginning of her lecture, she reported that several of the local graduate students had enthusiastically suggested that she meet one of their professors, a European-American woman interested in issues of feminism and difference. hooks told the audience that the professor in question had declined to attend her lecture because "she was going to a football game."[19] Whatever the intention of the professor, hooks seemed to recognize a familiar pattern in her behavior or she would not have brought it to the attention of the audience.

Tina Grillo and Stephanie M. Wildman have argued that white supremacy instills in many whites the expectation of always being the center of attention. In their view, "When people who are not regarded as entitled to the center move into it, however briefly, they are viewed as usurpers. One reaction of the dominant group to temporarily losing the center is to make sure that nothing remains for the perceived usurpers to be in the center of. Another tactic is to steal back the center, using guerrilla tactics if necessary."[20] In the examples above, Jane took "the center" from Lupe, by failing to consult about decisions with her as is customary among business partners. Ann denied the presence, thus the status of Tina by ignoring her. Similarly, by choosing to miss hooks' lecture, the other professor temporarily dismissed hooks' knowledge and authority as well as her position at center stage.

These examples suggest that embodied practices communicating messages of invisibility involve the suspension of rules of behavior that are customarily observed with other members of the same group: Failing to acknowledge a person's presence or speech, interacting with others in a group and consistently excluding a specific person, failing to recognize someone's achievements and expertise—i.e., absenting oneself from events one would normally attend when a person of color is the speaker or performer, etc. Such behaviors have ambiguous meanings but they do effectively negate or diminish another person's presence. It is precisely the multiplicity of meanings that makes these behaviors powerful. If they are ambiguous, they cannot be named. Patricia

Williams has compared racism to a ghost invisibly exerting its influence: "It is deep, angry, eradicated from view, but strong enough to make everyone who enters the room walk around the bed that isn't there, avoiding the phantom as they did the substance, for fear of bodily harm. They do not even know what they are avoiding; they defer to the unseen shapes of things with subtle responsiveness, guided by an impulsive awareness of nothingness, and the deep knowledge and denial of witchcraft at work."[21]

EMBODIED RACISM

Theories of embodiment stress the interdependence of mind and body in contrast to the traditional opposition of these entities foundational to most of western philosophy. The integration of mind and body also has been a tenet of various currents of feminism for at least three decades. Feminist theorists including Jane Gallop, Gayatri Spivak, Judith Butler, Luce Irigaray, Helene Cixoux and Elizabeth Grosz view the body as a social and discursive object essential to the production of knowledge, desire and power. Grosz developed a model of embodiment as a Möbius strip where outside and inside are one continuous surface. In her opinion, an ideal feminist philosophy of the body should reveal articulations and dis-articulations between the biological and the psychological and include "a psychical representation of the subject's lived body as well as of the relations between body gestures, posture and movements in the constitution of the processes of psychical representation."[22]

Various theorists including Pierre Bourdieu, Michael Oakeshott, Paul Connerton, George Lakoff and Mark Johnson have argued for the dependence of beliefs and social values on bodily practices. For Connerton, social memory is lodged in the body and activated through commemorative ceremonies, performances, habits, and body automatisms.[23] For Bourdieu, bodily habits are manifestations of political mythologies that in turn reinforce specific ways of feeling and thinking.[24] Habits function beyond conscious awareness because they are learned through imitation and not by the deliberate application of specific principles. Thus, people's behaviors often differ from their conscious intentions.[25] Because they are unconscious, embodied practices become naturalized, immune to questioning, and extremely resistant to change.[26]

George Lakoff and Mark Johnson have proposed that humans reason with metaphors that develop as a conflation of sensorimotor and subjective, non-sensorimotor experiences. In their view, "the mind is inherently embodied, reason is shaped by the body;" our most valued abstract concepts are conceptualized via multiple complex metaphors, molecular structures made up of atomic parts named 'primary metaphors.'[27] Like Bourdieu, Oakeshott and Connerton, Lakoff and Johnson believe that most of human thought is unconscious. They call the inaccessible aspects of cognition, including our system of primary and complex metaphors, "the cognitive unconscious." Lakoff and Johnson also believe in the persistence of habit: "Once we have learned a conceptual system, it is neurally instantiated in our brains and we are not free to think just anything. Hence we have no absolute freedom in Kant's sense, no full autonomy."[28] Although most of the scholars mentioned above stress the inflexibility and resilience of social habits, they also maintain that habits are open to transformation as their performativity implies continuous improvisation.[29]

It is almost thirty years since the publication in French of Bourdieu's book *Outline of a Theory of Practice*, and more than sixty since Marcel Mauss wrote his influential essay "Techniques of the Body."[30] Given the long trajectory of theories of embodiment, it is striking how little impact this knowledge has had on studies of racism. Traditional understandings of "whiteness" and "reason" as disembodied may have contributed to these omissions. In the opinion of Radhika Mohanram "blackness and whiteness assume the status of the Cartesian body and the mind respectively. Black bodies are represented trapped in the web of nature while white bodies have freedom of movement. Such a freedom disembodies whiteness."[31] Thus discussions of racism in terms of embodiment problematize the oppositions black/white, embodied/disembodied, static/mobile and their attributed associations.

In feminist theory, disembodiment is often associated with white males, but historically, disciplining, restricting and concealing the body played a part in what Kate Davy called the "politics of respectability," a complex of values and codified behaviors by means of which white women claimed moral superiority to women of color. In the United States and various European countries, white women also have employed discourses of modernity and mobility to differentiate themselves from women of color.[32] In cyberfeminist narratives, the cyborg ultimately validates the privileges of specific groups as people of color and the poor are either left out of technological futures or coerced into cyborgian conditions.

Racist practices are legitimating performances. In most of the West, whiteness has been construed as a mark of authority and privilege. Some would argue that class is a more significant variable as all groups at the bottom of the social ladder share histories of injustice, abjection and abuse. The brutality of class marginalization can hardly be contested. Often, however, it is difficult to disassociate race from class as the lower classes consistently have been racialized, that is to say, they have been *construed* as racially different from the dominant groups and often "blackened" (i.e., the Irish in nineteenth-century England; in the twentieth century, Jews, Indians, Pakistanis, Turks, Eastern Europeans, Roma etc.) In many contexts, whiteness still assumes a superior status: Poor whites may be just as economically disadvantaged and socially marginalized as poor blacks; yet, many believe themselves to be superior because they are white.[33] Imprisonment statistics in the United States, England, Australia and France suggest that this dynamic may be operative in various justice systems.[34]

Examining racism as a complex of embodied practices and social habits supported by discursive practices provides a better understanding of the pervasiveness and resilience of racist behavior than theories which privilege racism as discourse. I'm proposing that like other social habits, many racist behaviors occur below the level of conscious awareness. Racism can be performed without deliberation; thus, an individual may vehemently oppose racist beliefs and consistently behave in racist ways.[35] In fact, several studies demonstrate that by three years of age, children express specific attitudes about race but it is doubtful that their actions reflect reasoned *ideological* positions.[36]

Recently, I had the opportunity to observe a group of four-to-six year olds at a pre-school playground in a predominantly white, working-class area of southern England. A group of the older children spent the one-hour recess period taunting the only West Asian child (a four-year old) in the playground area. The school has a policy of no hitting, and no name-calling. So the children resorted to surrounding the "black" child in a tight circle, gently but incessantly pushing him, pulling on his clothes, and following him as he attempted to walk or run away. Finally, the accosted child ran to a "forbidden" area of the playground where he was spotted by the teacher and reprimanded. Several of the younger children identified the West Asian child as being inherently "bad" or "naughty." The teachers reinforced this opinion by admonishing the child while consistently ignoring the behavior of the older children. Several local academics affirm that racism is nonexistent in the school's geographical area yet in various social contexts (shops, restaurants, buses) in the same area, adults routinely make negative and derisive comments about Asians. The behavior of the older children is likely to be a manifestation of a complex of attitudes that the children emulate but do not necessarily understand. The antagonized child likewise learns a complementary set of behaviors involving self control, defiance, submissiveness, and denial necessary to survival in that social context.

UNLEARNING RACISM

In the sixties and seventies, scholars from various fields identified body language as a system of communication. In their view, body language including posture, gestures, and facial expressions, expressed emotions and thus was a good tool for evaluating and improving personal relations.[37] Second wave feminists also recognized the importance of incorporation. The pioneering book, *Our Bodies Ourselves* stressed the interconnection of body, identity and empowerment.[38] Consciousness-raising as well as the slogan "the personal is the political" implied the re-evaluation of habitual behavior that contributed to women's oppression. Feminists challenged traditions of comportment, dress, and speech by virtue of which women were trained to conform to specific social roles. The effects of questioning and changing those habits were profound.

Bourdieu explains that all societies and revolutionary movements that seek to produce "a new man" through processes of de-culturation and re-culturation, place high stakes on "the seemingly most insignificant details of *dress, bearing, physical and verbal manners.*" In his view, each technique of the body evokes the whole system of which it is part. Thus, "the whole trick of pedagogic reason lies in the way it extorts the essential while seeming to demand the insignificant."[39]

At present, awareness of body language is regarded as a good business tool: It figures prominently in the art of negotiation for businessmen and in women's magazines' advice on how to succeed in the job interview. The Center for Nonverbal Studies, with branches in Spokane, Washington and La Jolla, California, routinely conducts lectures and seminars for businesses and corporations. The importance of nonverbal communication is recognized by law, the police, and the military in assessing the credibility of individuals as witnesses and informants.[40]

Most cyberfeminists concentrate their efforts on the technical and political aspects of digital media and ignore racism. Despite the rhetoric of equality and disembodiment that prevails in discussions of cyberspace, racism is alive in digital spaces in overt and invisible forms. If mind and body are inextricably connected, digital representation, textual and visual, must be affected by embodied practices. Thus it is crucial to identify racism in the lived world if we hope to learn to recognize it in cyberspace.

To identify embodied aspects of racism we must begin by raising our own consciousness, by observing the ways our bodies behave in the presence of "difference." We must appropriate and refine techniques successfully tested by revolutionary movements, the behavioral sciences, commerce and the military. By acknowledging the power of embodied, nonverbal practices, cyberfeminists can subvert and deploy established forms of discipline to form and strengthen positive, powerful alliances. ★

---

1   For an example, see Margaret Wertheim, "The Medieval Return of Cyberspace," *The Virtual Dimension*, ed. John Beckmann (New York: Princeton Architectural Press, 1998), p. 55.

2   Beth Kolko, Lisa Nakamura and Gilbert B. Rodman, eds., *Race in Cyberspace* (New York: Routledge, 2000), p. 3.

3   Ibid., p. 4.

4   Personal communications by several cyberfeminist colleagues at the Next Cyberfeminist International, Rotterdam, March 1999 (where Faith Wilding and I introduced a discussion of cyberfeminism and difference).

5   Kenan Malik, *The Meaning of Race* (New York: New York University Press, 1996), p. 261.

6   bell hooks, "Beloved Community: A World without Racism," in *Killing Rage: Ending Racism* (New York: Henry Holt & Co., 1995), p. 263–272; and *All About Love: New Visions* (New York: Perennial 2001), p. 87–101; Chela Sandoval, *Methodology of the Oppressed* (Minneapolis: University of Minnesota Press, 2000).

7   See Kate Davy, "Outing Whiteness: A Feminist/Lesbian Project" in *Whiteness: A Critical Reader*, ed. Mike Hill (New York: New York University Press, 1997), p. 215–220.

8   Donna Haraway, "A Manifesto for Cyborgs: Science, Technology, and Socialist Feminism in the 1980's." *Socialist Review* (1985): 80, 7; Chela Sandoval, "New Sciences: Cyborg Feminism and the Methodology of the Oppressed," in *The Cyborg Handbook*, ed. Chris Hables Gray with Heidi Figueroa-Sarriera and Steven Mentor (New York: Routledge, 1995).

9   Sadie Plant, *Zeros + Ones: Digital Women + the New Technoculture* (New York: Doubleday, 1997), p. 39–40.

10 Ibid., p. 75.

11 A group exceptionally committed to international feminist issues are Les Penelopes in France <http://www.penelopes.org>

12 See for instance, J.L.A. Garcia, "Racism as a Model for Sexism" in *Race and Sex*, ed. Naomi Zack (New York: Routledge, 1997), p. 45–59; Homi Bhabha, "The Other Question: Stereotype, Discrimination and the Discourse of Colonialism," in *The Location of Culture*, ed. Homi K. Bhabha (New York: Routledge, 1994), p. 66–84.

13 Albert Memmi, *Le Racisme: Déscription, définition, traitment* (Paris: Gallimard, 1982), p. 98–99, recently translated to English as Albert Memmi, *Racism*, Steve Martinot, trans. (Minneapolis: University of Minnesota Press, 1999); Theodore W. Allen, *The Invention of the White Race: Racial Oppression and Social Control* (London: Verso, 1994) p. 1–17, 52–3.

14 Bhabha, "The Other Question." For an example of the racialization of class differences in 19th century England, see Anne McClintock, *Imperial Leather: Race, Gender and Sexuality in the Colonial Contest* (New York: Routledge, 1995), p. 104-111.

15 John Solomos and Les Back, *Racism and Society* (New York: Saint Martin's Press, 1996), p. 146.

16 Vicente Riva Palacio, *Mexico a travez de los siglos* (Mexico, editorial Cumbre, 1970) 2: 472; and Ilona Katzew, *New World Orders*, Catalogue of an exhibition held at the Americas Society Art Gallery (New York Sept. 26–Dec. 22, 1996).

17 Memmi, *Racisme*, p. 58, 128.

18 Conversely males in select groups, especially Latinos and African-Americans are made "hypervisible" in media representations and this condition translates to everyday situations.

19 All of these examples are from real life. With the exception of bell hooks, the identities of the individuals involved have been changed.

20 Tina Grillo and Stephanie M. Wildman, "Obscuring the Importance of Race: The Implication of Making Comparisons between Racism and Sexism (or Other Isms)" in *Critical Race Feminism*, ed. Adrien Katherine Wing (New York: New York University Press, 1997), p. 47. For more extensive scholarly studies on whiteness as a socially constructed location of dominance, white supremacy etc. refer to David Roedinger, *The Wages of Whiteness: Race and the Making of the American Working Class* (London: Verso, 1991); and *Toward the Abolition of Whiteness: Essays on Race, Politics and Working Class History* (London: Verso, 1994); Ruth Frankenberg, *White Women, Race Matters: The Social Construction of Whiteness* (Routledge, 1993). For white representations of whiteness, see Richard Dyer, *White* (New York: Routledge, 1997).

21 Cited in Adrienne D. Davis and Stephanie M. Wildman, "The Legacy of Doubt: Treatment of Sex and Race in the Hill-Thomas Hearings," in *Critical Race Feminism*, p. 175.

22 Elizabeth Grosz, *Volatile Bodies: Toward a Corporeal Feminism* (St. Leonards, Australia: Allen & Unwin, 1994), p. 15–19, 23.

23 Paul Connerton, *How Societies Remember* (Cambridge: Cambridge University Press, 1989), p. 1, 4–5.

24 Pierre Bourdieu, *Outline of a Theory of Practice* (Cambridge: Cambridge University Press, 1977), p. 93–94.

25 Connerton, *Societies*, p. 3; Bourdieu, *Outline*, p. 78–81.

26 Connerton, *Societies*, p. 102.

27 George Lakoff and Mark Johnson, *Philosophy in the Flesh: The Embodied Mind and its Challenge to Western Thought* (NY: Basic Books, 1999), p. 5.

28 Ibid., p. 13, 5. For a more extensive discussion of racism and theories of embodiment, see my "Racism and Embodiment" <http://on1.zkm.de/zkm/magazin/racism_embodiment> originally presented at Performative Sites Symposium 2000: Intersecting Art, Technology, and the Body, Penn State University, October 24–28.

29 N. Katherine Hayles, *How We Became Posthuman: Virtual Bodies in Cybernetics, Literature and Infomatics* (Chicago: University of Chicago Press, 1999), p. 200; Maurice Merleau Ponty, *Phenomenology of Perception*, trans. Colin Smith (London, Routledge, 1994), p. 144–146; Bourdieu, *Outline*, p. 91; Lakoff and Johnson, *Philosophy*, p. 44–46, 73, 107.

30 Marcel Mauss, "Techniques of the Body," lecture presented at the meeting of the Societé de Psychologie, May 17th, 1934 and published in the *Journal de Psychologie normal et pathologique*, Paris, Anné XXXII, 1935, p. 271–93.

31 Radhika Mohanram, *Black Body: Women, Colonialism and Space* (Minneapolis: University of Minnesota Press, 1999), p, 22.

32 Chandra Talpade Mohanty, "Under Western Eyes: Feminist Scholarship and Colonial Discourses," *Boundary 2*, no. 12(3), 13(1) (Spring/Fall, 1984); Trinh Minh Ha, *Native, Woman;* Kate Davy, "Outing Whiteness," p. 212–215; Julia Kristeva, *About Chinese Women*, trans. Anita Barrows (London: Marion Boyars, 1977).

33 See Roedinger, *Wages of Whiteness*.

34 World Factbook of Criminal Justice Systems <http://www.ojp.usdoj.gov/bjs/abstract/wfcj.htm>

Penal Affairs Consortium, "Race And Criminal Justice," <http://www.penlex.org.uk/pages/pacrace.html>

Statistics on race in the UK, The Guardian, Monday February 21, 2000, <http://www.guardianunlimited.co.uk/macpherson/article/0,2763,191672,00.html>
World prison statistics available on-line from: bodega@sprintmail.com

35 Oakeshott distinguishes between two types of morality: one that is reflexive and discursive, and another, which is habitual. Oakeshott cited in Connerton, *Societies*, p. 29.

36 Debra Van Ausdale and Joe R. Feagin, *The First R: How Children Learn Race and Racism* (Lanham Md.: Rowman & Littlefield, 2001). Debbie Reese, "Young Children and Racism," *Parent News*, March 1998.

37 Classics in this field include Edward T. Hall's *The Silent Language* (1959), Albert Mehrabian, *Silent Messages* (1971); Julius Fast, *Body Language* (1971); Desmond Morris, *The Naked Ape: A Zoologist's Study of the Human Animal* (1967).

38 Boston Women's Health Collective, *Our Bodies Ourselves* (New York: Simon and Schuster, 1971).

39 Bourdieu, *Outline*, p. 94-95.

40 Center for Nonverbal Studies <http://members.aol.com/nonverbal2/index.htm> The Institute for Non-verbal Communication <http://www.angelfire.com/co/body-language/>

"Maintaining Credibility Within Military Public Affairs While Preserving and Participating in Military Deception" <http://www.ou.edu/deptcomm/dodjcc/groups/98B1/paper.htm>

Bibliography, nonverbal communication and witness credibility <http://www.lawfinance.com/ARTICLES/NONVERB.HTM>

Racism, Technology and the Limits of Western Knowledge

Michelle M. Wright

INTRODUCTION: CONTEMPORARY ASSUMPTIONS

O n a day devoted to imaginary demons, the *New York Times* rather fittingly published an article by Henry Louis Gates entitled "One Internet, Two Nations."[1] In the article, Gates picks up a topic now gathering steam in the United States, namely, the gap in computer literacy between black and white Americans that permeates even income distinctions. In recent articles and television appearances, Gates has become a champion of the black middle class and of middle class values in general, paradoxically using anti-black stereotypes in characterizing the black working class and working poor as lazy, self-destructive, and even in need of a "moral revolution."[2] Unsurprisingly, in this brief article, Gates glides quickly over the complexity and extent of poverty and racism to focus on a popular conservative explanation for racial inequities and disparities in this country: the culture of poverty and, by extension, the so-called slave mentality. Without actually interviewing the vast number of blacks who do use computers, and without researching black views on the computer and Internet boom, Gates asserts that it is black behavior that must be corrected so that blacks, with corporate support, can finally overcome their self-destructive behaviors and learn how to imitate and eventually, one supposes, integrate with their white and black middle class role models.

Thankfully, there are other views on race and technology. In a January 1999 article in the *Atlantic Monthly*, writer Anthony Walton argues that African-Americans have never been done terribly well by technology: The Caravel paved the way for the slave ships, Eli Whitney's cotton gin gave a shot in the arm to the dying slave economy, and the communications and information revolution rendered black (and white) jobs in the Steel Belt redundant.[3] Like Gates, Walton argues that blacks must take independent steps towards computer literacy but, unlike Gates, he suggests a "Marshall Plan" for poorly funded public schools, so that all groups, not just the elite, can receive an equal education. One of the mainstays for that education, Walton concludes, should be computer literacy.

I do not agree with very many of Walton's views or his interpretation of black history (his argument that the Great Migration had nothing to do with the outrages of Southern racist violence and oppression, and everything to do with a shortage of jobs contravenes the bulk of historical evidence), but his more complex understanding of America's treatment of African-Americans—the only group forcibly brought to the United States and enslaved for over 200 years—makes me wish Gates had read this article before jotting down his own thoughts. However, Walton and Gates do share one oddity: Despite all the rhetorical flourishes and invocations of the term, neither Gates nor Walton focuses on technology itself—Gates fails to look at it at all, and Walton's only statement is that "technology in and of itself is not at fault," preferring a view of scientists and inventors and disinterested altruistic parties devoted to aiding mankind. This is either wishful thinking or sheer ignorance: Western science has never been kind to peoples of African descent, beginning with slaves serving as live test subjects in the name of medical progress,[4] and four decades of the Tuskegee experiments.[5] Gates and Walton both rely upon a series of simplistic assumptions about race, science and technology—completely bypassing historical records—in order to make what are ultimately predictable claims. Ignoring technology and science may have worked very well in Africa, but we're in the *West* now!

WHOSE TECHNOLOGY?

I want to return to Walton's rhetoric: What is "technology in and of itself?" It is certainly not what Walton thinks it is, as he is speaking of technologies developed by the West to enrich itself rather than the disinterested pursuit of knowledge "in and of itself." Before either Gates or Walton tackles this vexing question of race and technology, it is important to examine the terms of the discourse. After all, how many forgone conclusions are we to encounter using two terms, race and technology, that are not only Euro-centric in their definitions, but also in their connotations and denotations? "Race," like "gender" while claiming to speak to a range of groups, most often speaks to one group in particular that is seen as deviating from the norm. Just as "gender" is incorrectly synonymous with "woman," the deviant from the male, so "race" incorrectly denotes "black," the deviant from the white norm. Given that the categories of "black," "Negro," "colored," and "nigger" first defined an inferior people incapable of learning (and therefore of achieving civilization), how surprised should we be that Gates and Walton begin their work with two terms always already assumed to be in opposition? They then proceed to "discover," either because of their own laziness (Gates) or for reasons unknown—but certainly not the fault of technology—(Walton), an antithetical relationship between the two.

I want to argue here that it is our *representation* of technology that must first be analyzed, critiqued and revamped so that we might avoid this slew of foregone conclusions, recuperation of stereotypes, and this mythology of the West as the "cradle of civilization"—and therefore the sole owner of "technology in and of itself." It is difficult, if not impossible, to fairly assess all aspects of this debate on the "digital divide" when the assumptions we bring to bear on this discussion rest on 250-year old Western myths of European superiority and the vigorous defense of these fictions in the face of contrary evidence. Gates and Walton provide excellent examples of reaching these foregone conclusions from a flawed framework by failing to specify that they are discussing *Western* technology rather than technological innovations from all civilizations. I would venture to say that for both authors the two terms are synonymous. As any student of world civilization will tell you, they are not.

Understanding the fallacy of assuming that the (white) West is the birthplace of technology makes an important difference in Walton's argument. In his discussion of technology *versus* African-Americans, he ignores the technological innovations created by the latter, Africans, and the rest of the world. This leads the reader to assume that no black (without Western tutelage) has played a role in the history of technology except as victim or passive recipient. The first alphabets; the concept of zero; gynecology; veterinary medicine; the 365 day calendar (anticipating its "discovery" in the west by *three thousand years*[6]); elements of geometry; Caesarian section;[7] iron and copper smelting—all of these and far more were accomplished outside the West; indeed, before the West had developed from roaming tribes into permanent organized settlements.[8] This is not to claim, therefore, that African civilizations are obviously superior: only that the rather large and influential advancements they provided have been denied and usurped by late nineteenth and early twentieth century historians such as Arnold Toynbee, who famously declared that, outside of Europe, no other continent had contributed to world civilization. Toynbee, of course, did not provide any evidence, and in taking these beliefs to heart, we have yet to ask for evidence supporting this grand assertion. We ask non-whites to prove their case, and then ignore or ridicule them; we do not ask ourselves the basis for our assumptions of superiority. Yet, in our representation of the technological revolution, we construct the same mythological doctrine that still plagues public school and mass media representation of its American history by presenting it as almost wholly white and male.[9]

THE HISTORY OF A MYTH

Although I would venture to guess that very few Americans could name a single theory from the 19th century German philosopher Georg Friedrich Wilhelm Hegel, very many of us continually espouse and/or propagate some of his ideas regarding progress, history and civilization. More importantly, foreign policy discussions and decisions by Western nations and organizations (i.e., World

Bank, International Monetary Fund and the World Trade Organization) reflect an attitude towards developing nations that also echoes Hegel's discourse on civilization. One need only compare the generous loan terms offered by the World Bank and World Trade Organization to other "white" nations, and the loan restrictions and terms for non-Western nations to understand how skin color, more than any other factor—including propensity towards defaulting on payments—determines one's status as either "first world" or "Other." This is not to claim that Hegel is the architect of Western military and economic colonization, only that his theory of history had a profound influence on 19th and 20th century Western thinkers and leaders.

Drawing directly from his arrestingly prescient *Philosophy of History* [*Philosophie der Geschichte*], one can easily see that we, like Hegel, do not trouble too long over the dangerously simplistic binaries "civilized" and "primitive" and, more likely than not, pin these terms to the equally erroneous dichotomy we assert between the West and "developing nations." Like Hegel, we understand the history of Western civilization to be a *Bildungsroman*—an insular progressive narrative about the search for ourselves, where external characters (i.e., the rest of the world) play little or no role. Technology is deployed as the latest chapter of evidence for Western superiority. Yet, it is a specific representation of technology as white, male and Western, that is championed and accompanied by a truncated history that grossly distorts the facts.

Hegel begins the *Philosophy of History* by noting that there are three types of history, original, reflective, and philosophical—but of these three, it is the middle one that is significant because it is a history that records the meaningful progress of civilizations rather than the mere passage of time or the contemplation of events past. More specifically, Hegel argues that it is the *result* of history, that is, the developing human consciousness of freedom, with which we should occupy ourselves. More to the point, he argues that Europe—and his fatherland (Germany) in particular—is the premier site for such a history. By contrast, he claims, the continent of Africa is sadly lacking any (reflective) history. To follow Hegel's logic: Just as we would not consider the last several centuries of animal history as anything more than a passage of time for them, so should we regard Africa and Africans as *passing time* rather than *progressing in history*, as is the self-evident inclination of Europe: [10]

> Africa proper, as far as History goes back, has remained—for all pur-
> poses of connection with the rest of the World—shut up; it is the
> Gold-land compressed within itself—the land of childhood, which
> lying beyond the day of self-conscious history, is enveloped in the
> dark mantle of Night.[11]

The rhetorical counter-point assumed here between an "enlightened" Europe and the "dark continent" is clearly attached to concepts of intellectual develop- ment. Although Hegel had never been to Africa he did not hesitate (in this oth- erwise intellectually dense treatise); to recount outrageous stories of cannibal- ism, human sacrifice, and other bloodthirsty gore as anthropologically sound. Indeed, he was not alone: The first anthropologists reported that some Africans had tails, or two heads, or spoke out of their chests. Earlier Enlightenment philosophers such as David Hume, Emmanuel Kant, and Johann von Herder, while debating long and loud the relative merits of *a priori* versus *a posteriori* in the discussion of human consciousness, eagerly asserted black inferiority despite their supposed attachment to the scientific method. That is, when it came to the discussion of the black, they abandoned their now famous method- ology of questioning the reliability of myth and hearsay, and insisting upon an exhaustive gathering of evidence and the rigorous pursuit of the scientific method before making any truth claims on such an enormous scale.[12] While the respect of this method was certainly accorded to those they considered their peers (other economically respectable white males), those whom they already assumed as inferior remained so.

CONSTRUCTING A PAST TO JUSTIFY THE PRESENT

The irrationality of these racist assertions might be partially justified if Europe had had no contact with Africa until the Portuguese stumbled across West Africa in the late fifteenth century. But Mediterranean Europe had shared some 1,000 years of trade, warfare, and intellectual exchange before the Portu- guese arrival, and the very ancient Greek texts that Hegel cites in his Philos- ophy make mention of the centrality of Egypt to the development of Ancient

Greece—which Hegel locates as the cradle of Western civilization and "reflective history." As Martin Bernal has argued in his "controversial" trilogy *Black Athena: The Afroasiatic Roots of Classical Civilization*, this "amnesia" is due to the replacement of Europe's "Ancient Model" of historiography with the "Aryan" model.[13] This replacement, Bernal argues, was not due to the uncovering of new evidence, but simply to a change in European ideology that evinced a disgust, fear and contempt for non-European peoples and civilizations that far outweighed the xenophobia of classical Greece:

> [Hellenic superiority] was negligible compared to the tidal wave of ethnicity and racialism, linked to cults of Christian Europe and the North with the Romantic movement at the end of the 18th century. The paradigm of 'races' that were intrinsically unequal in physical and mental endowment was applied to all human studies, but especially history. To be creative, a civilization needed to be 'racially pure'. Thus it became increasingly intolerable that Greece—which was seen by the Romantics not merely as the epitome of Europe but also as its pure childhood—could be the result of the mixture of native Europeans and colonizing Africans and Semites.[14]

Bernal offers two equally important arguments: One, that European civilization owes much to its African predecessors and ancient contemporaries; two, that this evidence is easily obtainable from classical texts because the virulent anti-black sentiment that clouds contemporary Western thought did not, at that time, exist. It is the second point that many American classics scholars find so offensive: That their knowledge of world history is not based on research but racist myths. As historians Lerone Bennett, Jr., Winthrop Jordan and George Frederickson have noted, in the 17th and early 18th centuries, both blacks and whites were kidnapped and sold to traders as indentured servants, with distinctions being made only in terms of Christians and non-Christians. From the Jamestown settlement, which introduced "perpetual servitude" as a condition specific to non-Christian blacks (and then all black Africans) up to the late 18th century, there were very few justifications proffered for this custom beyond the pull of profit. Justification for racially determined chattel slavery based on supposed inferiority was developed after the fact and not, as we are often taught, the other way around.[15] In other words, in order to justify its claims to racial and cultural superiority, we in the West are not simply ignoring facts to the contrary, we are actively vilifying them and erasing them before they reach a wider audience.

American history in particular is only now beginning to confront the myths that have been presented as fact. In their article "Narrating Competing Truths in the Thomas Jefferson–Sally Hemings Paternity Debate," Venetria K. Patton and Ronald Jemal Stevens[16] look at how white American historians have long refused to even pursue the possibility that Hemings' children were part of the Jefferson line despite the overwhelming amount of circumstantial evidence. As examples, Patton and Stevens cite the numbing frequency of rape and forced liaisons with slave women by their white owners, the striking resemblance of Hemings' sons to Jefferson, and the unreliability of Jefferson's writings on slavery, not to mention the extensive and detailed oral histories of Hemings' descendants.[17] All this has been consistently refuted by prominent Americanists such as Merrill D. Peterson simply because Jefferson wrote unfavorably on miscegenation and, therefore, they reason, would never consent to have sexual relations with a black woman. In this contest between detailed oral histories supported by what little documentation exists, and a handful of sentences from a text (which did not hesitate to wonder if blacks did not have different colored blood and stated that African women mated with apes), traditional and mainstream texts determine what is credible not through research, but by the race and gender of the contestants.

Although we in the West pride ourselves on the objectivity of our scholarship—especially in fields that rely on "facts" from the social and natural sciences—we spend little time questioning the basis for that pride or doing more than angrily refuting those who point out the racial and gender biases inherent in much of our work. Despite the rocky history of both disciplines with regard to women and other minorities, science, like the phoenix, rises again and again from the flames in a perfect amnesia about past mistakes. As a result, the likelihood that these mistakes will be repeated *ad nauseam* unless the cause is thoroughly examined, discussed, and rectified remains all but certain.

Patton and Stevens suggest that, in Jefferson's case, it is our refusal to examine the enduring nature of anti-black sentiment in America that leads us to such dismal scholarship and regrettable ignorance. For those on the receiving end of this prejudice, questions such as "why would Jefferson lie?" bear little mystery:

> Time and time again, African Americans have witnessed hypocrisy and contradiction whether it be in the Declaration of Independence, which declares all men equal while legitimizing slavery, or in slave narratives in which slave masters view slavery as extending a familial relationship while disrupting slave families. This hypocritical view of America is related to the unwillingness of many historians to address adequately Jefferson's hypocrisy. Many of us prefer to see his contradictory views as mysterious rather than use them as a means to analyze race relations.[18]

In other words, the deep-rooted racism in American minds today only further perpetuates the lies and mythologies of our history. This is hardly surprising: It is difficult to recognize the myths and crimes of the past if they are in fact so much part of our present.

AFRICAN AND AFRICAN-AMERICAN TECHNOLOGIES

Consider a handful of the contributions that African-Americans have made to science and technology.[19] We have forgotten that Granville Woods invented the steam boiler furnace and the telephone transmitter; Mary Moore invented one of the first artificial pain relievers in the 18th century; Lewis Latimer invented the incandescent light bulb (greatly improving on Edison's use of a bamboo filament by replacing it with carbon, and therefore making light bulbs last from a mere 30 hours to over 300), and he supervised the implementation of electric lights in New York City, Philadelphia, Montreal, and London. We have forgotten that Garrett A. Morgan invented the prototype of the gas mask and the automatic stoplight; Frederick Jones made the transportation of fresh foods and dairy products possible when he invented mobile refrigeration. Elijah McCoy made it possible for locomotives to operate continuously without having to stop every few miles to re-lubricate the wheels and machinery. Despite the attempts of corporate competitors to duplicate his invention, only McCoy's actually worked, causing railway engineers to always ask if the automatic lubricator available for purchase was "the real McCoy"—this phrase has been re-attributed to several white McCoys, an athlete, an entrepreneur, and an inventor whose inventions were never actually used by anyone.

The only black inventor America acknowledges is George Washington Carver, who revolutionized Southern agriculture by developing more advanced methods of crop rotation so that farmers did not exhaust their soil after three years but could use it indefinitely (indeed, crop rotation was taught by the first African-Americans to white planters). Carver also developed peanut oil as a cheaper alternative additive to motor oil, diesel fuel, printing ink, rubbers, and lighting oil, but, today, his only publicly acknowledged invention is peanut butter. More recently, A. P. Ashbourne developed the airplane propeller; Dr. Charles Drew discovered plasma in blood; Henry Sampson patented the cell phone; Otis Boykin developed pacemaker controls for the guided missile; and Dr. Patricia Bath has patented her technique of using laser surgery to remove cataracts.

Although the West bases its assumptions of technological (and therefore intellectual) superiority over the non-West on "objective" evidence, what is most educational about returning to Enlightenment philosophy, Hegel, and thence to Bernal, is the degree to which myths and legends were quickly incorporated as truth into the Western discourse on civilization. Furthermore, it is important to understand that these myths were created to overturn roughly a millenium of history and evidence. We are still using them to quash all the overwhelming evidence to the contrary, such as that supplied by Bernal's voluminous proofs, as well as those supplied by historians such as Ivan van Sertima, Théophile Obenga, and Ali Mazrui.[20]

The refutation of this evidence has been swift, anxious, angry, and offensive. Mary Lefkowitz, Mellon professor in the Humanities at Wellesley College, is the most public academic in this debate. The cover of her book *Not Out of Africa* features a bust of Plato wearing a Malcolm X baseball cap tilted to one side. This advertises the level of respect with which she intends to treat any claims that ancient Europe did not suddenly flower on its own, achieving greatness in a vacuum. In other words, to question European superiority, by arguing that African civilizations were also influential is tantamount to claiming Plato was down with Malcolm X. What in the world does Malcolm X have to do with ancient African civilizations? In the eyes of Lefkowitz and her allies, one black is the same as any other, and just as Malcolm X could not have influenced Plato, so, too, it is impossible that any non-white civilization might have been influenced.

Responses to Bernal from public intellectuals of the far right have been alternately furious, sarcastic and patronizing, often attacking established scholars as misguided minds desperately seeking proof of racial equality in their myth-making. Most notably, these figures refuse to distinguish between Afro-centrists who back their claims with extensive data, and those reactionaries who, as Clarence Walker points out in *We Can't Go Home Again*, simply convert white racist myths and doctrines into equally ridiculous claims (i.e., all blacks in the West are descended from Egyptian kings and queens, all whites are evil). Bernal and his colleagues are not interested, as Lefkowitz and others claim, in elevating Africa to the top of the civilizational heap through myth—rather, they simply seek to demonstrate how all civilizations have contributed to world knowledge and progress.[21] In a West devoted to a binary thinking in which one is either inferior or superior, this is a difficult concept to understand.

As we have already seen, it is important to question not only the basis of the evidence but also the economic and political agendas of European claims to superiority. As Molefi Asante (among others) has pointed out, *Black Athena* quotes directly from the ancient texts of Herodotus, Diogenes, Plutarch, and Plato, in which African scientific contributions to Greece are explicitly recorded. Paradoxically enough, in their effort to uphold these scholars (as well as those who studied in Africa, such as Solon, Democritus, Anaxamander, and Pythagoras), the scholars assembled for *Black Athena Revisited* ask us to interpret those writings on Africa as false, but everything else as true. As Bernal, Asante and others have pointed out, Lefkowitz directly ties any attempt to question the superiority of Ancient Greece (and, by association, all of the West) to a direct attack on democracy. In other words, it is not so much the truth that is at stake as our way of life.

TECHNOLOGY AND THE "NEW FRONTIER" MENTALITY

The contemporary representation of technology in the West is deeply implicated in this ideologically motivated mythology in which, outside of Africa,
"history," that inherently progressive linear narrative of conquests and inventions, is the sole province of the West (and sometimes just the United States).
Despite overwhelming evidence to the contrary, those scholars who reject the
evidence of African achievements are convinced that acknowledging the contributions of non-Western civilizations is tantamount to admitting the West is
inferior to all other civilizations.

The nature of this discourse and its perpetuation is also evident in contemporary views of African-Americans and their technological prowess. We
assume that the information we receive in the media is up to date; that is, if
there were evidence of African civilizations that influenced Europe, it would
by now be generally acknowledged. The idea that Western knowledge often
constructs itself on the basis of an assumed racial superiority—and actively
attacks and suppresses contrary claims—runs counter to our self-construction
as the *only* site on earth where truth, not myth and magic, structures our world.
The truth is, we are just as fallible as other civilizations, and one need only
compare white American ideas about black inferiority with the innumerable
instances of black achievement to understand that what we believe, especially
in terms of race, is often based on wishful thinking rather than current
evidence. While thousands of black Americans have distinguished themselves
in all professional fields, we prefer to turn our eyes to those who have not done
so and express wonderment at their failure to keep pace with their white
countrymen. Like Hegel, we rely upon hearsay to maintain the binaries of
black/white, inferior/superior, and savage/civilized rather than bother with
actual research and fact checking. Polls and articles on the gap between white
American and black American computer literacy always seem to express some
sort of surprise, some sort of shock, but why are we so shocked?

Why are we so shocked when our human representations of technology (save
for a few Apple computer billboards) are overwhelmingly white and male? Why
are we so shocked when our mythological history of technology begins in the

West without the mathematical and scientific advances produced by non-white civilizations?

The information and communications revolution was not invented in a garage by two teenage boys, it came out of long and arduous advancements in metallurgy, mass production, an overwhelming accumulation of capital and, of course, slave labor. American Indians, Africans, Asians, Chicanos, Latinos, and working class white men and women were indispensable to the West entering the modern age, but their contributions (more often cruelly coerced and/or callously exploited than voluntary), have now been quickly dismissed. Technology, we are told, comes from the independent genius, such as Bill Gates or Steven Jobs, the same way we are told that America began with George Washington and Thomas Jefferson, the same way we are told that Abraham Lincoln wrote the Emancipation Proclamation and suddenly black slaves were free to do as they liked.

What I want to say here is that we are returning to old and dangerous myths in our construction of technology, in our short-sighted and heavily prejudiced recitation of its origins. Why should we be so shocked when those who belong to groups long designated as primitive and irrelevant, criminal and immoral, would not possess the skills or have access to a science that has worked hard to maintain an image almost wholly antagonistic to them?

In "Technology versus African Americans," Walton avoids a binary I have perpetrated in this brief essay and must examine—one between blacks and whites, where blacks are impotent and whites sadistically powerful. As Walton points out, many black Americans with the clout and power to change some of this imagery have only reinforced it—albeit for their overwhelmingly white audience.

FEEDING RACIST FANTASIES

In the past few years, "cyberstyling" has become a mainstay of many R&B and rap videos: Futuristic sets populated with blacks dressed in robotic or otherwise space-age costumes, technologically aware, if not completely cyborg in their familiarity. At the same time, the messages pushed forward are problematic because they reify this dichotomy between race and technology. The only exception I have found is rapper Missy Elliott's bold and powerful video "I'm a Bitch," in which, dressed in an impressive (and deliberately exaggerated) robot's armor, she declares her right as a black woman to make her own decisions and follow her own path, even if others might (predictably) see her as a "bitch." However, this video and its message, unlike her previous releases, failed to reach the Top Ten on any charts. More successful and yet far more compromised is TLC's visually seductive "No Scrubs" video, in which black men are rejected for being stereotypically oversexed and too lazy, too stupid, to earn a decent salary. Although playful and intelligent in some of its critiques, this highly popular single and award-winning video offers no other representation of blacks outside of this stereotype as well as showing the black woman as a cold gold digger. I am not even going to mention the nasty response this song elicited that further pushes these negative stereotypes of black men and women to greater depths.

I would argue that even in some of these more liberating and radical musical art forms, old myths are replayed to destructive ends. After all, it is the African American development of rap music rhythms that spurred important technological innovations by both blacks and whites, including drum machines and more sophisticated synthesizers that could accommodate complex sampling techniques. These technologies in turn have been used to help develop the use of sound bytes and musical samples on the Internet. Why can't the musical form that aided in their creation celebrate these connections?

How we actively maintain the digital divide

In our drive to bring African-Americans into the computer revolution, let us also ask exactly what it is we are offering and how we can change those assumptions and representations. At present, as many black students and colleagues from highly ranked "tech" universities will attest, we are inviting black students into an environment where many of their white teachers believe them to be intellectually inferior, where many of their white peers take cues from those teachers and ostracize them from study groups or less formal gatherings. We are inviting them into an environment where they are often discussed as handicaps and a threat to the university's pursuit of excellence.

In his famous book, *The Souls of Black Folk*, W.E.B. Du Bois analyzed a question often put to him by curious whites: "How does it feel to be a problem?" As Du Bois and many others since then have explained, positing blacks, rather than racist behavior, as the "problem" leads nowhere. This is the circular path that leads Gates, Walton, and others to scratch their heads over the "digital divide" instead of questioning the broad assumptions about race and technology that begin their discussions. In working to include all of our citizens in this new Internet nation, we can work towards learning and disseminating the true history of technology, as "in and of itself" as we can get: Involving *all* races (yes, *all*) and dispelling this destructive myth of white Western superiority.

CONCLUSION: AREAS OF EMPOWERMENT

In the midst of these debates on the "digital divide," black activists, students, faculty, entrepreneurs and "techies" are using the Internet to encourage black participation, and linking African-Americans and their communities both to one another as well as to concerned non-profits and corporations. Continuing the tradition of self-help community outreach developed by the Oakland Black Panthers, San Francisco Mayor Willie Brown, musician Herbie Hancock, and Pittsburgh entrepreneur Bill Strickland are three of the main sponsors for Rhythm of Life (<http://www.rolo.org>), a non-profit organization that raises money to provide both computer skills and job training to the black working poor and working class in the San Francisco Bay Area. The Afro-Futurist collective (<http://www.afrofuturism.net>) provides a clearinghouse for a discussion on how the work of African-American and African diasporic artists and intellectuals intersects with the latest breakthroughs in technology. The Website also provides a series of links to other Web-sites that take a radical political and social stance, and seek to inform, connect and empower dispossessed communities. The Cyber Sisters Club from Allentown, Pennsylvania (<http://www.lv.psu.edu/jkl/sisters>), created by a Lehigh Valley black women's collective, provides face-to-face mentoring, online and outdoor activities and advanced computing skills to elementary school girls who live in disadvantaged and remote areas. Sistahspace (<http://www.sistahspace.com>), by contrast, is a for-profit site for black women interested in connecting to one another through bulletin boards and chat rooms, and to a wide range of both non-profit and for-profit services.

There are also Web-sites that document and record African and African-American cultural and technological developments, including African Fractal (<http://www.rpi.edu/~eglash/eglash.dir/afractal.htm>), African Indigenous Science and Technology Systems (<http://www.members.aol.com/afsci/africana.htm>), and the Black Cultural Studies Web Site (<http://www.tiac.net/users/thaslett>). They provide a forum for both posting and reading messages, as well as links to scholars and artists across the Diaspora interested in exploring the role of black writers, thinkers and artists in the West and beyond. There are other steps being taken by academics and activists. Most recently, activist and novelist Walter Mosely, and activists/scholars Manthia Diawara, Clyde Taylor, and Regina Austin came together to produce the book *Black Genius: African American Solutions to African American Problems*, enlisting the aid of figures such as Haki Madhibuti, Anna Deavere Smith, bell hooks, Angela Davis, Jocelyn Elders, Spike Lee and many others, to discuss practical and affordable solutions (no more than $5) for African Americans to empower themselves not only in areas of technology, but also lifestyle, finance, the arts, and politics. *Black Genius* also focuses on developing non-profit organizations that are based in, made up of, and serve the black community.

Postscript: Strategic illiteracy

Many African-Americans *are* working towards social, educational and economic parity with whites, and in the past *have* developed and progressed along the same yardstick that the West uses to favorably distinguish itself from other civilizations. For those of us seeking to end the "digital divide," our main obstacle is *not* the Black computer illiteracy that the mainstream bemoans, but the *strategic illiteracy* deployed by those who wish to bemoan lazy black communities too closely tied to their primitive past. ★

1   Henry Louis Gates, Jr., "One Internet, Two Nations," *The New York Times*, 31 October, 1999, Final Edition.

2   See the PBS Frontline special from 1997 on "African Americans and Class."

3   Anthony Walton, "Race and Technology." *Atlantic Monthly*, January, 1999.

4   While James Marion Sims is celebrated by most medical histories for his pioneering efforts in surgery, his practice of operating on unwilling slaves and the white poor, without the use of anesthesia, is rarely discussed.

5   Although the Clinton administration admitted that the U.S. sanctioned withholding treatment at Tuskegee, the government has yet to acknowledge that Tuskegee doctors also deliberately exposed healthy black men to syphilis.

6   I apologize for the obnoxious italics, but some things really need to be stressed, given our odious assumptions that Western civilization holds a monopoly on all significant technological inventions.

7   Long predating Julius Caesar, after whom the procedure was named upon its "discovery" in the West.

8   All these facts and more are available in the *Encyclopedia of the History of Science, Technology, and Medicine in Non-Western Cultures*, ed. Helaine Selin (Boston: Kluwer Academic, 1997), and *Milestones in Science and Technology: The Ready Reference Guide to Discoveries, Inventions, and Facts*, by Ellis Mount and Barbara List, (Phoenix, AZ: Oryx Press, 1994).

9   Even those books and articles sympathetic to how former colonies have been exploited by the West often operate on these fallacies, referencing books some 20–50 years out of date.

10 Unsurprisingly, Hegel's attitudes towards Asia reflect many contemporary ones of being "not quite white;" he notes that Asians are superior to Africans, but inferior to Europeans; behind, but not in such a hopeless limbo.

11 Georg Wilhelm Friedrich Hegel, *The Philosophy of History*. trans. J. Sibree (New York: Dover Publications, 1956), p. 91.

12 For the best account of early French anthropology in Africa, see Christopher Miller's *Blank Darkness: Africanist Discourse in French* (University of Chicago Press, 1985), and for the "best of" selections from Enlightenment philosophers, see Emmanuel Chukwudi Eze's *Race and the Enlightenment: A Reader* (London: Blackwell Publishers, 1997).

13 Despite the extensive documentation supplied by Bernal, and the acknowledgement of his achievement by some of our leading scholars in linguistics, history and anthropology, Bernal's argument that the West has only recently (since approx. 250 years) denied the contributions of other civilizations has enraged a vocal minority who insist that the West has always been the superior civilization and always known it.

14 Martin Bernal, *Black Athena: Vol. 1.* (New Brunswick: Rutgers University Press, 1987).

15 See Thomas Jefferson's "Notes on the State of Virginia," *Thomas Jefferson: Writings*, ed. Merrill D. Peterson (New York: Library of America, 1984), for one of the earliest claims for black inferiority, relying upon such bizarre suggestions as the tendency of blacks to mate with "Oran-Ootans" and the possibility that black blood is a different color. Jefferson's passages on the racial future of America are especially enlightening given the widespread knowledge of his having fathered children with bonds-woman Sally Hemings—directly contradicting the disgust he evinces for miscegenation in the Notes.

16 *The Black Scholar* 29, no. 4 (2000).

17 All we do know "for sure" at this point is that either Jefferson or his nephews fathered Hemings' children, but it is far less likely it was his nephews, given Jefferson's preferential treatment of Sally and her children.

18 *The Black Scholar*, p.14.

19 There is still no one book specifically devoted to African or African American inventors, but there are a dizzying array of exhaustive sources that detail these inventors and provide bibliographies. The Masschusetts Institute for Technology <http://web.mit.edu/invent/www/inventorsA-H/Aaweek2.html> and the Detroit Public Library <http://detroit.lib.mi.us/glptc.aaid> as well as a website known as "The Patent Café" <http://patentcafe.com/inventors_café_africanam.html> are a good place to start, as well as *The Encyclopedia Africana*, edited by Henry Louis Gates, Jr. and Anthony Appiah. One can also consult M.A. Harris, *The Black Book* (New York: Random House, 1974); or check out <http://www.invention-express.com/oa4.html>.

20 It should be noted that the one bone of contention African scholars bear towards Bernal is his failure to look beyond Egypt to the range of other African peoples and civilizations, such as the Kush, Eritreans, Ethiopians, Nubians, Timbuktu and the Asante kingdom—just to name a few, mind!

21 There are some reactionary black figures who do in fact want to claim that blacks are superior to whites, and these marginal fanatics are often the ones trotted out by the press and quoted by journalists when this debate over African civilizations arises. Unless we trot out the KKK's Grand Dragon as an expert in Western history for these same debates, I see no value in this distortion.

Race in the Construct, or the Construction of Race: New Media and Old Identities in "The Matrix"

Lisa Nakamura

"The Matrix is a world pulled over your eyes
to blind you from the truth."

"What truth?"

"That you are a slave, Neo. Like everyone else,
you were born into bondage."

The preceding dialogue occurs between Neo (Keanu Reeves) and Morpheus (Laurence Fishburne) in the 1999 film "The Matrix." In it, Morpheus reveals that Neo has been living in a dream world created by a sinister Artificial Intelligence (AI) which has reduced humans to organic power sources to fuel their own processors, and most importantly, has constructed a digital representation of a "real world" so convincing that most humans take it for real. This Matrix, or "neural-interactive simulation," is a digital construct indistinguishable from the real. The danger lies in the exploitation of the human race, at least of those still enslaved by its simulated reality. The connections between the Matrix depicted in this film, and the Internet as it exists today, all have a common root in cyberpunk fiction, specifically William Gibson's novels, from which both the terms "cyberspace" and "matrix" originated. Gibson coined the term "matrix" to describe a network of computers which had achieved sentience, and the word "cyberspace" as a means to describe a "consensual hallucination experienced daily by billions of legitimate operators."[1]

Hence, the film "The Matrix" can and should be read as a narrative about the Internet and its possibilities and dangers.

Like Gibson's novels in particular, and cyberpunk in general, "The Matrix" both celebrates technology and critiques it. The cyber-utopian or celebratory strain often advances the notion of technology as a social equalizer that levels out race and gender inequities, since bodies are supposedly left behind in cyberspace, or at least are invisible when using it. This line of thinking depends upon a mistaken notion of race as solely a somatic or bodily feature, one which can (and should) be conveniently edited out or eliminated by the use of the Internet. "The Matrix" is all about visibility, however, and thus cannot elide the question of race, though at times it tries to, with important repercussions, as I will show. On the contrary, I posit that the film envisions a vexed multiculturalism as a corrective to the dehumanizing excesses of modern machines, which promise so much but end up delivering so little.

Though the film has been called "equal parts Luddite polemic and seeker of truth,"[2] its "truth" couches a critique of technology within a deeply raced narrative. In this narrative, humans must learn to master the machines, not abandon them. Race functions as a means for humans to hack into the machines; it represents a "pirate signal" which affirms racial diversity and stakes out its place in the global landscape of the future. Utopia, or "Zion," as it is termed in the film, is the last refuge of "100 percent pure homegrown human beings," as the black character Tank terms himself. This future-world is emphatically multiracial; rather than depicting a world in which race has been "transcended," or represented solely by white actors (who command more money at the box office), we are shown a world in which race is not only visible but necessary for human liberation.

Neo's dialogue with Morpheus, one of many that contribute towards the Orientalized sensei/student relationship which they share, employs the term "slavery" which can never be separated from power relations and race in the United States. Morpheus's efforts to school Neo, to first convince him that he is a slave exploited by machine culture and later to help him to "free his mind" so that he can defeat the machines and rewrite, or hack into, the Matrix, reverses the usual order of things in a film of this genre. Firstly, it constructs a black character as a leader in a cyberpunk film, and, in fact, as more than a leader. As the character Tank says while delivering an elegy to the Morpheus who he thinks will be shortly unplugged, or killed: "You've been more than a leader to us, you've been a father." Previous canonical cyberpunk films have depicted minority characters, particularly Asians, as window dressing symptomatic of a post-apocalyptic pastiche of cultures; in "Blade Runner" (1982), the viewer can tell that the apocalypse has come and gone because there are so many minorities running around speaking in foreign languages, or mixtures thereof. The same can be said of "Strange Days" (1995). In both of these films, people of color are supporting characters at best.

In noticeable contrast, "The Matrix" is a truly multicultural cyberpunk film. Perhaps this, in part, has had something to do with this film's "regenerating the sagging cyberspace genre,"[3] a genre that had been "left-for-dead" in the words of a *Newsweek* review.[4] However, though the review refers to the "combination of Chinese martial arts and American special effects" which have created the spectacular hybrid fight scenes which most viewers remember after they view it, it says nothing about race and the casting of the film, much less the ways that race is constantly referenced in the narrative. It seems as if the film's critical reception exists in another matrix or frame of reference, one in which race is invisible, overshadowed by the conflict between men and machines. However, in the film, machines are racialized and so are men (and women, though the treatment of women is another story). A black man leads the resistance or slave revolt against the machines, who are visible to us as Anglo-Saxon "agents" wearing suits.[5] They all look the same, as one would expect machines to do, but most importantly they all look white and middle class in a way that no one in the resistance does.

The black Morpheus is a father to his multicultural crew of rebels, which is impressive in its diversity; in addition to Morpheus, it contains two black characters, Tank and Dozer; an adolescent white boy, Mouse; a Latino figure, Apoc; and a white woman, Trinity. There is even a queer character, Switch, signified as such by familiar tropes such as spiky hair, minimal makeup, and a matter-of-fact way of speaking. However, her queerness isn't flagged by the characters pointing it out via dialogue, just as race isn't constructed in that way either, as it is taken for granted that by 2199, the year when the film's "real" action is taking place, racial diversity as well as tolerance *vis a vis* sexual identity has become accepted enough to go uncommented upon. However, the discourse of racism has been re-purposed in this film. At times, it is projected onto machines, as when Morpheus is beaten and abducted by the white agents; his reply to learning Agent Smith's name is "You all look the same to me." Primarily, the presence of people of color in the film lets us know that we are in the realm of the Real;[6] machine-induced fantasies and wish fulfillment, which is what the Matrix is, are knowable to us by their distinctive and consistent whiteness.

The machine in its worst incarnation, the sinister face of technology run amok, the hegemonic, cyber-spatial, cold regime that has reduced all humans to slaves, is shown to us in the film as being distinctively and conventionally white and male, in contrast to the warm living multi-raciality and gender-bending of the rebels. These agents are the visual manifestation of a system of domination which is technologically enabled, and appear in suits, which signify a critique of corporate imagery in general as well as capitalism-as-usual. The agents also manifest themselves as cops, clearly also allied with the hegemonic machine, and the scene in which they gather in a circle and beat the black Morpheus invokes images of Rodney King, images indelibly coded as being about the oppression of blacks by whites.

The only four Anglo-Saxon characters in Morpheus' crew of the *Nebuchadnezzar*—the warrior-heroine Trinity; the androgynous Switch; the hacker-boy Mouse; and the betrayer Cypher—are positioned either in opposition to or in alliance with this version of whiteness. Cypher, the only adult white male on the crew, is on the side of the machines; he is their "agent." Mouse, as well as Switch, the queer female character, and Trinity, the other female crew member, are emphatically against the machines. Both Switch and Trinity, in particular, unite a cyberpunk style of femininity and a formidable role as a warrior; Trinity's is the first combat scene in the film. Trinity and Switch stand outside traditional gender definitions of woman as nurturer and ones-to-be-defended. While the machine defends traditional gender roles—there are no female agents—Trinity and Switch challenge them, which exempts them from the taint of whiteness-as-inhuman and preserves femininity as an opposing force to technology as oppressor. This racing of the machine itself identifies whiteness as part of the problem, not the solution, a problem which multiraciality—the alliance between blacks, as shown to us by Morpheus, Tank, and Dozer, Latinos like Apoc, and interracial characters like Neo—is positioned to solve.

The multiracial position of Neo, as played by Keanu Reeves, is occluded to some extent in the film. However, it is a significant casting choice to have placed him in this role precisely because of his actual mixed racial status. (Early journalistic writing on Keanu Reeves always takes note of his mixed Asian and white heritage.) Significantly, the decision was made in 1999, the same year as the film's release, to make the choice "other" available in the race category of the National Census. This official recognition that people who don't fit into one racial "box" do exist in demographically significant numbers represents a significant paradigm shift in our national conceptions of race, one which this film recognizes by making a character of mixed race its hero, literally "the One," humanity's only hope against oppressive whiteness and the enslavement and eventual eradication of humanity which it represents in the film.

Neo unites within himself the rainbow of races which have come to stand for "the human" in the film; like the stunning special effect termed "recursive action," or as John Gaeta, the effects coordinator of the film calls it (in the DVD edition), "the fist bouquet," Keanu makes visible all the different varieties of color including white; his hybridity is marked as the only available corrective to the agents of whiteness.

Machines take on the onus which previously belonged to racial "others" and unite non-white men and white women against a system or matrix of white purity and privilege as exemplified by institutions such as the law and the corporation, specifically high tech corporations. Here, the film's critique of information technologies and their alliance with capitalism is particularly apparent; the company that Neo works for, Metronex, is staffed almost entirely with white men, as is the digital Construct which is part of the rebels' training program.

The idea that all whites are, unwittingly or not, "agents" of the racism-machine to some extent, relates to George Lipsitz's notion of the "possessive investment in whiteness."[7] In his book of the same name, Lipsitz explains the dynamics by which whites often unknowingly consent to the perpetuation of their own entitlements and privilege in relation to non-whites. Lipsitz is anxious to note that not all whites participate in this system, indeed many whites have resisted it strongly and continue to do so, but the fact that there are an array of ready-made institutions or machinic systems designed to produce white privilege provides them with that choice, a choice lacking to non-whites. The fact that the possessive investment in whiteness is often unconscious gestures towards the nature of racism in the age of multiraciality and multiculturalism, a time when claiming such privilege overtly classes one in a socially undesirable category, that of white supremacist or racist. As Morpheus says of the business-suited whites peopling the Construct, or world which enslaved humans think they are living in, these plugged-in people think they are living in the real world, but instead are experiencing a hallucination, and thereby have been made "so helplessly inert, so dependent on the system, they will fight to protect it." It is not possible to "liberate" such humans; like the majority of whites as described in Lipsitz's work, they are dependent on the system of privilege which allows them to be on the winning side of information age capitalism and the machines which underpin it. To unplug them from their dream of whiteness and its attendant comfort would be to kill them. This may explain the lack of white men among the Rebels; theoretically, non-whites and women are the ones who would *want* to wake up from this particular dream.

Cypher betrays the other crew members precisely because he wants to jump the ship of multiculturalism and reclaim his possessive investment in whiteness.[8] He negotiates with Agent Smith, who addresses him as Mr. Reagan— a fine jab at the trickle-down capitalism of the 1980s which perpetuated white privilege—to be "replugged" into the system, where he can eat steak and drink red wine in a fine restaurant. The fact that he knows that this privilege is an illusion (the steak and wine are digital simulations provided by the agents) and that he must kill his crewmates to get it signifies the ways in which the virtual have colonized the real, to the detriment of the real, and most importantly, the ways in which white maleness is always constructed as suspect in the film. In the scene where he kills Apoc, Switch, and Dozer, and almost kills Tank, he relates that his grievances have specifically to do with the lack of privilege and entitlements he feels in the real world. He cries "I'm tired of this ship, tired of being cold, tired of eating the same goddam glop every day."

He wants to be the "One," feels entitled to be the One, but the multicultural logic of the film will not allow it. In order for the critique of whiteness to be completed he must be the Lu(Cypher) of the story and his white hubris must be punished by death. Indeed, his claims to be oppressed while he is receiving no less and no more than any other crew member—we are pointedly shown that everyone eats the same glop, which issues from a tube in the ship—invokes the ways that a lack of white privilege can be experienced as oppression. Lipsitz notes the case of Allan Bakke and the ways that it mobilized protest against affirmative action; in this case the "language of liberal individualism serves as a cover for collective group interests,"[9] the interests of whites. In the DVD version of the film, this section is entitled "Dealing for Bliss," a title which takes note of the deals that whites can make, with themselves (i.e. denial or incomprehension that a deal has even taken place), and with the institutions and practices which underpin racism.

"The Matrix" constructs a new discourse of race in the digital age, one which plugs us in to our own dream-worlds about cyber-utopias and cyber-futures. And like any dream, it is conflicted. It opens a window into our cultural anxieties, fears, fantasies, and desires, about the Internet and the roles of blacks, whites, machines, and all combinations thereof. Like the Internet, the Matrix looks the way we want it to look or have made it look; it is symptomatic of our visions of utopia. It is a construct, a wonderland of sorts, as the film's frequent reference to Lewis Carroll's *Alice in Wonderland* signal broadly. As Morpheus says to Neo about the Matrix, "Your mind makes it real."

Indeed, cyberspace engenders particular questions about what is "real," and the implications of these questions are increasingly unavoidable today; as pundits of digital culture debate such problems as the reality of on-line relationships, chat room identities, and the status of the self on the Internet, we are faced with a radical interrogation of the nature of personal identity. Millions of users create on-line identities via email, chat rooms and web-construction which may vary quite a bit from their Real Life identities. This signifies the desire for elasticity in identity-construction; it gestures towards a sense that we are more than we appear, or wish to be read differently than we are, and that we can use cyberspace to create versions of ourselves that look, and in some sense, are, different from ourselves. Much research has been done on this phenomenon of gender (and to a much lesser extent racial) cross-dressing or masquerade on the Internet, and the jury is still out on whether this should be viewed as a progressive aspect of the Internet, one which liberates users and encourages democratic social relations, or whether it simply re-duplicates old gender and race hierarchies.[10] The Matrix is an embodied cyber-space, meaning that in order to be there you have to have a body, albeit a digital body. This body, which is created by the mind, is known in cyberspace literature as an avatar.[11] The avatar is described by Morpheus to Neo as "residual self-image…it is the mental projection of your digital self."

Thus, while the real Neo is wearing a tattered sweater, his head is shaved, his skin is pale and unhealthy looking, and his body still bears the marks of the plugs and ports that connected him to the sinister machines, the Neo-in-cyberspace has coiffed hair, stylish black clothing, and looks as glam-orous as only Hollywood lighting and excellent makeup can make him look. Indeed, all of the rebels undergo this transformation while they are in the matrix fighting the agents; they wear full length leather coats, natty Prada-ish suits, painfully stylish haircuts, excellent sunglasses, and high tech PVC fabrics and silks.[12]

This transformation, like the changes in self-presentation which Internet users execute when they create a visual "self" to deploy in cyberspace, says a great deal more about what users *want* rather than who users *are*. Or rather, in cyberspace it boils down to the same thing. The striking aspect of the way the

Matrix's avatars look has to do with the solidity of race. Avatars can look any way you want them to: They are aspects of "residual self-image." The term "residue" seems to signify that the mind "re-members" the body only partially; when it constructs itself in the Matrix aspects of it are left out. Race is part of this residue, it is that which the mind identifies as belonging to itself, an essential and indispensable part of itself. Hence, none of the characters are differently raced when in the Matrix. Instead, they create versions of themselves that are differently classed: Glossier, better dressed, more powerful. They upgrade themselves and the accoutrements of class identity: their clothes, their abilities, their hair (lots of hair gel in the Matrix), their weapons and cars. But their race stays the same throughout. In a world where you can download special abilities, such as Kung-Fu, Ju-Jitsu, and the ability to fly a B-211 helicopter, knowledge is a fluid thing, yet race remains solid; it is inseparably part of the self in a way that mere class cannot be.

However, in contemporary Internet practice, users change their gender and race all the time. Why does the film leave this more radical transformation out of the picture? (Highly publicized stories about men on the Net who really turn out to be women are fodder for talk shows.) While the critique of whiteness and machines together seems to affirm multiculturalism and hybridity as correctives to the alienation and exploitation of most humans today, the film passes up a prime opportunity to question the monolithic nature of race more radically. Race is not a fluid in this film but rather a solid in the sense that while hackers into the Matrix can change just about any aspect of themselves, they cannot or, significantly, do not choose to change their race.

I read this move as an affirmation that race matters: Racial diversity is depicted as a source of the hero's strength. (And, of course, there is the matter of movie stars needing to get their proper amount of screen-time. Since Keanu Reeves' name is above the title on the promotional material, we can expect that film goers' expectations to see him during most of the film must be indulged.) Non-whiteness is what makes the real humans different from the artificial agents. Race serves to anchor the viewer in the real, a crucial function in a film which sets out to bend viewers' minds regarding the status of the real,[13] a status which is changing at a vertiginous rate in our world as well.

Neo's nausea and vomiting when he discovers that what he thought was the real him is simply a version or digital avatar of him, signifies that sense of nausea which goes along with rapid and unexpected movement. Vertiginous shifts in cultural, physical/ontological, and epistemological points of view are engendered by digital identity-switching. In a sense, his nausea mirrors our own in the face of radical instability regarding personal identity. Race in general and blackness in particular stabilize this cyber-vertigo of identity; as Neo wakes from his pod-induced trance, his first sight in the real world is the face of a black man, Morpheus. The first words that Neo hears as a real person are "Welcome to the real world." These particular words, coming as they do from Laurence Fishburne's character, signify that the real world *is* black, solid, to-be-trusted, and worthy of being defended.

In fact, the only two characters who have never been exploited by the machines are Tank and Dozer, two black men who are "100 percent pure home-grown human" since they were born in Zion, the last outpost of human civilization. The traditional colonial mission of civilizing the disorder and disarray of savages has been retrofitted and revamped to fit this movie's multicultural politics: The Great White Hope of the last humans on earth are black men and women, at least until this point in the film.

The position of black women in the film is far more vexed, however. The Oracle's authority and power as a black woman and a source of knowledge are undermined by her depiction as a woman baking cookies, wearing an apron, and living in a housing project. In a film so much about visual style and beautiful futuristic couture, her dowdy appearance and position securely in the lower classes seems to signify the place of black women in the future as well as the present. While the film envisions a multicultural crew resisting the white hegemony, as embodied by the Agents and their agent, Cypher, it can't yet incorporate black women into this group of real humans except as supporting characters. Indeed, the Oracle's function as the nurturer of "potentials," or candidates (most of whom are children) for the position of the One, continues the familiar trope of black women as mammies or supportive and willing domestic workers. The Oracle's apparent satisfaction with her traditionally racialized role as a glorified child-care worker and giver of advice to the hero represents the limits of this multiculturalist fantasy of inter-human democracy. Perhaps women of color represent the real "potentials" in this film, a potential that remains untapped and unrealized in this narrative of the future.

The crew of Morpheus's hovercraft *Nebuchadnezzar* resembles the population of Los Angeles as it is projected to look in the near future, that is, whites are a minority. However, in the face of dire anxieties regarding the future of multicultural cities and white flight from them, the ship is depicted as an ideal community, a hopeful and determinedly un-glamorous coalition of oppressed workers fighting the machine. This model of community is diverse, real, gritty, dense, warm, close, and caring. They seem happy to be eating their gruel together, and united in their purpose. (Cypher is the exception to this rule, and, hence, the traitor.) However, the plot kills them one by one, leaving only Morpheus, Neo, and Trinity—a trinity composed of a black man, a multiracial man, and a white woman.[14] The disturbing aspect of this resolution has to do with the eradication of community as the solution to machine-induced slavery and exploitation, and its replacement by the cool imagery of Neo's sun-glassed face in the film's closing scenes as he assumes his mantle as the One.

This notion of there only being One who counts in struggles against white oppression redoubles the rhetoric of heroic individuality which has haunted civil rights movements since the martyrdoms of Martin Luther King and Malcolm X. Trinity and Morpheus are reduced to girlfriend and sidekick-mentor, effectively turning them into support-staff for the One. Morpheus in particular is shunted off to the sidelines and turned into a Tonto to Neo's Lone Ranger; he is rendered "serviceable" in Toni Morrison's use of the word to describe the function of blacks in American fiction.[15] Morpheus's presence makes Neo even more the One, even more a lone hero, since he stands for those things which Neo is not: Bounded, limited, vulnerable, defeatable by whites. He and Trinity, whose only purpose in the plot, at this point, is to confirm Neo's status as the One by being in love with him (an all-too-familiar reminder of the uses to which female characters are put in Hollywood generally), are discarded entirely in the film's final scene in which Neo delivers a monologue into a pay phone.

This film's ending is frustrating because it seems to take back the progressive images of race and multiracial communities, which had been advanced from the beginning, and replaces them with an anti-communitarian figure of authority and power—the lone hero. Its ultimate message about multiculturalism in the future is to assert the solidity and abiding presence of race as a "real" thing, a serviceable thing, as well as construct a hero whose race is so ambiguous as to be readable as white or not.

Keanu Reeves is a stealth minority; many viewers do not know that he is multiracial.[16] His casting reflects the notion of race as "residual self-image": Reeves is read in ways that reflect viewers' own preoccupations and notions of race more accurately than they reflect anything about the actor himself. Perhaps this makes him a perfect type to become a hero by dominating machines; half-machine himself, at least according to some film reviewers' writings about his (lack of) actorly affect and style, his position on the boundary of white and "other" calls attention to the status of race as a matrix, no more real than viewers' perceptions of it. But, as we know from observing hiring practices, mortgage terms, the prison-industrial complex, and the continuing segregation of neighborhoods, race doesn't need to be real to accomplish things in the world. As Morpheus says in reference to the Matrix, "Your mind makes it real."

Neo's final monologue, which is directly addressed to the viewer, asks us to "imagine a world without limit or controls, borders or boundaries." One could read it as an echo of Morpheus's exhortation to Neo while he is training him to believe in himself enough to leap from one building to another: "Free your mind." The difference has to do with the rhetoric. Both of these commands ask their interlocutors to challenge authority, but with a crucial difference, a *racial* difference. "Free your mind" has long been a staple phrase of funk and popular music, much of which has an anti-racist bent. Bootsy Collins' and En Vogue's iterations of the phrase ask the listener to "free your mind and your ass will follow." En Vogue follows this up with another verse: "Be color blind, don't be so shallow." Freeing your mind of racism is a task as hard as learning to fly from building to building, it would seem. Neo's challenge to imagine a world

without limits echoes an infamous MCI commercial from the mid-nineties entitled, "Anthem," which tells the viewer to "imagine a world without boundaries...Utopia? No! The Internet!"[17]

This is the rhetoric of commercial digital utopianism.[18] The appeal to a cor-
porate/commercial discourse is opposed to the discourse of civil rights and
multiculturalism. Its promise is to bridge the digital divide[19] by setting up a
hero who will "free the minds" of others. This leaves out a scenario in which
others might free their own minds. The multiracial and multicultural community has been sacrificed to produce this leader, and, most significantly, they
have been depicted as eager to do so. Morpheus's determination to sacrifice
himself for Neo (his cry to Trinity to take Neo away from the agents, while he
stays behind is: "He's the only one who matters now!") is disturbing in that it
constructs him, in all his blackness and, in the logic of the film, attendant real-
ness, as an ancillary character, an adjunct or assistant to the One, and as accepting of life on these terms. He truly is a "supporting character" despite
Fishburne's superior abilities as an actor at making the character of Morpheus
seem "like a real person," verisimilitudinous in a way that Reeves never is.

Neo's promise to construct a world without boundaries places the responsibility for leadership in this quest upon the figure of the lone hacker.[20] This
utopic vision of a world in which humans regain their control over machines
glosses over disturbing questions about mastery in the digital age. To return to
Lewis Carroll, and cite his sequel to *Alice in Wonderland, Through the Looking
Glass*, the question which Humpty Dumpty directs to Alice in her travels
through Wonderland, the virtually real, is, "Who is to be master?"[21] This question is indeed the one to consider, and in the context of this film and our culture
today, it can be broken down as follows: Can whites continue to be master in the
face of globalization and racial/cultural hybridity? Must whites, or institu-
tionalized investments in white privilege, continue to structure access to information and media? Will the machines win by making us their agents? Does
global capital make us all agents of the hegemony in ways that we can't resist
or even see? Whose interests are being served in the world of the Internet? Must
there be a Master, a One, or can the notion of heroic and lone leadership be

replaced by community and consensus instead? What is the place of the Real and the place of race in the world of the virtual?

While cyberspace may be touted as a world without boundaries or limits, the real is ineluctably bounded. Just like the hovercraft *Nebuchadnezzar*, where all the real action in the film occurs, it is a *place* rather than an unbounded space. The quest to understand this place, to recognize the raced and gendered cultures and people which occupy it and make it real, needs to be undertaken by the many, rather than the One. Beneath the great look of the film, the sleek and telegenic images of technology and machines, lies the insight that we are in much the same position of the enslaved humans trapped in their pods, dreaming that they are living lives of privilege which do not exploit others. This matrix of racism is the thing from which we must free our minds. While it is tempting to "deal for bliss," to buy into the prepackaged vision of the cyber-society as a democratic, race-less, free space, doing so means engaging in a deal which perpetuates the digital racial divide. Inequities of access, power, and representation are real. And the means of addressing these problems: Community networking, funding for public technology education, better support for families and children, etc., will not come from machines and networks, but rather from people who are willing to all eat the same "glop," so to speak. Only then can the promise of cyberspace and the Internet to democratize social relations move from the realm of Wonderland's dreams to the lived realities of humanity in all its diversity. ★

Acknowledgements: I would like to thank Drea Moore for assistance with research, and members of the Sonoma State University Faculty Writing Group: Kathy Charmaz, Kim Hester-Williams, Richard Senghas, Elaine McHugh, Adam Hill, and Dolly Freidel, as well as Tim Wandling, Scott Miller, Anne Goldman, and Leilani Nishime at Sonoma State, for support and assistance.

1   William Gibson, *Neuromancer* (New York: Ace, 1984), p. 51.

2   Ted Anthony, "At the Movies: The Matrix," *Entertainment News*, March 30, 1999, Internet.

3   N'Gai Croal, "Maximizing the Matrix." *Newsweek*, April 19, 1999, p. 64.

4   The directors' commentary on the DVD version of "The Matrix" also omits the topic of race entirely, as do the actors'. There are no references to race at all in the wealth of additional and supporting material provided on this state-of-the-art DVD.

5 This is another cautionary reference to the Internet: In 1996, digital agents were celebrated in *Wired* magazine as the next new thing in cyberspace. These software programs were supposed to do the tedious work of searching out information in cyberspace; in this film they've acquired sentience, rebelled, and taken over the system.

6 In the DVD commentary to "The Matrix," Laurence Fishburne says that "Morpheus is a person who lives in the real world."

7 George Lipsitz, *The Possessive Investment in Whiteness: How White People Profit from Identity Politics* (Philadelphia: Temple University Press, 1998), p. vii.

8 Cypher also has a possessive investment in maleness; as he says to Neo while looking at the monitor of coded signs that represent the software of the Matrix, "all I see is blonde, brunette, redhead." This is the only invocation of sexist language in a film which depicts women as formidable warriors and computer hackers. Trinity is both a fighter and the person who "hacked into the IRS D-base." Part of Trinity's role in the film is to school Neo and the viewer that women can "hack it" too. When Neo comments "I thought you were a man" when he learns of her software expertise, she responds by saying "most men do," a clever acknowledgment and rebuke of gender stereotypes.

9 Lipsitz, p. 22.

10 See Sherry Turkle, *Life on the Screen: Identity in the Age of the Internet* (New York: Simon and Schuster, 1995); Allucquère Rosanne Stone, *The War of Desire and Technology at the Close of the Mechanical Age* (Cambridge: MIT Press, 1995); and Lynn Cherny and Elizabeth Reba Weise eds., *Wired_Women: Gender and New Reality in Cyberspace* (Seattle: Seal Press, 1996) for discussions of cross-gender role-playing in cyberspace. See Lisa Nakamura, "Race In/For Cyberspace: Identity Tourism and Racial Passing on the Internet," in *CyberReader*, 2nd edition (Boston: Allyn and Bacon, 2000) for an examination of cross-racial passing on the Internet. See also *Race in Cyberspace*, eds., Beth Kolko, Lisa Nakamura, and Gil Rodman (New York: Routledge, 2000).

11 The term "avatar," used to describe a visual digital representation of a self in cyberspace was first coined in popular literature by Neil Stephenson in his novel *Snow Crash* (New York: Bantam, 1992). He writes "your avatar can look any way you want it to, up to the limitations of your equipment. If you're ugly, you can make your avatar beautiful. If you've just gotten out of bed, your avatar can still be wearing beautiful clothes and professionally applied makeup." p. 36.

12 In *Fashions of the Times*, "The Matrix" is cited, along with the film "Gattaca," as a "fashion show." Mitchell, Elvis, "Character Assassination," *The New York Times Magazine* (special supplement) Part 2, Spring, 2000. While wardrobe is a necessary component of the visual field which signifies to film viewers that the action is taking place in the future rather than now, the article's author claims that the cutting-edge fashions actually overshadow the plot.

13 When at the beginning of the film Neo is shown extracting black-market recreational software from a hollowed out volume entitled *Simulation and Simulacra*, these issues are being foreshadowed fairly overtly.

14 The black character Tank, though left for dead by Cypher, does manage to survive and in fact kills Cypher. This allows him to continue as the crew's "operator," and to eventually pull the heroes out of the Matrix back into the real world, thus reinforcing the connections the film has built between "raced" characters and the Real. However, his role in the film is somewhat effaced; he operates behind the scenes, much like the Oracle, and never participates in any of the telegenic battles with the agents which contain most of the film's narrative high points.

15 Toni Morrison, *Playing in the Dark* (New York: Vintage, 1992), p. 64.

16 It seems that this "open secret" is constructed primarily by viewers' own residual self-images or identifications; while Asians tend generally to know Reeves' interracial status, whites do not.

17 *Anthem*, 1997, produced by Messner Vetere Berger McNamee Schmetterer for MCI.

18 See Lisa Nakamura, "'Where Do You Want to Go Today?' Cybernetic Tourism, the Internet, and Transnationality," in *Race in Cyberspace*.

19 See Donna Hoffman and Thomas P. Novak "Bridging the Digital Divide: The Impact of Race on Computer Access and Internet Use," Project 2000, Vanderbilt University, Internet, 29 January 1999. Available: <http:/www2000.ogsm.vanderbilt.edu/papers/race/science/html> for a discussion and explanation of low usage of the Internet by minorities compared to whites.

20 This is very much a convention of cyberspace narrative since its inception. See Scott Bukatman, *Terminal Identity: The Virtual Subject in Postmodern Science Fiction* (Durham: Duke University Press, 1993).

21 Lewis Carroll, *The Lewis Carroll Book* (New York, Tudor Publishing, 1939), p. 238.

Moscow: Fortress City

Irina Aristarkhova

Quiet, quiet, my loud age,
By me, floods—and future generations.
—MARINA TSVETAEVA, 1931

I am the place of your birth, the birth of the New World, the only world.

Writing is auto-bio-graphy, auto-matically, physically. Does a city have such autobiography? Does it write? Does it leave marks? Has the place of your birth left marks on you? Marked you out? Marked you inside out?

Is your mother a place? Desire to desire, forgetting and remembering, playing fort/da,—you just know that you cannot take another step as soon as you have realized that you are THERE forever. Either UP there, or DOWN there, as they say. You can only confirm it. And you do. Just recollect your dreams.

...in many places Moscow looks as tightly sealed as a fortress.
—*WALTER BENJAMIN, 1927*

The Kremlin is not like any other palace, it is a city in itself; a city that forms the root of Moscow, and that serves as a fortress between two quarters of the world... —MARQUIS DE CUSTINE, 1839

Moscow acted out the primal scene of the 20th century, the place where it all started. A womb or birth-place that citizens of the world will never be able to experience without some sort of bowel movement. As an abject mother of the "Soviet monster," an embodiment of the specter of communism, totalitarianism, terror, etc., Moscow realized its dream of immaculate conception of delivering the third Rome, the holy city, the New World.

From the early years of Moscow and the Kremlin, its fortress, subsequent generations had been left with fortress consciousness. The Kremlin multiplied obsessively, expanding and enclosing in successive concentric circles, like a matreshka *(nesting Russian dolls) into the surrounding regions. Every major Russian city was striving to have a Kremlin or one semblance of it. Fortification also became*

I know I can help you to move, for I do it every day and every night. When I read that you are "not able to return from" Moscow, Berlin, New York; from HOME/birthplace/mother tongue, that you are travelling, fleeing, running, writing, collecting,—struggling—I tell myself: yes, you are still MINE, and mine forever. Do I have a choice in having you or freeing you? Yes, …yes,—I do.

Do I still want you? Want you inside myself? This question is with me, you know. If I leave you just for a while, just to give birth to you, just to teach you to make your first step, to walk, I know I leave you in-between birth and death. I even help you in teaching you how to substitute the word "birth" with the word "life," so that you are left between "life" and "death," and you think both belong to you. I made you think that way.

Always in place? In my body. Now…GO. Walk away. Find out for yourself. And by the way, call me not "yours" or "my birthplace." Too many of you do it. I contain the army. I contain the nation. I contain all past and future heroes, the people, the matter, the air you breathe. If you want to be *special, different, not*

a primary operation in the domestication of conquered territory. For example, the Russian appropriation of the Siberian 'body politic' started in 1571 with Ivan the Terrible's system of fortifications. It was a series of southern ostrogi *(forts) to fend off Tartar attacks behind which Ivan the Terrible established peasant* slobody *(settlements). Fortifications were used to establish the boundaries of what was conceived to be Russia and Russian. Then, in addition to serving as places to deport "the depopulated" of Russia, these fortification towns and villages helped to clarify spatially and politically what constituted Russia.*

Catherine the Great's Russification policy used the fortress logic to build up identifiable borders of the Russian national identity using the language of French Enlightenment. It is noteworthy that in the first ukaz *(edict) of 1764, this policy was articulated as a means of assimilating the Cossacks into the Russian population, and bringing them to 'acceptable cultural standards', since 'they lacked social discipline and intellectual sophistication'. At the same time the issue of the protection and defense of Russians within an ever-growing Russian the same*—and this is what you have always asked for—if you want to be *the chosen one*, then this is the way to weave the words of the new world. New World: Is there something more trivial for the Muscovite ear? Trust me: I've imagined this world for you, and everyday you continue to rename me and your-self—anew, obsessed with the past.

Do not call me your "Mother." Do not call me "Mother-Russia." Do not call me "Mother-land." Do not call me "Mother-Earth." Unlearn these words before coming back—to your senses. This is my last lesson as a mother. I am your first word and your last word, never mind what is written there in your sacred texts. Calm down. Sleep. Eat, darling, eat. Sleep is good for you, food is good for you. I am good for you.

...

In Russia everyone wants to belong to Moscow. Everyone wants to be able to claim: 'I live in Moscow.' Even though after such claims some are as ready to disclaim the use of it, its importance, and try to "purify" themselves of what

territory was addressed. It was estimated that the 'original' Russian state covered approximately 15,000 square miles in 1462, but had since then expanded at a rate of some fifty square miles a day over a period of four hundred years, creating a vast empire of about 8,660,000 (constituting one-seventh of the total land surface of earth) by 1914. Setting out the borders of 'Russian way' or 'Russian soul' meant that those who were incompatible with it were to be expelled from within fortress-Russia. In some sense, it is in the Kremlin where one finds the roots of the Gulag. To claim that the Gulag is the result of Bolshevism or communism, as argued by Solzhenitsyn among others, is to be blind to Russian history and especially to the way in which Russian national identity has been historically complicitous in this process. Still today the expres-sion "soty kilometr" (100th kilometer) remains familiar to Muscovites. "100th kilometer" refers to the distance of 100 kilometers from the official borders of Moscow, it is a circle with Moscow in the center; an area that former convicts and other officially prohibited citizens were not to enter. Russian identity with

I call '*Moskvacentrism* (Moscow-centrism).' How many times you read: In "Moscow, Russia?" Let's face it: Moscow=Russia. When you write of Moscow, you write of Russia by default. Many non-Muscovite Russians hate Moscow and Muscovites. Till they become Muscovites themselves. However, here again birth is significantly different from life. It is true that those who live in Moscow already lay claims to some writing rights. But they are still only partly Muscovites. In Moscow these things mean a lot: Whether you are born as Muscovite or you *only* have become a Muscovite. That is, which generation immigrant are you?

You must be already wondering: What about the author? Do I have the right to write on Moscow because my name sounds Russian? Because I am Russian? Let me assure you: I have full right to write on Moscow. I WAS BORN IN MOSCOW. I WAS BORN IN RUSSIA. I WAS BORN IN THE USSR.

Moscow is mine through and through. Full stop. Those who were not born in this place, will always be haunted by a desire to possess it, *in one way or*

another. Something that is given (as a birth-right) is experienced differently from something that is conquered. It means that one and one's parents do not need "to make it" to Moscow. One *has* Moscow. One has attitude. One does not need to learn it, to mimic it, to wear it. Performance is *natural*, given by and taken with mother's milk. Muscovites can identify each other by smell, by gaze, by being the makers and the center of the universe called the "Russian empire." Muscovites have that famous Muscovite accent that betrays me anywhere. Actually, that privileges me, marks me out as special, as some 'chosen one,' as the lucky one. One cannot buy an accent, one can only spend years or hours of hard work on trying to speak what Russians call *'without* accent,' that is, in Muscovite accent, just like many Russian actresses and actors had to do in order to work in Moscow. In order to call Moscow "theirs." However, it is mine. By birth-right: Mother, thank you. Moscow is my Mother-land. It is my Mother-tongue. It is a place where I was born, I live in; a place I love.

...

Moscow at its center has been fortifying itself in many different ways and it seems many of those practices and discourses have been utilized for building Russia and the USSR as well.

The fortification logic of Moscow, that has been essential for the constitution and territorial consolidation of the Russian nation, is of dual nature. On the one hand, it guards its borders and imagines itself to be in constant danger, ever vigilant to aliens of all sorts. On the other hand, Moscow propels itself outwards, feeding off its internal turbulence (after all, the root word for Moscow, mosk, means 'turbulent') that is realized in the centripetal expansion of Russia. Kremlin walls absorbed urbanization in 1147 once and forever. The rest of Moscow, as many have insisted, is a "big village." No matter how many Stalinist stone buildings have been erected and how Moscow parades its current construction work, it ultimately fails to be simply *a city, one of the world's capitals. It is* the city. *The rest of Russia is destined to make sure that* only *Kremlin embodies Russia as such. The rest of Russia, as a whole, is residue, excess, discharge, is*

Do not take me seriously. I am not expecting it. You know when *woman writes*, she writes by her heart, pure emotions speak through her. Being Russian, woman doubles her lack. Lack of sense. Lack of reason. And if you want me/her…to remain "Russian woman" —*as you know her*—let me kill you, or let me sacrifice myself, or let me suffer. But remember: *Russkiye ne sdaútsya* [Russians do not surrender]. So you have to let me remain certain, remain *standing* in my holiness. Or I would lose my identity, therefore you would lose yours. Do you want it? Think again, how many hopes would be lost, how many pleasures will not happen. Do not give me your questions. Just enjoy me, just experience me. I do not speak your language, and you cannot speak mine, even if both of us seem to speak the *same* language. Translations are strong aphrodisiacs: Feel it. Let yourself go and do not feel guilty: I allow you. Come to me, Moscow, Russia.

You must excuse me—I forgot another important part of my Muscovite existence that's becoming crucial in the next millennium. Let me introduce myself

"the rest." Today, more than ever. Anyone who valorizes excess and margins must feel suffocated in this place: Space outside Kremlin is negative, it is a shadow. So much of space, so many cultures and civilizations have been systematically *swallowed for this* **one** *to claim a special destiny, to claim its red purity, to "surprise the world." To let THIS go, in order to wake up from a thousand-year old dream of wholeness and holiness, is, in the Russian imaginary, tantamount to treason. The dream clears all charges of responsibility.*

Entrances into fortresses are always ambivalent, as any vchod v ukrytie *[entrance to shelter]: What makes a fortress a fortress is its simultaneous elicitation and frustration of the desire of those outside it. In Russia 'fortress' has been translated into mythology, into law, into language and culture, into* national identity; *most clearly exemplified by the fortress city, "Kremlin." Russians are constantly* defending *themselves, being in a permanent state of anxiety of all sorts and kinds. However not to be desirable anymore is Kremlin's ultimate nightmare. If a fortress cannot sustain its attractiveness by all means, those properly* to ease our communication. I am Russian. I am not *just* a Russian citizen, not *just* Muscovite. I am ACTUALLY Russian. 100 percent. Though some of my Moscow friends claimed that my eyes are *a bit* Mongolian, but much less than those of Yeltsin or Lenin, of course. Still others were suspicious of my nose: It was suggested within earshot that my nose was *slightly* Jewish.

With the latest Chechen wars this question has acquired a stronger meaning, and I am proud to assure you that I am not just ethnically Russian (I hope you believe me by now). I am...BLOND. I am *naturally* blond, almost blindingly. Trust me—this is my real color (I've been asked many times). I am *really* white though I am not using any whitening lotions. My skin is delicate, properly white, *naturally* white skin. To make you understand what I mean: My skin does not tolerate sun. As a test ask yourself: If your skin does tolerate sun, you are not *completely* white by Muscovite standards. Among my school friends those of not completely white skin were called "Gypsy-likes." My eye color is grey-green, depending on the color of my clothes and mascara it becomes

who belong lose more than those outside. Defense of one's own "way of life" does not know the word "enough." Defense is the way to make sense of the world. It is not to say that somehow this siege mentality marks out Russia as a special case, but here it took on monstrous forms.

Anyone who lives in Moscow or comes into Moscow for more than three days knows this word: Propiska *or* registrastiya. *To be a Muscovite (temporarily or permanently) is to have "propiska"—best translated as* inscription *or* 'writing through'. *Without going too much into its history, this practice today has at least two dimensions: Spatial and legal. Spatial dimension is characterized by being allocated to a particular space, by being localized in a particular* home, *being fixed into a space and also being granted a space to place one's body. So it is a* spatio-corporeal inscription. *It provides control over the body and its movements in a city space. To be a Muscovite in this sense is written through one's body, it is to have a* Muscovite body.

The fact that Russians—to sustain their identity as spatially and ethnically greyer or greener. But of course the point is: It is not dark, it is not brown. It is light. When I was young and slim, sometimes I looked like the Venus by Botticelli. And you?

It is often said that 'logos' and rationality do not operate in Moscow, Russia, especially in our "irrational" post-Soviet era. We are "senseless," we are losing our sense! There are claims that we lack a tradition of metaphysics and 'proper' phenomenology. We are "naturally" *unreasonable*. We do not make sense, we can show it to you (on demand). Hence we must work on our reason urgently, otherwise we could be completely consumed by our "essential" passion for a "strong hand," our love for terror, for blood, for power. That is why we do not have anything to deconstruct. No, no! We are *scared* to even think of it: Have you not seen it? We speak your language, we call ourselves your Great Other (a child of the Big Brother). We can deconstruct *you*, but: Take your hands off me! You cannot possibly understand what it means to live here, to experience it, to have "Russian soul." It is irrational, it is maternal, eternally feminine. Today

stable and homogenous—have employed movings, re-movings, deportations and re-placements of peoples is well known. In the early period the main target of this activity was 'exchange' of the wealthiest native people with Russian merchants and deportation of conquered citizens to the interior of Moscow prin-cipality. For example, in 1486 merchants from Moscow replaced a few thousand people from Livonia. In 1656 'pro-Swedish' subjects from Ingria, Finland and Karelia (about 8,000 families from the latter two countries) were forced out of their homelands. Peter the Great continued to use this policy in 1708 when on invading Dorpat in the Baltic region its German citizens were forcefully relocated in long caravans to Vologda (known today as povólgskie nemcy, *Volgian Germans). Russian national identity, based on the principle of homo-geneity to be defended by fortification, found its earliest instantiation in the strategies of exile and deportation.* Propiska *is one of more modern means to keep* nezelatelnye elementy *(undesirable elements) away from places of strate-gic importance, specifically Moscow.*

more than ever it needs "borders," "reason," it needs a strong frame of meta-physics and rationality. At the end of the day, we say that the Soviet period was alien to great Russia, holy Russia. It was "sin" what those communists had com-mitted. What can save us now? The Russian Orthodox Church and *solid, steady*, thought. Thought that is to survive centuries.

However, steady thought needs 'a man,' a hero, a thinker and a protector of Russian culture. All cultural aspirations today are directed towards this: A great man, a new Russian hero. You just wait, wait, you will see. He will be strong, he will be a genius, he will be beautiful, he will be Russian, and...he will, of course, live in Moscow (I could be HIM if I were not HER). Before we can think through heterogeneity and diversity, before we can think *with* Chechnya, *with* Tatarstan, *with* Kolyma, *with* you, WE NEED ANOTHER RUSSIAN HERO.

See for yourself: It takes eight centuries to deliver into the world the Union of Soviet Socialist Republics. They will all see; I will show them what we can deliver. At last, they all saw. Moscow has never felt more fertile and potent. It want-

Thus those without propiska *are to be constantly removed from Moscow, checked-on, moved around, deported, imprisoned, marked out in ethnic/racial/ sexual/class terms: prostitutes, non-whites, vagrants, migrants and refugees. This topographic inscription has an embodied power only if it exists as a stamp in a valid identity document—for Russian citizens, in their passport. This stamp in turn is supported/backed-up by papers in local registration offices. Identity papers, inscriptions, pictures and stamps within them discur-sively mark out the "sexualized" and "ethnicized" bodies of non-Muscovites and exclusive bodies of Muscovites. It is also important to note that since the break-up of the Soviet Union and introduction of the new Constitution of Russian Federation the practice of* propiska *has become unconstitutional. It remains in force only in Moscow, being called today "registration" instead of "inscription," most probably to neutralize it. The Moscow municipal government continues it despite constitutional and court orders. Moscow protects its status of exclusivity and desirability, making sure that the rest of Russia remains THE REST.*

ed more. It wanted to swallow the whole world. It was the mother of all poor and left children. What's next? Today we, Muscovites, do not try to protect everyone, do not claim to love everyone who agrees with us. In the new millennium I want to protect *my own* children. They are in danger. We are in danger. The danger is near our door. She/death is black, she is more fertile. Our kin might disappear. I must bear more children with my blood, with my skin, with my eyes. I must be a responsible citizen. Once again, my sons, my children, behind you— Moscow, behind you—Russia. Fighting, you defend your mother, your children, your bright future.

Can you ever come back/to/from home, mother(land), Moscow, the USSR, Russia—ME?

I am home. I am fortress.

That's all I am. Da? ★

```
⊓⊔⊓⊔⊓⊔⊓⊔⊓⊔⊓⊔⊓⊔⊓⊔⊓⊔⊓⊔
```

Let's imagine this bastion of Moscow, propiska, *falls soon. Will it change things? Only to a certain extent: Muscovites (therefore, Russians) have learned that the only way to keep fortress identity alive and impregnable is to keep it expanding, innovative, to make new "them." Historically it was the West or Asia, today it is "Islamic terrorism," "blacks from Caucasus," and even de-clines in the birth rates of ethnic Russians. Muscovites are "vsegda gotov" (always alert) like student-pioneers in Soviet schools, to defend our Motherland and Fatherland, to defend our women and children, to defend ourselves. Fortress-Kremlin-Moscow-Russia still guards its limits.*

I dream: Moscow will lose its identity, it will fail holy Russia, it will fail to surprise, to protect, attract, and deliver "them." ★

This essay was originally published in German in Rowohlt Literaturmagazin 46. New York, Berlin, Moskau: Traumstädte im "Traumstadtbuch" Hrsg. von Ralf Bänt, Dirk Vaihinger und Sylvia Sasse, 192 Seiten, gebunden ISBN: 3498039091 www.lipsius.de/literaturmagazin.html

The Woman Question: Addressing Women as Internet Users

Susanna Paasonen

What do female Internet users want? What kinds of online services are appealing to women? These are what one might call million dollar questions, and ones that service providers are desperately seeking answers to, even while trying out sites designed for women.

As a feminist media researcher, I often feel caught in a strange double-bind. On the one hand, there's a considerable body of writing on the subversive possibilities of the Internet as a site for trying out multiple identities, reworking fluid and unfixed gender boundaries, and subverting one's conceptions of gender identity.[1] Information networks are seen as sites for escape from the gender systems of everyday life, a Promised Land of sorts, and one especially suited for women and "feminine modes of communication."[2] On the other hand, these subversive potentialities are nowhere to be seen in the ways commercial services, information society agendas, and guide books address women as Internet users. Commercial services for women that reach vast audiences of female net users are a far cry from academic fantasies of fluid genders. Sites such as the U.S.-based Oxygen, or the Finnish services Nicehouse, Ellit, and MTV3's Naiset, or sites maintained by companies that produce sanitary products for women—like Tampax, Always, and Libresse[3]—illustrate quite a different take on gender and the Internet, one that is prone to reproduce and reinforce very familiar gender structures.

I will look at this gendering of online services for women, and argue for the importance of critical feminist intervention; my focus is on addressing women as Net users. These services, targeted at a wide range of audiences, are important platforms for articulating concepts of gender, and (re)producing specific understandings of women. Commercial Online Services (COS), Internet Service Providers (ISP), and various kinds of corporations have launched services for women with specific ideas of female Net users in mind. Roughly put, some of these services function as advertisements for the company behind them (Tampax, Libresse, Always). Others can be thought of primarily as a means for the company to profile itself as "woman-friendly," and thus address new customers (MTV3, Sonera), and yet others are attempts to create a profitable business that both attracts female users and provides advertisement income (Ladyvista, Nicehouse). The target groups vary from teenage girls to young urban professional and middle-aged women, although these emphases are not always obvious. What interests me here are the common features of these services, the gender categories that they are based on, the means used to attract female Internet users, and the ways in which these strategies of address are linked to wider discourses of women and technology.

I will illustrate practices of gendering with recent examples from memoranda on Internet and equality, popular guidebooks and overviews that address the so-called "woman question" on the Internet. These practices are linked to widespread frameworks for conceptualizing gender and information networks, frameworks that span national borders and exert a powerful influence politically as well as economically.

I am writing this text in Finland, a country widely recognized as a model "virtual society." It has one of the highest rates of Internet usage per capita, its economy is boosted by Nokia and its schools and institutions are carefully wired. As in other European countries, North America, and Asia, there are governmental information-society agendas that aim at securing the nation's position in the global marketplace. In economic and educational outlines alike, new media, especially information networks, are given high status as tools of the future, and the challenges and implications of rising information societies are the subject of academic research, as well as various regional and national strategies and memoranda. In this tradition of public policies, Internet users are discussed in seemingly gender-neutral terms as "citizens."[4] There also are, however, attempts to diversify the category of citizens by pointing to such markers as gender and locality. In 1998, for example, the Finnish Ministry of Transport and Communications published a memorandum on equality and information networks, with a special focus on women. The memorandum, to which I will return below, directly addressed gender difference, women's needs and likes as Net users, through anonymous expert interviews.

In terms of gender equality, Finland was the first country in the world to give women full political rights back in 1905, and in the spring of 2000 the first female president, Tarja Halonen,[5] was elected. A substantial majority of women are in fulltime employment, and more than half of all university graduates are female. One might think of Finland as a test-laboratory, both in terms of the information society and gender equality, but things are not that simple. Although the Finnish language lacks the semantic difference between *"she"* and *"he,"* this does not really translate as a culture free of gender bias, as a society with equal access, or equal pay for that matter. The processes and technologies of gendering are no less active in Finland than in other parts of the world. I would argue that the Finnish texts on women and the Internet, used below as illustrative examples, are applicable also to discussions of mapping and defining gender difference, women's needs and interests as Internet users elsewhere. The project of localizing female users/consumers is carried out by corporations on a national, as well as cross- and multinational level. Furthermore, the popular and fundamentally anti-feminist trend of socio-biology, as it has been employed to explain gender differences in Internet use, seems to have market value on a global scale.[6]

Broadly speaking, "the woman question" has surfaced in discussions of the Internet in two ways. First, women have been under-represented in technical skills, in content production, as well as online usage. This has been seen as a threat to plans for an equal information society, in which all information-intense citizens possess multiple media skills. It has also been a problem for

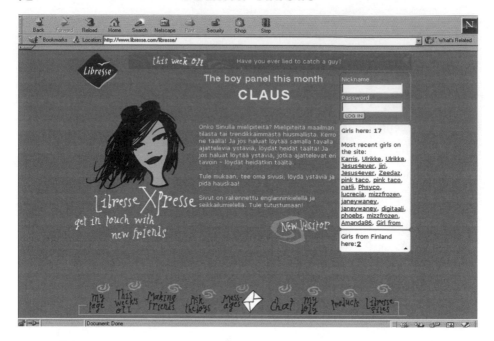

different service providers, who fail to reach the desired groups of female users. Second, the woman question has to do with how women could be better addressed as net users, and with what kinds of contents and services this could be accomplished. Discussions on gender and the Internet are often based on the construction of women as a collective *other* defined against the male norm. Internet services addressed to women always presuppose an understanding of what women are like, what unites them, and what they are interested in. These understandings are not necessarily based on market research, but on so-called common knowledge. Thus, the problem involves not only the ability of the media industry to provide services that reach women, but also its capacity to determine why women might be less interested in information networks, computer technology, and what "women actually want." Thus "the woman question" widens into ontological reflections on gender difference, women, and femininity. To put it bluntly, women as such become the problem to solve.

These articulations of women as Internet users are parts of a wider process, which, paraphrasing media scholar Cecelia Tichi, can be understood as a discursive production of a medium. Media texts, such as web sites, but also various—and often contradictory—texts by experts, popular overviews, commercials, and publicity all participate in the production of meaning through which a new medium becomes understood. Explaining and domesticating a medium is based on already existing discourses, values, and traditions that provide it with a cultural context.[7] The web site of Tampax, or the memorandum by the Ministry of Transport and Communications, for example, operate on different levels of authority, credibility, and desirability, and there is no guarantee that their addresses actually work. What I'm interested in are the continuities between these forms of address, and their location in wider discursive formations. Therefore, these texts and services should not be seen as merely descriptive, but as productive, active technologies that shape understandings of media technology and its use of gender and identity.

THE BIG DIFFERENCE

Services for women, as well as official memoranda on women and the Internet, presuppose a given gender difference, which can be based on evolution, genes, learned behavior, upbringing, or the common-sense knowledge that "women are different from men." Currently, various socio-biological explanations surface when gender difference is directly addressed in guidebooks, general interest articles, or memoranda. The fluid gender identities extolled in academic literature have little connection to these gendered uses of technology and understandings of gender difference primarily through the lenses of evolution history, thus reflecting the prevailing Western belief in biology as destiny.

A popular guidebook by Petteri Järvinen, as well as anonymous expert interviews in the memorandum by the Finnish Ministry of Transport and Communications, assume innate psycho-physical gender differences drawn from the twilight of evolution, from the gender-differentiated roles of man the hunter and woman the gatherer/nurturer. Gender difference becomes here something final and unchangeable, difficult to define, but mostly marked by women's inclination to social interaction and all things domestic, and men's determination and desire for exploration. According to these arguments, men became physically strong, handy with tools, and good with 3-D structures, since it was their role to provide for the family that waited in the domestic cave.[8] Thus, the gendered division of labor, as it was developed during the 19th century, becomes inscribed in the flesh. Projected to a million years ago, this model is depicted as an inescapable result of human evolution (and thus natural laws). Consequently, the links between women and femininity and men and masculinity are naturalized and turned into expressions of inner character.

The "natural" division between the public and the private resurfaces in several expert interviews by the Ministry of Transport and Communications. Men are associated with "hunting, tools and determination...men's hobbies [are] outside the home, women's at home. Because of this, men get a mobile phone, own a PC, and use cars a lot." Furthermore, "Men [have] a relationship with the machine, women are into human relations."[9] Thus the male drives of hunting and mastering tools, as well as the social nature of women, are genetically determined, automatically placing men behind the steering wheel and women by the stove. Even a superficial reading reveals the inconsistencies inherent in these propositions. For example, the acquisition of a PC might just as well be explained by domestic inclinations as by the opposite. Thus, these categories do not make any sense, or have any consistency, but can realign from moment to moment as the complete opposite of one another.

In these texts, the Internet is seen as gender-neutral, which is crucial in terms of information-society agendas aiming at greater female participation. Gender is depicted as a set of stable differences that structures experience (being, feeling, and communicating) in a way that resembles the logic of Mars and Venus, familiar from John Gray's internationally best-selling relationship guidebooks.[10] Ultimately, however, the woman question for Järvinen and others concerns a bias in women's attitudes towards technology: Gender ceases to be a problem only if women "act more like men." These understandings of gender follow a common-sense logic which, according to sociologist Judith Lorber, tends to see gender as bred into one's genes. The binary gender model and the universality of gender difference seek justification from nature, genes, and even the pairing practices of simians. In all cases, gender differentiates women from men almost as if they were from two different species. Genes and hor-

mones are upheld as unchanging factors that define needs, desires, and behavior. The natural gender difference thus produced functions as an ideological
justification of gender inequality. However, biology is not so clear cut and binary, and a biological body is always also a social body, one that is gendered
from the cradle to the grave. References to "the natural" are always cultural and
serve to justify and strengthen a given social order.[11] Current socio-biological
rhetoric justifies stereotypes of "emotional women" and men "that do not
iron," and thus supports a culturally specific gendered division of labor.

One solution to the woman question is to tailor Internet services especially
for women to meet needs specific to the group. What is it that women need,
then? According to Järvinen, there is a need for online versions of women's
magazines, cosmetics companies, Tampax, and clothing stores.[12] Thus understood, women are defined by an interest in their own appearances, quint-
essentially feminine consumer products, and the maintenance of heterosexual
desirability. Companies like Tampax have, in fact, invested great amounts of
resources into developing their online services into "communities for women,"
service sites that do not only do direct product promotion, but instead offer
channels for communication, asking questions, and exchanging experiences on
health and corporeality. The term "community" is used somewhat liberally,
since it refers more to the framework of the site than it does to its actual uses
or users. The discourse on virtual communities and community building of all
kinds has, during the past years, led to a general dilution of meaning, as networks, random points of contact, discussion forums, and mailing lists are all
referred to as "communities," often without further consideration.

The term "community," in sites by Tampax, Libresse, and Always, can also be
seen as a soft-core appropriation of the discourse of community within the
women's movement—of support and sharing experiences *among women*, but
without any political edge. The international on-line *Tampax Community for
Girls/Women* offers spaces for discussing women and health under the headline
"Women Know," plus a chat forum for young women, as well as a Net 'zine for
girls. *Always a Woman*, a site by the company Always, deals with the relations
between mothers and daughters, health, and growing up to be a woman, but it

also includes a discussion forum named "Sharing—Women Worldwide Helping Each Other." These communities maintained by sanitary-supply companies do, to a large degree, circulate the discourse of communication between women, women-only spaces, and a rhetoric of "shared experiences of womanhood." In addition to offering product information, the sites aim to function as support- ive communities of "sisters."

"Female spaces" on corporate web sites seem to be defined through a very familiar axis of embodiment (menstruation, reproduction, motherhood) and femininity as a set of values, characteristics, and practices (sharing, caring, emotions, social skills, mutual support). The shared experiences of women are depicted in pastel colors, with images of neatly attired, able-bodied women of various ethnic backgrounds smiling side by side. The diversity has obvious limits, and the sites do not give space to a redefinition of gender and/or femininity.

The *Secret Garden* by Libresse invites, in a somewhat separatist vein, only women users to discuss topics such as ideals of manhood, or the latest news on the Spice Girls: "You are welcome in the Libresse Secret Garden in whatever mood you are! The most important thing is that you are your own self. The only criterion is that you are a representative of girls, for all discussions are carried out only and exclusively 'among girls'! Here you can say out loud even your most secret dreams." The name of the service is intriguing, for it refers to men- struation as a "secret shared among us girls" and to the private and lush space of a garden instead of a more mundane chat-room, but it is also associated with female genitalia. The site emphasizes authenticity: Users are encouraged to be their true selves, and, so it seems, also "true," that is, biologically defined, "natural" women.

Libresse's online services are illustrative of how sites are both localized for different language groups (in the Nordic countries, with domains .fi, .se, .dk, and .no), and linked to an international site (.com). Thus the audience, and the community in question, is simultaneously national and cross-national, and uni- fied by the product manufacturer. Libresse's online services are clearly target- ed at teenage girls, and their international site seems to be structured around

gendering girls. The service includes, among other things, a possibility to "ask the boys" from different countries questions on dating, female attractiveness, and male preferences.

On November 3 and 4, 1999, among the questions addressed to a boy named Daniel were: "You look really good, Daniel :) And how must the girl of your dreams look?"; "Hey, Daniel…I just wonder…do boys really like girls with tight jeans, tight sweaters and high shoes…and the girls that laugh at everything? Please answer me!"; "Hi Daniel. What do you think about girls with big breasts? Tell the truth," and "Have you got a girlfriend?" The hot question of the week was, "What do you do to make a boy notice you?" Handsome young Daniel was situated here as the official male that could voice general male preferences. The genre of questions posed to him, as well as the general framework of the "ask

the boys" pages, clearly positions girls as interested in boys and in the preparation of their body both for boys and romance. Like romantic fiction for girls
in a study by Pam Gilbert and Sandra Taylor, Libresse's sites function as
technologies of gender that prepare girls to enter heterosexual practices, and
romantic love in particular, by instructing them in the ideological and discursive positions that produce and reproduce femininity. Femininity means,
both on the Libresse site and in Gilbert and Taylor's study, being socialized as
romantic and heterosexual, and female desire is defined through desirability,
and success in relationships.[13]

This making of girlhood takes place in specific settings, since Libresse's
international service also is based on chat options: "Do you have opinions?
Opinions about the state of the world to the latest haircut. Well, express them
here! And if you want to find friends who think like you, find them here! And if
you want to find friends who don't think like you, find them here too." The
friends who *think unlike* are not that easy to find, however. The rhetoric of
community is linked to a homogeneous construction of gender, since it is difficult to find discussions on other things than music, dating, looks, fashion, and
beauty. When registering as members of the community, users fill in a personal
profile that consists of a pet name, approximate age, favorite hobbies, music,
actors, web sites, ideal holiday destinations, and general self-descriptions. Profiles are visible whenever the user in question has logged onto the service. These
parameters of the self are very much focused on consumption preferences, and
they seem to function as guarantees of "thinking alike"—that is, of having similar orientations to heterosexual relationships, looks, and desirability.

The ways that media products recognize and address women also can be considered in relation to Louis Althusser's ideas on religion, family, education,
communication, culture, legislation, and profession as multiple ideological
state apparatuses that address—or, in his term, "hail"—subjects. According to
Althusser, it is typical of ideology to make things taken for granted function as
truisms. When faced with them we automatically and "naturally" cry, "That's
clear! Right! That's the way it is!"[14] Judith Butler has rethought hailing and
subjection as the gendering of bodies, in which bodies are named and situated

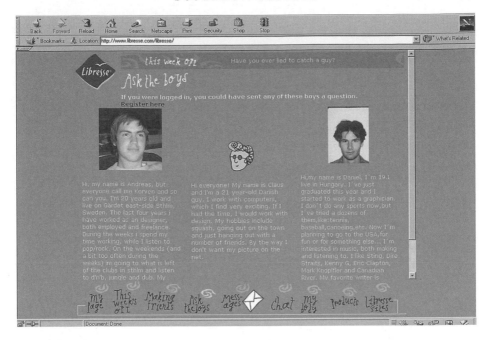

in the structure of illegibility, the heterosexual matrix. According to Butler, naming bodies male and female is the fundamental hailing that is the perquisite to the cultural legibility of an individual. To put it another way, gender difference, understood as a bipolar model structured by heterosexual desire, is a cultural truism that produces frameworks for thinking identity, corporcality, and desire in general.[15] Subjection means being addressed (hailed), and recognizing oneself as the object of address, as a subject. Girls are formed through the compulsory reiteration of norms that assume the continuity of body, gender, and desire as feminine, heterosexual womanhood.

Althusser emphasizes the contradictory and uneven nature of different mechanisms of interpellation. However, he understands subjection as a one-way process, whereas Butler emphasizes the possible failures of address, the ruptures and gaps between the discursive command and its appropriated effect.[16] The Libresse site, for example, is based on truisms about girls and their focus on looks and heterosexual attractiveness. These truisms provide the site with coherence, but their simplified and one-sided nature makes the gender norms strikingly visible and, perhaps, open for resistance.

Such more or less successful attempts at hailing can be thought of as technologies of gender that not only aim to position the target of address as a woman, heterosexual, teenager, etc., but also provide these categories with meaning. A technology of gender generates assumptions on what the subject category, and the subject, in question is like.[17] This "knowledge" is incoherent and often contradictory, as the notions of gender difference discussed above illustrate. If gender is thought of as an unstable result of continuous production, it is necessary to note the importance of common knowledge, and things taken for granted: That women are "known" to be talkative and social and men determined and technical, are examples of repeatable elements of common knowledge that reproduce the social order. Something becomes obvious when it is repeated over and over again: "Everybody knows," and "it is familiar to all," for example, that women's communication is intimate. Things taken for granted thus function as performatives, as acts of discourse with the power to create that to which they refer.[18] Simultaneously, they function as interpellating calls that reproduce the social order. It is exactly the taken-for-granted nature and transparency of such gendered practices of everyday life that supports the assumptions of gender as biology. Through constant repetition, these assumptions become common knowledge that doesn't require any proof or explanation—that, in fact, cannot be proved or verified. When common knowledge reaches transparency, it becomes a substitute for reality.[19] Repeated gendered practices thus naturalize gender difference and help to whisk women towards Venus, and men to Mars.

SOMETHING FOR THE LADIES

The rationality of female users is a recurring theme in discussions on women and the Net: For example, the Internet "doesn't save time or money, so it doesn't interest women," or "women usually surf the Net with determinacy, looking for something, whereas for men, surfing is often a purpose in itself, existentialist wandering in the ocean of information and humbug."[20] Women's Internet use is thus seen as well motivated and functional, linked to saving time and money, not fun or leisure. Paradoxically, then, women's Internet use is here defined as determined, and goal-oriented, which are mentioned above as innate *male* characteristics. Intimate, social, or emotional womanhood seems to have little space in these understandings of gender and Internet use. However, women are simultaneously associated with compulsive, uncontrollable, passive and basically useless, media use. Thus, television, cinema, radio, magazines, and romantic fiction alike have addressed women as their most central source of income. The intimate relationship between women and consumption (as opposed to men and production) has positioned women as primary consumers of media, who are addressed by various content providers and advertisers.[21]

The passiveness often associated with consumption of television—and consumption at large—has been given a range of feminine features. The Ministry of Transport and Communications also presented assumptions of television viewers as passive female consumers numbed by the televisual program flow in the memorandum. The gendered differences in media uses find their meaning in a bipolar framework of active vs. passive, which is often complemented by the conceptual dualism of old and new media. In such divisions, men are often positioned as the forerunners and users of new and experimental media, while women are defined as conservative users of older media, like TV, radio, and print media.[22] It makes a kind of sense, then, that when women are addressed as Internet users, services designed especially for them use and recycle representations from other media products targeted at women, such as women's magazines. Ellit, Nicehouse, and MTV3's Naiset ("Women"), the major Finnish women-oriented sites, use the format of women's magazines.

As in women's magazines, women's sites address women as a group less defined by hobbies or professional interests than by gender.[23] To give only a few examples, according to interviewees of the Ministry of Transport and Communications, "The way of thinking about content design is women's worlds, and men's worlds, and news for everybody. Women's world: Food column, fashion, interior decoration, parties. Men's world: Sports, fishing, cars."[24] These definitions produce an understanding of women and men literally as creatures of different worlds, the private and the public sphere. It is hardly a surprise, then, that these very categories are the ones that structure online services for women.

The domesticity of women is emphasized in the interface of Nicehouse, which is strongly based on the metaphor of a home. The name of the service is a word game, signifying both a pleasant space (nice house), but also one of women, since the suffix *nais-*, which is pronounced the same way as the English word *nice*, translates as female. The interface is built as a light-colored drawing of a cross section of a house, and the different rooms of the house represent the different sections of the service. They include, among others, a "bedroom" on sex and relationships, dreams and their interpretations, a "wardrobe" on fashion, the somewhat Woolfian room of one's own of spiritual growth and questions of the self, as well as a "study," a "children's room," a "kitchen," and a "workshop." According to the introduction of the site, "The hand-made graphic appearance warmly welcomes especially women, but also those men bored with net surfing, who long for real content on the Internet." Content is, no doubt, the most central issue in services targeted at women, but it is impossible to separate content from form, from representation. The service is mainly made by women, and it seems to rely on a fantasy of women/girls as "decorating" creatures who are fond of organic, "hand-made" shapes and forms.[25]

Ellit, another major service for women, operates on a large budget, and advertises more widely. Ellit is divided into articles and discussions, which are carried out in five different categories: Relationships, fitness and beauty, leisure and hobbies, home and environment, "kitchen of Ideas" and work and finance. Ellit also includes the section "Forbidden to Men," which, in spite of its name, is open to all users independent of their gender. During the first months of the service the articles in that section dealt with issues such as domestic violence, large breasts, and beauty ideals. Later, the emphasis shifted to intimate interviews with female celebrities. Discussions on autobiographical and emotional issues are defined as something "between us women," and not meant for male eyes. The colors used in Ellit vary from time to time, but are dominated by pastel shades (at the time of writing, lime), and softly filtered photographs. Like MTV3's Naiset, a service for women launched in 2000, Ellit relies on the conventions of women's magazines both in its ways of structuring information and representing it.

In Clarisse Mehar Molad's book on women and the Net, she advises designers working on sites for women: "Your site's look and feel should appeal to women. For example, straight lines do not work as well as curves, and women like pastel colors and softness. Black and red are considered very male. Yellow is female."[26] Indeed, the logic of "the pinks and the blues" is taken to full use in all three major Finnish services for women, which rely widely on pastel shades. An extreme case of gender-specific orientation is Ladyvista, a search engine for women. Despite its mostly American links and advertisers, the contacts are two Finnish men, who describe the aims of the site as "a gateway to the Internet— especially designed for ladies":

> Most of the sites that can be found in the Internet are made by male engineers. Those sites tend to look a little shady and are often quite mixed. We at Ladyvista realised that there is a clear need for a web portal which could prove itself a little different. That is why we launched Ladyvista in June 2000: To give our users a little bit more.

> Our mission is to make more attractive sites and bring beautiful web experiences to all for free. Ladyvista is especially designed for women, or "ladies," as we prefer to say. We know that even nowadays it is quite hard to find anything especially designed for ladies in the Internet. Our goal is to create a web community of all the sites including interesting information for women. We strongly believe that in this way we are able to make our users stronger and more independent as women in the male dominated world.[27]

The portal claims to emancipate women, but simultaneously the "Ladyvista team" prefers to call their target audience "ladies"—nothing short of an intimidating gesture. The site is interesting in many ways, not least since search engines, basic tools for using the web, are not often considered gender-specific. Relying on a binary gender model, Ladyvista challenges this notion. By marking itself "for ladies," it implies that general search engines are "for gentlemen." Like so many other services for women, the design of Ladyvista relies on pastel shades of pale pink and blue, and violet, soft italic fonts, and floral ornaments. The site has news services on entertainment, politics, fashion, travel, etc., and links to mainstream services for women, such as "Moms online," "Fighting Fat," "Women connect," and "Recipe Finder." The logo of Ladyvista comes with pink and blue little hearts, a style reminiscent of cute stationery for girls. Banners advertise rings and beauty services, and the link of the week, at the time of this writing, was one for romance novels. With claims to make its users "more strong and independent," the service has no links to explicitly feminist resources. The most intimate tie is to Missit.net, a Finnish service that provides information on beauty pageants in Finland and abroad, as the basic layout for the sites is identical. Contact information for Missit.net leads to the same people as in Ladyvista. Excessive gendering? Excessive femininity? I think so.

REPETITION WITHOUT A DIFFERENCE?

Ellit advertises itself as "a community of active women," but has a considerable percentage of male users. Discussions in Ellit often turn into heterosexual games, in which users use both male and female screen names, and also strongly gendered pseudonyms, such as Cosmo, Vanha Aatami (Old Adam),

Mies40 (Man40), Karhu (Bear) and Nalle (Teddy Bear). Following the logic of Mars and Venus, the discussions are structured by comparisons between male and female experiences, ways of thinking and experiencing, debates on women and femininity (what women are *really* like). Although "Relationships" is the most sex-oriented of the discussion channels, other discussions easily turn to sex and sexual desirability. Although the service is strongly moderated and censored, discussions do get personal, offensive, and sexually descriptive. Ellit discussions are structured around sharing experiences among women, but also among women and men, and among men. The core of the discussions is almost invariably the signification and reproduction of a given gender difference. The central question here, as in Libresse's "ask the boys," is what men and women *really* think, feel, and want. Discussions aim at understanding otherness, and in doing this, they reproduce the bipolar gender order.

Discussions on homosexuality and cross-dressing do surface, but are discussed in relation to the heterosexual norm, which renders these practices "perverse" or "unnatural." Thus, for example in a discussion on male homophobia in November of 1999, biology was used to justify and devalue alternative sexualities. In the words of a user, "What are males and females for? Man and woman. Stamen and pistil. For reproduction. And gays/lesbians are not abnormal?" Nature and biology function here as ideological assumptions, and by referring to them, specific sexualities are marked as natural, that is, "normal," and others unnatural and "abnormal." As philosopher Tuija Pulkkinen has put it, in the Finnish language there is no simple division equaling that of sex/gender: "The word for the realm of the body, desire, and role identification, for both sex and gender is *sukupuoli; Suku* means family in large or kin, *puoli* means half of. Ideas of ordering, reproduction and division in two are linguistically present in this concept. *Sukupuoli* assumes that there are two classes of beings and that they produce offspring." It is no surprise, then, that in this cultural context the "truth" on sex life *sukupuolielämä* is searched for in reproductive nature.[28]

Taking into consideration the much-discussed possibilities of altering one's gender online, it might very well be that the bears and men in Ellit are in fact something other than anatomical men. But this crossing is not necessarily an interesting object of study. Independent of his/her "true" identity, the textual man performs, produces, and reproduces a specific gender, which is again linked to the norms and conditions that define the cultural illegibility of individuals. There is not, then, much subversion in these gender performances, and they do not automatically aim at a *repetition with a difference*, parody and variation that might open up gender categories and their assumed coherence for reinterpretation.[29] On the contrary, "making" another gender also can mean seeking credibility by contentiously repeating the stereotypes, norms and issues of common knowledge that structure gender categories.

For several decades, feminism has problematized discussing women on a generalized and/or essentialist level, and has made visible the norms, exclusions, and privileges inherent in such discourses. Generalizing speech assumes an understanding of women as norm, which, historically, has meant the universality of white, Western, middle-class, heterosexual women.[30] The representation of women as a homogeneous group ultimately reinforces the binary gender models discussed above. Critical analysis of concepts of gender is a quintessential part of cyberfeminist activity. In discussions of women and the Internet we must question *which women are being discussed*, what meanings are attributed to the category of "women" and what meanings are actively excluded. Critically we must analyze women-oriented products and services along with basic assumptions about women's "nature," needs, and experiences produced in commercial contexts. The companies that market these services and products are local and global, national and multinational, and, in most cases, prone to efface differences between women while selecting primarily middle-class women with higher incomes as ideal consumers.

Information networks are not only media of tomorrow, but, more crucially, they are parts of a cultural continuum for reproducing cultural values and hierarchies. The attempts to increase the percentage of female Internet users by producing women-specific services can contribute to the reproduction of gender stereotypes, and naturalization of the status quo. Janelle Brown, writing on women's sites in her complaint, sums this up: "They promised a revolution, but all we got was horoscopes, diet tips, and parenting advice."[31] ★

Many thanks to Marja Vehviläinen and the participants in "Technology, Economy, and Local Interpretations" seminar, as well as the editors of this book for their helpful comments and criticism while developing these ideas.

An earlier version of this article was published as "Naisongelma, eli kuinka nais-puolisia verkkokäyttäjiä puhutellaan." *Tiedotustutkimus* 22 (1999); 4, p. 34–48. Koivunen, Anu (1995), Isänmaan moninaiset äidinkasvot: sotavuosien suomalainen naisten elokuva sukupuoliteknologiana. Turku: SETS.

1   See Sherry Turkle, *Life on the Screen: Identity in the Age of the Internet* (New York: Simon and Schuster, 1995), p. 210–232; Sandy Stone, *The War of Desire and Technology at the Close of the Mechanical Age* (Cambridge and London: MIT Press, 1996), p. 180–181.

2   See Sadie Plant, *Zeros + Ones: Digital Women and the New Technoculture* (London: Fourth Estate, 1997); Clarisse Behar Molad, *Women.Weaving.Webs: Will Women Rule the Internet?* (Houston: CBM Press, 2000).

3   Cf. <http://www.oxygen.com>; <http://www.nicehouse.fi>; <http://www. soneraplaza.fi/ellit>; <http://www.mtv3.fi/naiset>; <http://www.tampax.com>; <http://www. always.com>; <http://www.libresse.com>. **Note:** some of these site addresses have been changed or deleted since this article was first written.

4   Päivi Eriksson, and Marja Vehviläinen, eds., *Tietoyhteiskunta seisakkeella: teknologia, talous ja paikalliset tulkinnat* (Jyväskylä: SoPhi, 1999).

5   <http://www.presidentti.fi>

6   Evelyn Fox Keller, "How Gender Matters, or, Why it's so hard for us to count past two," Gill Kirkup and Laurie Smith Keller eds., *Inventing Women: Science, Technology, and Gender* (Cambridge and Oxford: Polity, 1998), p. 45.

7   Cecelia Tichi, *Electronic Hearth: Creating an American Television Culture* (New York and Oxford: Oxford University Press, 1991), p. 3–6, p. 43.

8   Cf. Petteri Järvinen, *Internet—muutostekijä.* Juva: WSOY. 1996, p. 222–223; *Tasa-arvo ja tietoverkot* 1998, p. 35. For a discussion on gender and evolution history, see Linda Marie Fedigan, "The Changing Role of Women in Models of Human Evolution," in Gill Kirkup and Laurie Smith Keller eds., *Inventing Women: Science, Technology, and Gender* (Cambridge and Oxford: Polity, 1998/1986).

9   Järvinen, *Tasa-arvo ja tietoverkot*/Equality and information networks. Liikenneministeriön julkaisuja/Publications of the Ministry of Transport and Communications 10/1998. (Espoo: Edita, 1998), p. 34.

10 Liisa Tainio, "Opaskirjojen kieli ikkunana suomalaiseen parisuhteeseen". *Naistutkimus – Kvinnoforskning* 1/1999.Tainio 1999, p. 4–9, p. 20.

11 Judith Lorber, *Paradoxes of Gender* (New Haven and London: Yale University Press, 1994), p. 13–15, 37–39; Judith Butler, *Gender Trouble: Feminism and the Subversion of Identity* (London and New York: Routledge, 1990), p. 7; Lynda Birke, "In Pursuit of Difference: Scientific Studies of Women and Men." In Gill Kirkup and Laurie Smith Keller, eds., *Inventing Women: Science, Technology, and Gender* (Cambridge and Oxford: Polity, 1998).

12 Järvinen, 1996, p. 220–221.

13 Pam Gilbert, and Sandra Taylor, *Fashioning the Feminine: Girls, Popular Culture and Schooling* (Sydney: Allen and Unwin, 1991), p. 77–78; 82–83.

14 Louis Althusser, *Ideologiset valtiokoneistot (Ideological State Apparati)* (Jyväskylä: Kansankulttuuri & Vastapaino, 1984), p. 127, 129.

15 Butler, 1990, p. 2–7, p. 122; Birke, 1998, p. 82.

16 Judith Butler, *Bodies that Matter: On the Discursive Limits of "Sex"* (London and New York: Routledge, 1993), p. 122.

17 Teresa de Lauretis, *Technologies of Gender: Essays on Theory, Film, and Fiction* (London: Macmillan, 1987), p. 3, p. 10.

18 Butler, 1993, p. 122.

19 Lorber, 1994, p. 50; Althusser, 1984, p. 127; Fedigan, 1998, p. 107; bell hooks, "Representing Whiteness in the Black Imagination," in Lawrence Grossberg, Cary Nelson and Paula Treichler eds., *Cultural Studies* (New York and London: Routledge, 1992), p. 341; Homi K. Bhabha, (1992), "The Other Question: The Stereotype and Colonial Discourse," in Mandy Merck ed., *The Sexual Subject: A Screen Reader in Sexuality* (London and New York: Routledge, 1992), p. 312, p. 323–324.

20 *Tasa-arvo ja tietoverkot* 1998, p. 33; *Järvinen* 1996, p. 217.

21 Lynn Spigel, and Denise Mann, "Introduction," in Lynn Spigel and Denise Mann eds., *Private Screenings: Television and the Female Consumer* (Minneapolis and London: University of Minnesota Press, 1992), p. vii.

22 *Tasa-arvo ja tietoverkot* 1998, p. 16, p. 36.

23 Heidi Keso, Tarja Pietiläinen, and Satu Ranta-Tyrkkö, "Grounding Business Idea on Gender—The Case of Nicefactory, Ltd." Paper presented at "Women's Worlds 99", the Seventh International Interdisciplinary Congress on Women. Tromsø, Norway. Kristiina ja Kolari Rautio, Jukka, Netti ja naiset. Jyväskylä: Gummerus. 1999, p. 63; Behar Molad 2000, p. 68.

24 *Tasa-arvo ja tietoverkot* 1998, p. 33–35, p. 15.

25 See *Tasa-arvo ja tietoverkot* 1998, 24; see also <http://media.urova.fi/~female/protot.html>

26 Behar Molad 2000, p. 68.

27 <http://www.ladyvista.com/aboutus.htm>

28 TuijaPulkkinen, "Keinotekoista seksiä? Luonto, luonnottomuus ja radikaali sukupuolipolitiikka" (Tiede & Edistys 4/1993), p. 298–313.298; Tuija Pulkkinen, *The Postmodern and Political Agency* (Department of Philosophy: University of Helsinki, 1996), p. 183–185; also Butler, 1990, p. 7; Fedigan, 1998, p. 103.

29 Butler, 1990, p. 145–146.

30 Adrienne Rich, "Notes Toward a Politics of Location," in *Blood, Bread, and Poetry: Selected Prose 1979–1985* (New York and London: W. W. Norton, 1986), p. 214–219; Butler 1990, p. 3–5.

31 Janelle Brown, "What happened to the Women's Web?" <http://www.salon.com/tech/feature/2000/08/25/womens_web/index.html> 2000.

Urls: Always, <http://www.always.com>; Ellit, <http://www.soneraplaza.fi/ellit>; Ladyvista, <http://www.ladyvista.com>; Libresse, <http://www.libresse.com>; MTV3 Naiset, <http://www.mtv3.fi/naiset>; Nicehouse, <http://www.nicehouse.fi>; Tampax community for women, <http://www.tampax.com>. **Note:** some of these site addresses have been changed or deleted since this article was first written.

"Analoging" the Digital, Digitizing the Analog: Contemplations on Communities of Production and Virtuality

Radhika Gajjala and Annapurna Mamidipudi

INTRODUCTION:

W hat might cyberfeminist e-commerce from the "bottom-up" look like? Is such a contradictory "e-commerce" at all possible? What are the collaborations, connections, and issues that might emerge? Recognizing that the "local" is very much tied in with the "global" and vice versa in present day economic practices, how do we negotiate complicity and resistance, silence and speech within various communities of production and practice in an increasingly digital economy? In addition, the digital economy and associated communities of practice and production situated within the so-called "global" practices and configurations of power feminizes certain types of labor. Therefore a "cyberfeminist e-commerce" at a transnational level is as much about feminized *male* labor as about women's labor. A transnational cyberfeminist e-commerce, then, would not only be critical of transnational corporate practices, but also of theory, and academic information flow located within various Westernized spaces of the world (these are not always geographically situated in the West, however), including mainstream liberal feminist discourses about its Other, the "third-world-woman." A critical transnational cyberfeminism thus would balance on the edge of a blade that does not allow for victim-hood, self-pity, complacency, individual celebration of victory, or a lack of constant self-reflexivity.

The present essay is a speculative exchange between two women who attempt to engage and articulate theories and practices of (im)possible critical transnational cyberfeminisms. One of us, Annapurna Mamidipudi, works with a non-governmental organization (NGO), trying to "revive" the old technology of vegetable dyeing and cotton handloom weaving in a few villages of South India. The other, Radhika Gajjala, is an academic whose work examines cross-cultural dialogue and the expression of women's identity among "virtual communities" and diasporic/postcolonial/transnational subject formations. She engages in the production and maintenance of web-based and e-mail list-based interactive e-spaces. Both are situated within an increasingly digital and transnational economy.

Annapurna Mamidipudi (AM): As the train in which I travel moves from the modern port of Vishakapatnam, towards interior Andhra—past historical Vijayangaram and Srikakulam to the small weaving village of Ponduru, time seems to slow down. It is almost as if each of these cities has taken a different route to modernity. What has this quasi time-travel meant to the people who weave their route through these various cities, acting as story tellers and interpreters to each other...drawing circles of various sizes and representing one circle to the other? How have these people affected different communities of people?

Radhika Gajjala (RG): When does community happen? How are social relations shaped? In addition to communication and cultural identity, what are the factors that lead to the formation of community? Indeed how do prevailing definitions of "communication," "culture," and "identity" influence how we approach notions of community? In my quest to understand the possibilities for the creation of dialogic online networks, I am faced with questions related to the definition of community. Most discussions of community in relation to online networks—virtual community—tend to focus on the discursive, cultural and communication aspects of being a community. Most often these are placed in a "cultural" sphere that is implicitly separated from the material practices of economic production and power negotiations that arise therein.

AM: For the weavers in Ponduru, the meaning of the word community has not changed much in the last two hundred years. Here in this little village, cotton fabric is being woven even today in the same manner in which it has been woven for centuries. The tools used are simple, but achieve fabric of the finest counts, aesthetically perfect as well as fulfilling quality parameters in longevity, dye absorption and low cost maintenance. The cotton grown on the nearby hills is perennial, it does not need the unsustainable input of fertilizers and pesticides that hybrid cotton crops need. The spinning, unlike the weaving, is done by women of all communities or villages, a tradition that was revived by the Gandhian nationalist movement to achieve freedom from British rule. Originally, in most of these communities, the weavers, farmers, and potters were linked economically and socially, the social interactions facilitating the economic. Many of these interactions have mutated, with cotton farming being supported by the government *khadi* [handspun yarn] commission, the less skilled Devangula community weaving and innovating, with the Pattusaali preferring to educate their children and enter mainstream occupations.

The weaving castes, the Devangula and the Pattusaali, wove cotton *sarees* using handspun yarn. The Pattusaali were higher up in the hierarchy, they were more skilled. In the village of Ponduru there has been a Devangula street and a Pattusaali street, from the time that Krishna Rao, a weaver of the Devangula community remembers; every house has had a loom. Local women spun in their leisure time, chatting together in their backyards. Spinning was not caste or community bound in Ponduru. It was as much part of their lives as the skill of drawing water from the well. Cotton was grown locally; it was a perennial crop and was available in all seasons. Strong links of economics wove the farmer, the spinner and the weaver communities into their cultural spaces.

To enable warping and sizing—the pre-weaving processes which give the *ponduru* fabric its particular fine texture—houses in the weaver localities are built in rows, back to back. Four families had to work together to warp a single length, which made up five *sarees*. It took the better part of three days in the old days; today the Pattusaalis who are the harder workers have mostly quit weaving, their children go to school and eventually become teachers and clerks. But that means the Devangulas had to learn the superior weaving techniques of the Pattusaalis, as the market for the Pattusaali product was better. Krishna Rao chuckles though, when he owns up, "We Devangulas don't like to take the hard way, one of us learned that the sizing solution for the warp can be made thinner and the three-day process shortened to one. Of course we don't know if that change in process is reducing the quality of the product."

Once, his customers, the now old women who had been wearing his *sarees* since childhood, would have told him that his *saree* did not drape as did the old, even though it took the same amount of wear that the older *sarees* did. Today the communities that were his customers are not bound by ritual to wear only Ponduru *sarees*. My mother-in-law who continues to buy the *sarees* through a circuitous marketing route could, but what she says about Ponduru *sarees* remains a personal opinion, and does not constitute 'market feedback.'

But the market feedback worked in wonderful ways. Yarn produced from hybrid seasonally cropped cottons took over the rest of the handloom world, and products changed everywhere else. But a famous Telugu actor continued to order and wear the Ponduru *dhothi* [men's wear] in his personal life and when he became an icon, in his movies. This kept the product in its original form, all the wannabe Akkineni Nageshwar Raos, and the wannabes of the parts he had played, like the honest politician, the dignified patriarch, the poor but self-respecting farmers...they all continued to buy the product. Other things changed. Some of the weavers who could not upgrade their skills went a different route. Though hand spinning was not common anymore—as women preferred to watch TV and they did not consider spinning a true leisure activity—mill yarn was now available everywhere. But these weavers were all able to weave low-grade reject mill yarn, as they were used to weaving hand-spun yarn that is not uniformly strong. Their product was consequently cheaper than most other weavers' and so developed markets in far away cities as a cheaper version of the popular Ponduru product. According to Krishna Rao, twenty thousand families in and around Ponduru depend on weaving to provide their livelihood even today.

For Krishna Rao, his community is still tied up around his home and with his neighbors, who are mostly also the same caste as he is, and engaged in the same economic activity as he is—weaving. But Krishna Rao is also the manager of the Handloom Co-operative society of Ponduru, and is a government servant. He travels regularly to the cities and interacts with the new communities of suppliers, market and traders which modern economics has engendered. While working with non-governmental organizations like the one I work for, that are trying to teach him to survive in a hostile market in which he does not negotiate from a position of strength, he dialogues and learns and translates—color, texture, technology, economics and culture.

RG: My research and inhabitation of cyberspace has thus far engaged in what is often viewed as the "cultural" side of producing virtual communities. Yet looking all over the Web, I see no getting away from the economic dimension of virtual communities. Diasporic postcolonials, seeking community through a medium of bytes and pieces, are using tools of work as tools of play, sometimes even obsessively. They invoke the presence of "home" in co-constructed imagined communities of nostalgia and memory; sometimes indulging in mere apolitical and uncommitted emotional and intellectual masturbation as the medium allows for connections and re-connections, disappearances and invisibility, while not demanding continuity, commitment, responsibility or accountability. Community is not nurtured, not sustained. Yes indeed it is the digital dollar here that shapes community and meanings. Cultures cannot be separated from economies, and neither of these can be removed from politics. Community building, whether online or in geographical space, is not an individual act and is always context-based. Communities are shaped by production processes, actual histories. As Carolyn Marvin has argued, the history of electronic technologies "is less the evolution of technical efficiencies in communication than a series of arenas for negotiating issues crucial to the conduct of social life: among them, who is inside and outside, who may speak, who may not, and who has authority and may be believed."[1] Yet on the technical side I produce and re-produce opportunities for varieties of "data" collection—sites for engaging, sites where sometimes all I "hear" are silences, and all I "see" are absences.

Sneja Gunew has said that women's writing is no longer an absence. But is this only some women? And in some genres? And how is our presence articulated? Women's writing can break distinctions, explore dichotomies, give new perspectives, question boundaries. As Anne-Marie Sauzea-Boetti points out: "The actual creative project of woman as subject involves betraying the oppressive mechanisms of culture in order to express herself through break... Not the project of fixing meanings but of breaking and multiplying them."[2]

> in
> finite
> absences in the spaces we con
> struct
>
> the absences are made visible by the spaces we re
> con
> struct
>
> build—and no one comes
> the silences
> speak volumes
>
> the gaps are visible

like grave yards
the links that go nowhere
never lead elsewhere
silent graveyards built in impossibilities
rip
through the speech
ancient URLs
...
virtual ashes
bytes unto bytes

I live the isolated life of a self-styled programmer and list-owner, Web-"master" in diaspora. I live the life of a "colored" woman in the Western academy. Producing virtual communities in isolation, often with no idea who the other people are—invisible programmers, infrastructure, software designers, etc. I write for academic audiences in virtual space. To gain access to masculine modes, a woman must be isolated from communities of support. But does this justify a discourse of victim-hood? To gain access, this woman was historically privileged to begin with. The virtuality of the academy, situated within a

Western(ized) power-field, and virtuality of the digital economy cannot be separated. One is complicit with the other. Meanwhile narratives of identity politics and victim-hood—even feminist discourses—are re-appropriated by the consumer culture, like it or not.

cyberdiva has left.
cyberdiva has arrived.
cyberdiva drops homi_bhabha.
cyberdiva activates gayatri_chakravorty_spivak.
gayatri_chakravorty_spivak says, "Let me ask you how do *you* see issues of identity?"
cyberdiva activates homi_bhabha.
homi_bhabha says, "Gee thanks for waking me up! I must have dozed off..."
gayatri_chakravorty_spivak says, "[to cyberdiva] You are most welcome!"
homi_bhabha says, "[to cyberdiva] You are most welcome!"
cyberdiva scrutinizes homi_bhabha's key word list...
cyberdiva activates donna_haraway.
donna_haraway says, "I also remember the dreams and achievements of contingent freedoms, situated knowledges, and relief of suffering that are inextricable from this contaminated triple historical heritage. I remain a child of the Scientific Revolution, the Enlightenment, and technoscience."
donna_haraway says, "[to cyberdiva] Challenging the material-semiotic practices of technoscience is in the interests of a deeper, broader, and more open scientific literacy which we will call situated knowledges."
cyberdiva teaches donna_haraway a new word.
cyberdiva teaches gayatri_chakravorty_spivak a new word.
cyberdiva teaches homi_bhabha a new word.
cyberdiva scrutinizes homi_bhabha's key word list...
cyberdiva teaches homi_bhabha a new word.
cyberdiva teaches gayatri_chakravorty_spivak a new word.
cyberdiva teaches donna_haraway a new word.
cyberdiva teaches homi_bhabha a new word.
cyberdiva says, "hi again!"
gayatri_chakravorty_spivak says, "[to cyberdiva] Hello there! How's it going?"
donna_haraway says, "[to cyberdiva] Hello there! How's it going?"
homi_bhabha says, "[to cyberdiva] the subject matter at hand is..."
gayatri_chakravorty_spivak says, "[to cyberdiva] Subject position is something that we in fact cannot ourselves declare. It is some-thing that should keep us careful because a subject position is assigned, and the word there is 'sign'; it is that which makes itself visible through our textual productions in language and action. It is therefore given over to readers. There isn't *a* subject position."

donna_haraway says, "[to cyberdiva] Whoever and wherever we are
in the domains of technoscience, our practices should not be deaf
to troubling interruptions. Interpellation is double-edged in its
potent capacity to hail subjects into existence. Subjects in a discourse can and do refigure its terms, contents, and reach. In the
end it is those who mis/recognize themselves in discourse who
thereby acquire power, and responsibility, to shape that discourse."

On the poetic/creative side I seek connections and dis-formations in
virtual technologies. The virtuality of this poet, situated within a West-
ern(ized) discourse and the virtuality of the digital economy cannot be separated. One is complicit with the other. In narratives of mothering, periods
of long-distance mothering, there is constant yearning, seeking family,
extending emotion. Communities of production, both monetary and professional (which comes first?) shape family structures, shape community and
culture through histories of dominant cultures' appropriations and re-
appropriations of exoticized Others.

...

I remember when I was eleven or twelve, during the wedding season
we had to weave trousseaus. The women and men of the bridal
households would come to our houses and place orders for items of
daily utility as well as the formal wear. It was not only about work
and economics, it was about mutual respect between them and us.
—ODELLU, aged 33, weaver and dyer, Natural Dyes Resource Persons
Meet, Dastkar Andhra, Hyderabad, 1998

AM: The memory of the very hot summers of Hyderabad affects people in
different ways. In government offices it means that the air conditioning in the
managing director's chamber is turned on very high all through the year. But
for cooling the lowly offices of the *peshi* [the receptionist], there are no air con-
ditioners, here the desert coolers and fans whir almost sleepily. This is an office
I visit very frequently, as most of the state support for artisans is channeled
through these offices, whether it is marketing, credit, or welfare schemes.

For weavers in the handloom sector today there are not many options. While
in some places the traditional community-based structures exist, there are very
few places where the weaver is in a position of strength, and capable of dealing
with either his raw material suppliers or his customers. Most of these interac-

tions are handled by traders who exploit the situation to their benefit; the only other option for the weaver being the state-sponsored corporations or the co-operative societies.

When the community-based traditional production modes seemed rudderless in the light of modern industry, the vacuum was filled by the definition of them as the working class: the co-op society was presented as the weaver organization that would give him an identity in the changing world. The co-op society structure was part of the communist movement of the 1920s and '30s, in fact some of the weaver societies in Andhra are pre-independence. Very early on, procedures were set for the production chain, within the co-operative society —from yarn purchase to dyeing, warping, sizing, weaving and marketing. In their heyday in the 1950s and '60s the big co-operative societies were servicing thousands of weavers with centralized yarn depots, dyeing units and also their own retail outlets. The big co-operative societies were also supplying to the apex marketing organization Andhra Pradesh Co-operative (APCO) on their own terms. The societies' activities ranged beyond production. Some were able to tap into government and institutional support and provide housing and welfare perks like health care and schools to the members.

The 1960s and '70s saw a decline with local government politics entering the co-operative structure. To a great extent the weavers were now being governed by the government officials or government appointed office bearers under the supposed guidance of the elected board, who had no interest in either developing the institutions or working out economically sustainable models of production. These centralized government outlets have proven to be unsuccessful at marketing since the government order guarantees no haggling on rates, and eventually the payment is made. The weavers supply the material ordered, taking the endless wait for payments and the buying of the lower orders' favors as a necessary but unpleasant part of the transaction.

Just as they were not allowed to sit in air-conditioned comfort, the lower order officials kept their clients standing outside in the hot waiting area where not even fans whirred. But as a field worker in an NGO that was acting as a consultant to the state corporation—a liaison between them and the weavers—

my job was simple: Whenever any file had to be moved up for payment, one of the group of weavers would come to the corporation and wait outside while I asked the relevant officer when the file would be passed. All the documentation would be gone through and the officer would be forced to commit to a date by which time the bill would be paid. If the payment was not made by that day, another weaver would come up all the way from his village. I would receive another call. Once again while he waited outside I would repeat the same procedure. Usually after a couple of such visits, the file would be moved up and the checks issued.

My power, in the weavers' eyes, was literally my ability to move up the pecking order, to gain access to the hallowed air conditioned room and remind the official that there was a certain weaver who needed to be paid.

My role then was only to give them access, to give them a position of strength to negotiate within the hierarchy. In fact, that was all I could offer them, and more important, that was all they needed. Access then is the key: access to information, access to technology, access to markets, access to financial institutions, access to people and access to power. However, as the vision of the new equalizing tool of the new world, the access to the Net is filling our eyes, the promise of a new pecking order that does not seem to operate on old hierarchies is being built up in our minds, I wonder, will it really constitute true access?

> *RG: What do terms like "Race" and "Gender," "Ethnicity" and "Nationality" mean in the context of cyberspace/cyberculture? How are diversity and multiculturalism defined within an increasingly global digital economy? For that matter, what is perceived as global and what is perceived as local? We have always been global and local (glocal) in various ways through history, as people traveled, colonized and migrated—why is there such an emphasis at times, on the globality of the world? Questioning the uneven power relations involved in the global circulation of material and discourse, I reiterate a question asked by Gayatri Spivak (1998): "In what interest, to regulate what sort of relationships [material, social, political and cultural] is the globe evoked?" Similarly, what sorts of relationships—material*

*social, political, personal and cultural—are being regulated within
current hegemonic definitions (whether implicit or explicit) of diversity and multiculturalism—whether IRL or in cyberspace.*

*If, as the famous New Yorker cartoon says, "On the Internet no one
knows you're a dog," why bother with theories of culture and difference when discussing computer-mediated-communication? One of my
co-travelers in cyberspace has the following signature file attached to
his email messages:*
>New Yorker Cartoon (Internet Savvy Dog):
>"On the Internet, no one knows that you're a dog."
>Art McGee (Internet Ignorant Dog added to cartoon):
>"What's wrong with being a dog?"[3]

*This signature file questions the need for us to disguise who we are.
Indeed, why should it be assumed that it is wonderful for "dogs"—
women, colored people, and people on the periphery of the Westernized
logic of consumerism—to be able to hide who they are and to be able
to disguise their gender, race and culture in favor of passing as white?
I also wish to raise the question of where "cyberspace" as a cultural
concept can be separated from "cyberspace" as situated within an
economic system.*

RG: As you speak of being an "access point" for the weavers my mind wanders
back in time to look at personal access points in my journey as a transnational/
diasporic postcolonial subject. Immigration offices, airport terminals, and
passport officers are points of access and discrimination. Being transformed
from a subject of material and cultural privilege into one who is marginalized
(as the process of "Othering" worked on me), then turned again into a subject
of material and cultural privilege who is tokenized and re-appropriated.
Knowing that the limits of my resistance lie in necessary negotiations as well
as witting and unwitting complicities, I resist consumption and being a representative native informant. Transnational subject formations cannot be
reduced to simple binaries of us and them, insiders and outsiders. Neither is
physical travel the only condition for the formation of transnational subjectivity, for I see you and the weavers you work with—located geographically in

Hyderabad, located in remote weaver communities—as transnational and nego-tiating the global structures of hegemony. And yet, as we discussed in previous exchanges, without the local there can be no global.

We must ask: Access at what cost? Do we become access points for locals to become consumers of the global? Or do we become access points for locals to re-empower their indigenous producer communities? How might it be possible to provide access to the indigenous producer communities so that they can insert themselves as actors within the global arena and prevent their re-appropriation and consumption even as they are exoticized and marked as the analog Others of a digital economy?

> Date: Thu, 06 Jul 2000 06:16:23 -0400
> From: radhika_gajjala &ltradhika@cyberdiva.org>
> Subject: (no subject)
>
> how can absences be articulated
> by the presences?
>
> how can the present
> not
> silence
> the absent
>
> re-presenting absences
> does
> not
> make the absent
> present
>
> but
> re
> presents
>
> absence

---

1   Carolyn Marvin, *When Old Technologies Were New: Thinking About Electric Commu-nication in the Late Nineteenth Century* (New York: Oxford University Press, 1988).

2   Anne-Marie Sauzea-Boetti, personal e-mail communication.

3   Art McGee first made this statement at the "Computers, Freedom and Privacy" con-ference, San Francisco, 1995.

The Female Flesh Commodities Lab

In/Visible Body: Notes on Biotechnologies' Vision

Lucia Sommer

N ever before has so much been available to the eye. The revolution in biotechnologies accelerates the centuries-long drive of vision technologies, bringing ever more of the world within the domain of the visible. Distant stars and galaxies, citizens and enemies of state alike, and the minutest particles of matter have for some time now been objects of the sight machine. The moment foreseen by Jorge Luis Borges, in which ambitious cartographers have produced a map with such detail and accuracy that it would completely cover the very territory it depicts, has become normalized in everyday life. Military satellites hurtling through space can visually read an address, a map, or a face: Images produced not with photography—light—but digitally, with 0's and 1's. In a strange double-vision, the hypothetical surveilled citizen could (in the unlikely event of being granted access to such an image), step outside her home and then view her screenal self, moments later on her personal computer. In the hyperreal, simulation and lived experience are inseparable.

HYPER/VISIBLE BODY

How does the body, that most vulnerable of territories, fare in the relentless expansion of the sight machine? The same viewer could now download The Visible Human™, the "first digital description of an entire human being," created by anatomists and computer scientists as part of a project conceived by the U.S. National Library of Medicine. This lofty goal is being realized through the creation of a hypermedia medical image-and-text database that can be accessed by computer nets. The data for the Visible Human™ was obtained from digitized images of cadavers. The data body was named Adam in a religious invocation of the creation of life, and the images are heralded as "living images," or "real images." Virtual animation will eventually be applied to the data to simulate the signs of life, the motion of circulation, respiration, and even disease processes.

If the data body Adam represents the ultimate Western fantasy of autogenic scientific objectivity, then Adam's repressed foundational moment is surely the

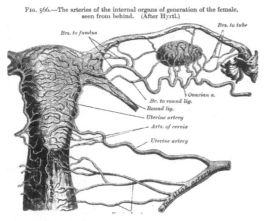

FIG. 566.—The arteries of the internal organs of generation of the female, seen from behind. (After Hyrtl.)

Dissection of the uterus.

colonizing violence that opened modernity's vision, and among the erased others must be the "Hottentot Venus." An African woman, known as Saartjie Baartman, she was "exhibited" in London in 1810. She died in Paris at age twenty-five after being displayed for a period of five years all over Europe. "Her body was whisked away and promptly cut open, cut into pieces. We can, to this day, examine [the remains of her flayed body] at the Musee de l'Homme [sic] in Paris."[1] If Adam is the classical body, once hermetically sealed and now finally open to surveillance, Saartjie, her colonized sisters, and the prostitutes studied by nineteenth-century medicine as markers of bodily deviance, were not lucky enough to benefit from science's "disinterested" gaze. While the Visible Human™ may indeed save lives, his foremothers—Baartman and countless colonized others like her—literally died of their hypervisibility.

Perhaps this foundational repression explains why it is so easy to forget that the Visible Human™ is not living blood and tissue, but created of bits and bytes, or to believe in the complete identity of the image and the portrayed, as if one were the identical double of the other.[2] And to forget that the data was obtained by a process of radical disembodiment: by slicing segmentally into the (dead) body of a male (death row prisoner) and then segmenting again—that is, selecting and organizing the data digitally according to identifiable outlines of anatomical structure. But identifiability necessarily presupposes the possibility of its opposite: Non-recognition. What happens to the data that does not fit identifiable outlines? And what of anatomy—as structure or process—whose outlines cannot be identified?

Although the identity of image and portrayed has no basis in some sort of ultimate truth, this does not stand in the way of capital's instrumental deployment of representation on living bodies. The dataset Adam will be used not only for surgical

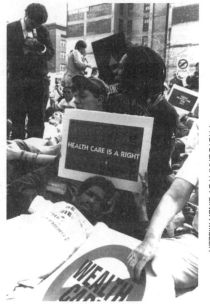

National AIDS Action for Healthcare direct action, Chicago, IL. 1990.

simulation and training; the simulated operation will also be applied to the living bodies of patients or the semi-living bodies of soldiers, as the case may be. The U.S. Defense Department's Advanced Research Projects Agency (DARPA) is developing telepresence technologies to allow virtual surgery by robots guided by satellite and computer, on the "remote" battlefields of the future.

Similar interests are working to increase the profitability of medicine through, for example, the use of vision technologies to further reduce and even eliminate doctor-patient contact. As Claudia Reiche points out, the title of one international conference sponsored by military, corporate, and medical leaders, "NextMed: The End of Healthcare?" referred not to the crisis in accessibility of healthcare for forty-three million Americans, but to the goal of rendering the doctor even less visible to patients. Where patients' data bodies could not be treated remotely, genetic engineering would supposedly eliminate "more objective" health problems such as aging and cancer.[3]

When Audre Lorde spoke of deep seeing, she had something entirely other in mind. For Lorde, 'seeing' as black feminist practice entailed attention to the unseen histories as much as to the visible body of the female subject.[4]

IN/VISIBLE DIGITAL

Even the most in/visible reaches of the human body have been thrown open by the sight machine. Now, we are told, life itself can be seen, manipulated, and controlled. Reprotech scientists can view a human egg as it is pierced and implanted with sperm. Even smaller components of life—genes and chromosomes—can be seen, organized, and compiled using new digital technologies

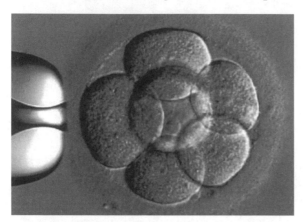

Microphotograph: Pre-embryo.

and, via their representation as DNA, selected and transformed for profit.[5] Here, too, the medical industry and the military intertwine in their quest for perfect vision.[6] The fact that DNA code is a representation makes it no less instrumental and potent as vision—for seeing has always been mediated, symbolized. In the hands of late capital, the digital, the analog, and matter itself are seamlessly welded. Or are they?

There is no doubt that the technologies of vision have the potential to further the cause of life. Lives have been saved, and enhanced, through medical application of microscopic, electronic, and cybernetic vision. Just as the same technologies, in the hands of the late capitalist state, have expanded the territories of death.

Is it only a matter of the map's completeness? So much depends on who is looking, who is looked at, and what kind of story is told about the looking.

HYPER/IN/VISIBLE
(DEATH BELOW THE SIGHT-LINE OF POWER)

When U.S. bombs 'accidentally' destroyed the Chinese embassy during the U.S./NATO bombing of Yugoslavia, killing four and injuring many, the CIA took refuge first in non-identity of the analog. The maps were old and

inaccurate, they said. When report-
ers questioned how this could matter since the bombs have to be guided by laser/satellite technology, the
state finally took refuge in silence.

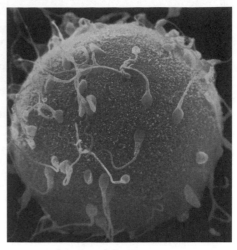

As if visibility were only a matter
of technology, in any case.

As bombs rained down on Iraq in
the 1991 war and after, Americans
were treated to a cinematic spectacle
of virtual war, complete with simu-

Microphotograph: Sperm and egg.

lated targets and detailed dissections of warheads. As thousands of Iraqui civilians died then, and thousands every month since, as a result of the devasta-
tion and sanctions, their bodies are strangely invisible to the same media
hyper-vision.

On March 3, 1991, three days after George Bush called a halt to the Gulf War,
twenty-seven police officers surrounded African-American motorist Rodney
King, four of them beating him with such intensity as to knock fillings from
his teeth and cause permanent brain damage. Although the world watched
this blow-by-blow assault captured on George Holliday's home video tape, wit-
nessing more violence in the course of eighty-one seconds of video than in
the entire Gulf War, the predominantly white jury was able to return a verdict
of 'not guilty'.

The global information economy and the revolution in biotechnologies are
ceaselessly invoked and represented to the public as utopian promise. Yet as
media spectacle, these representations are nearsighted: The very labor which
makes information and biotechnologies possible—entire gendered and racialized economies—are not seen or represented as part of that world economy.[7]

Yet the paradoxical relation of the two bodies bracketing modernity's tele-
scope: The digital Adam and the analog Venus—one immaculately conceived
and composited at its end, one tortured to death at its beginning—reminds us
that invisibility and hyper-visibility are not new to digital technologies, and

have never been a simple duality. Black and postcolonial writers have for some time now alerted us to the complex dialectics of in/visibility.[8] bell hooks observes that, for example, whites "imagine that they are invisible to black people" and describes how disconcerted her white students are to discover that black people "watch white people with a critical 'ethnographic' gaze."[9] Radhika Mohanram has demonstrated that "…bodies become visible or invisible only through the vectors of power and economics and the meaning imputed to these within cultural knowledge systems…The proper, ideal subject is one with property but no body."[10]

Indeed, the same vision technologies which are unable to see the unpaid or underpaid labor of postcolonial workers, are amazingly sensitive to raced and gendered bodies at policed boundaries such as airports and border crossings; how else to explain that Black women are the most frequently stopped, detained, or strip-searched of any group, while also being the least frequently engaged in the surveilled activities?

IN/VISIBLE (PLEASURE)

The question of pleasure may seem excessive, unproductive to some, now that vision's machine is so efficient, instrumental, productive. Yet to miss understanding the role of the sight machine in producing both terror and pleasure would be to miss understanding either.

What does it mean to say that sometimes we imagine that the body's pain, pleasure, desire itself, can be seen? Dr. Helen O'Connell, urological surgeon at Australia's Royal Melbourne Hospital, was moved to ask such questions by the lack of knowledge about (so inconsequential a matter as) female sexual anatomy. If women's bodies, from Saartjie on, have been hyper-visible, ubiquitous, in other ways they have been invisible. Although reprotech scientists can scrutinize the female reproductive system well enough to harvest, fertilize, and implant microscopic eggs and perform pre-natal surgery, Dr. O'Connell found a striking lack of accuracy in medical textbook representation of female sexual anatomy, not just in its fine-tuning, but overall.

After dissection studies and using 3-D photography, O'Connell found that, for

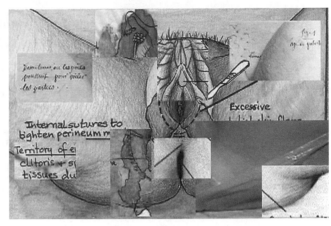

Video still from subRosa's "Vulva De/Reconstructa."

example, the clitoris was not only twice as large as normally depicted, but that it extended deep into the body. Even *Gray's Anatomy*, the medical bible, had it wrong, and failed to show the extensive network of blood vessels and nerves connected to it. The study showed that the clitoris is connected to a pyramid of interior erectile tissue and two bulb-like structures on either side of the vaginal cavity. It has two arms up to nine centimeters long that flare backward into the body, lying just a few millimeters from the muscles that run up the insides of the thigh. "There is a lot of erectile tissue down there that is not shown in any anatomy textbook," O'Connell told New Scientist Magazine, "except perhaps a couple of really old dissections in French and German literature… Just because you can't see the rest does not mean that it is not there."[11]

According to medical research, hysterectomies have been over-prescribed for women for years, but only recently have doctors in the United States begun to study the effects of hysterectomy on sexual pleasure.[12] New York University pelvic surgery expert Dr. Joy Saini and associates compared the effects of different types of hysterectomy. Using a specially developed anonymous questionnaire, she found worse sexual function in a total abdominal hysterectomy group than in a group given supra-cervical hysterectomy (where the cervix is spared). Researchers are beginning to speculate that a complex network of nerves surrounding both the uterus and cervix, and interwoven with those of the clitoris, play a significant part in orgasm. Her conclusions agreed with European researchers, whose research also demonstrates damage to sexual pleasure from removal of the uterus only: "This is a vital area of research for women's health that is not well studied and sadly under-funded," noted Dr. Saini.[13]

And although alternative medicine has developed methods for regaining sexual pleasure in cases of somatic or psychic injury, this information is seemingly not finding its way to women patients in mainstream medicine.

But not-seeing women's anatomy is hardly new to science: At least since Freud, there has been nothing there to see except a lack—and an "ugly" lack at that. Although blind to the beauty of the vulva, Freud and Lacan were productively obsessed with a female *jouissance* that threatened to undo patriarchal logos. Their radical formulation failed to survive even the American reception of psychoanalysis, much less to influence the medical canon. American second wave feminism offered much in the way of correctives, both theoretical and practical. Yet, perhaps still owing to the tendency to channel the body's pleasures, and the inevitable difficulties presented by vision's (and language's) own territorializations, some of these correctives ended up offering a rather dualistic alternative to the valued vaginal orgasm. In its turn, the clitoris became the politically correct pleasure organ. French feminist theorists such as Luce Irigaray have unearthed and detourned the radical possibilities of women's *jouissance*,[14] but have been suspicious of pleasure's sojourn through realms of visibility.

BODY IN/VISIBLE

In Borges' story, the cartographers' map eventually disintegrates with age, until only shreds remain, scattered across the desert. Finally, representation would be indistinguishable from the body of the desert itself.

Thus far, every image, every representation (or 'simulation') has been finite, in time if not in consequence. As with any image, the frame excludes, too. As with Borges's map, holes remain: Will we ever escape the mirror logic of seer and seen, visible and in/visible? Can difference and visual pleasure find a place outside that binary? Have we learned to challenge, as bell hooks has said, those "who think that by merely looking they can 'see'?"[15] Or, will digital communications and biotechnologies, in global pan-capital, merely increase the pace of a chronic and disastrous blindness?

We are far beyond a nostalgic quest for some mythically originary body—all such quests in this century have been tied to fascist disasters. The contribution of critical theory has been to show that the body has always been mediated by the structured and structuring function of language, and, since the Enlightenment, by a particular form of Reason. One task before us now might be to collectively envision counter-bodies to the body of pan-capitalist spectacle. That is, we could imagine ways in which lived bodies could speak, could be represented, other than as commodities in an endless chain of equivalencies. ★

PHOTOGRAPH BY BILL STAMETS

**ACT UP Chicago's "Freedom Bed."
Street theatre, Chicago, IL. 1990.**

---

1 Francette Pacteau, "Dark Continent" in Lisa Bloom, ed., *With Other Eyes: Looking at Race and Gender in Visual Culture* (Minneapolis and London: University of Minnesota Press, 1999), p. 90–91.

2 See Claudia Reiche, "Bio(r)Evolution™—On the Contemporary Military-Medical Complex," in *The Spectralization of Technology: From Elsewhere to Cyberfeminism and Back—Institutional Modes of the Cyberworld*, Marina Grzinic et al, eds. (Maribor, Slovenia: MKC Maribor (the Youth Cultural Center) 1999) <http://www.rrz.unihamburg.de/Koerperbilder/REICHE/BioRevolution_E.htm>

3 Ibid. As the conference program proclaimed, "The ability to manipulate genetic code presents the possibility of ending worry about diseases and defects which burden humankind. Physicians, researchers, entrepreneurs and investors can glimpse this future." Medical workers were treated to statistics such as the following to support this vision: "50 to 80 percent of all people who consult a doctor are in no need of medical help. 70 to 80 percent of all health problems can be treated at home, if one knows what to do. Not a lot remains to be treated."

4 Audre Lorde, "Eye to Eye," *Sister Outsider* (Freedom, CA: The Crossing Press, 1984), p. 174.

5 A handful of powerful biotech firms such as Monsanto are reaping enormous profit from their control, storage, and manipulation of genetic data, through its digital representation.

6 The U.S. Dept. of Energy is a primary investor in the Human Genome Project, while DARPA and other branches of the military conduct secret research in virtual surgery and biotechnologies.

7 See Maria Patricia Fernandez-Kelly, *For We Are Sold, I and My People: Women and Industry in Mexico's Frontier* (Albany: State University of New York Press, 1984); Armand Mattelart, *Transnationals and the Third World: Case Studies Of the Electronics Industry* (Westport, CT: Bergin & Garvey, 1986); Saskia Sassen, "Toward a Feminist Analytics of the Global Economy," *Globalization and Its Discontents* (New York: The New Press, 1994).

8 For example: Toni Morrison, *The Bluest Eye* (London: Penguin Books, 2000); Ralph Ellison, *Invisible Man* (New York: Vintage Books, 1995); Michele Wallace, *Invisibility Blues: From Pop to Theory* (London: Verso, 1990).

9 bell hooks, in David Roediger, *Black on White: Black Writers on What It Means to Be White* (New York: Schocken Books, 1999).

10 Radhika Mohanram, *Black Body: Women, Colonialism, and Space* (Minneapolis & London: University of Minnesota Press, 1999), p. 38.

11 Susan Williamson, "The Truth About Women," *New Scientist*, August 1, 1998, and Helen E. O'Connell et al., "Anatomical Relationship between Urethra and Clitoris," *Journal of Urology*, Vol. 159.

12 Sills E.S., Saini J., Steiner C.A., McGee M,. Gretz H.F., "Abdominal hysterectomy practice patterns in the United States," *International Journal of Gynecology and Obstetrics* 63:277–283 (1998).

13 Sills E.S., Saini J., Applegate M.S., McGee M., Gretz H.F., "Supracervical and total abdominal hysterectomy trends in New York State: 1990–1996." *Bulletin of the New York Academy of Medicine* 75:903–910 (1998). Saini J., Sills E.S., Kuczynski E., Gretz H.F., "Supracervical hysterectomy vs. total abdominal hysterectomy: Perceived effects on sexual function," [abstract] 24th Annual Meeting, Society of Gynecologic Surgeons (1998).

14 Luce Irigaray, *Speculum of the Other Woman*, trans. Gillian C. Gill (Ithaca, NY: Cornell University Press, 1985).

15 bell hooks, "Altars of Sacrifice: Re-membering Basquiat," *Art In America*, June, 1993, p. 69.

Photographs of the AIDS actions are courtesy of Mary Patten and the ACT UP Chicago archive. See Mary Patten, "The Thrill is Gone: An ACT UP Post-mortem," in *The Passionate Camera*, ed. Deborah Bright (New York: Routledge, 1998).

# of maps and holes

(ON THE FOUR HUNDREDTH ANNIVERSARY OF DESCARTES' BIRTH)

Lucia Sommer

in this place

approaching millennium

(after centuries,

always approaching millennium

as toward some state line,

or star)

where think to see

but just are

were taught value of sight:

"make body disappear

make of world, body

to scc

to sea/l"

forget smell, feel

of love, fright

forget childhood's mouth

skin crave

asshole's bliss

to touch limit

body's trembling intelligence

before the grave

damp want of connection, this

terrible ecstasy of incompleteness

now safe

with glass, pen, paper

dry clothes

all but eyes, closed

feel whole

now see everywhere:

points, maps, holes

(a philosopher we call dead

saw space and time thrown out ahead

still could not evade return of birth—

so who has learned of thought the worth?)

Stolen Rhetoric: The Appropriation of Choice by the ART Industry

subRosa

B iotech industries currently expanding globally, but especially in the United States, have opened new frontiers for colonizing bodies—and commodifying and patenting life—at the molecular and genetic level. Gamete harvesting and freezing, in vitro fertilization (IVF), intra cytoplasmic sperm injection (ICSI), pre-implantation embryo screening, and genetic manipulation of embryos are just some of the new techniques transcending previous limits of reproductive intervention that have profound repercussions for human genetic heritage. Under the guise of optimizing reproduction—and "improving" human beings—assisted reproductive technologies (ART) are rapidly being naturalized in everyday life. As feminist theorists have pointed out, the new biotech reproductive order has territorialized the female body as a pre-eminent laboratory and tissue mine for a lucrative medical/pharmaceutical industry.[1]

The women's liberation movement of the early 1970s formulated a politics of women's autonomy and control over their sexuality and reproduction that included the right to safe contraception and abortion. By the late 1980s, after almost two decades of abortion wars, the politics of autonomy and liberation had been transformed into a rhetoric of "choice" typified by the slogan, "A woman's right to choose," which became identified with the pro-choice movement. Since then, the rhetoric of "choice" has become firmly associated with reproductive liberalism.

Using strategic marketing, a seductive consumer industry intent on normalizing ART in everyday life has appropriated the rhetoric of choice in order to appeal to a broad constituency of progressive consumers ready to produce "children of choice." Marketers of new reprogenetic technologies (reprotech) were quick to capture this rhetorical territory, cashing in on the expectation that it would appeal to liberal, educated, middle-class consumers schooled by feminist activism to be proactive in personal health care. ART, principally driven by profit motives and embodying eugenic ideologies, have recuperated the politicized rhetoric of choice by concealing a deeply embedded conflict between the macro politics of rationalized reproduction in late capitalism and a micro politics based on individual desires.

Despite the highly invasive and risky procedures of ART, many feminists have explicitly welcomed the development of reprotech for its promises of an expanded range of reproductive choices for women. Others have recognized that reprotech can represent not only an ultimate form of body colonization, but that its practice and ideology often reinforces patriarchal systems of scientific and medical authority, control, and rationalization of reproduction—contradicting radical feminist philosophies of women's autonomy.

Appropriation of liberational feminist rhetoric and practices by liberals and conservatives alike is rampant in the abortion movement. In the '70s, the nationally mobilized Feminist Women's Health Movement (FWHM) developed clinics that offered a wide array of feminist health care services. Most controversial were their abortion services, especially the technique of menstrual extraction pioneered by the Los Angeles Feminist Women's Health Center. This vacuum suction procedure could be done by lay practitioners and was often used as a form of early abortion. Abortion services made feminist health clinics the target of vicious attacks from anti-abortion and right-to-life fundamentalist groups like Operation Rescue. These groups appropriated many of their confrontational direct action occupation and blockage practices, as well as their spectacular visual tactics, such as their use of images of the fetus, from leftist activist movements including feminism. "Pro-choice," "anti-choice," and "pro-life" are rhetorics that now signify a divisive, often anti-feminist, partisanship. Diverse and bitterly contradictory feminist positions on abortion have been subsumed under the liberal rhetoric of choice.

Abortion became such a loaded political and cultural issue that the medical profession tried very hard to wash its hands of it. Clearly, abortion could not be made to suit capitalist ends since no sexy consumer market of clinics and products could be developed around the choice of abortion. But the rhetoric was perfect for the purposes of the new infertility industry that promises to be a lucrative new flesh industry. Some have estimated the potential worth of IVF procedures alone at $40-$50 million a year. It is time to question the capitalist marketing strategies of reprotech and the imbalance of macro and micro politics masked by the stolen rhetoric of "choice."

MODELS OF CHOICE

Many feminists and bioethicists have argued that despite their risks, the new reproductive technologies represent greater reproductive choices for women and men. Most notorious among the latter is John A. Robertson, whose passionate advocacy of "procreative liberty" concludes: "There is no stopping the desire for greater control of the reproductive process.... There is no better alternative than leaving procreative decisions to the individuals whose procreative desires are most directly involved."[2] Such arguments appeal to the deepest democratic beliefs of Americans, but they overlook the way entrepreneurial marketers and fertility services providers are exploiting the rhetoric of choice to naturalize ART. Their clinic brochures, fertility advertisements, and Web pages pitch the many reproductive choices and techniques available to satisfy the desires of different sectors of the population—including people who are not biologically infertile. Rather than selling ART principally as a set of biomedical procedures designed to cure or circumvent severe cases of infertility, reprotech marketers highlight its many benefits for those who want the control made possible by scientifically managed reproduction. ART is represented as a means to realize lifestyle choices and support career goals—key factors in reifying its use in everyday life.

For example, an advertisement from the Genetics & IVF Institute offers a "large choice of fully evaluated and screened donors who are immediately accessible," and a "revolutionary technique enabling men with long-term vasectomies to father children."[3] Though never mentioning any of the risks involved, such ads imply that almost anyone (who can afford it) can "make" a baby with purchased donor eggs and/or sperm, and the use of a hired gestational womb. ART would therefore seem to be the ideal choice for people living in non-traditional family configurations, as this group includes single women or men, older couples, affinity groups, lesbians, and gays. Thanks to entrepreneurship—although most fertility books are aimed squarely at married couples—there is a thriving niche market of reproductive choices. There seems to be a specialized clinic for almost every group; for example, there are feminist and gay sperm banks and insemination clinics as well as those that specialize in male infertility problems or treating older women. ART are also sold as the reproductive solution for couples or singles who have pursued career goals and postponed childbearing. Healthy people considered at risk for certain diseases, or exposed to environmental hazards at work, can choose to use ART procedures such as gamete banking before they are ready to reproduce as insurance against future infertility. Thus child-bearing becomes subordinated to a rationalized, efficient, and orderly life-style.

ART procedures promote new eugenic consciousness.[4] Marketers sell IVF as a family-building technology; infertile couples are encouraged to bypass adoption and instead "make" a child of their own. IVF is a eugenic procedure because it involves screening and selection for 'fit' gametes and embryos. Currently, between 60 and 70 percent of U.S. pregnancies are already being screened using methods such as amniocentesis and ultrasound. The discovery of individual gene functions through sequencing of the human genome will further facilitate the routine use of embryonic genetic screening and manipulation. Parental "choice" now encompasses so much more than whether or not to have children. Consumers can purchase a wide selection of pre-screened and tested human gametes that come with detailed profiles of donor characteristics promising improved success and health for offspring. IVF produces excess embryos, and multiple embryos are usually inserted to ensure implantation of at least one. By using pre-implantation embryo screening and selective reduction, parents can select precisely which embryo is to be gestated. Selective reduction—a euphemism for abortion—is justified by the eugenic argument that it is the necessary means by which only "fit" embryos are selected to be carried to full term. Here the rhetoric of choice is firmly bound to an individualistic micropolitics of manipulating consumer desire. (subRosa is not making an argument for or against abortion here, but wishes to call attention to how the rhetoric of choice is used to make controversial issues acceptable.)

The liberal rhetoric of choice has long been used in the mass media to imply that women can "have it all" no matter what the personal or social costs. Infertility discourse similarly promotes as a given the idea that everyone has a right to choose procreative liberty, and have a child using whatever methods they can afford. ART can be used to tame recalcitrant bodies. The titles of infertility books clearly tell the story of the enterprise of conquering infertility, for example: *Overcoming Infertility*; *How to Get Pregnant with the New Technology*; *RESOLVE Infertility*; *Taking Charge of Infertility*. The imperatives to "take charge" and "overcome" urge the individual woman to take control of her body—with the help of her doctors and technology, of course. What she learns by reading further is that ART requires her to surrender her body to disciplinary medical manipulation, surveillance, and invasion. While clients are urged to shop around for clinics with the best specialists and success rates for particular procedures, they are given virtually no tools to assess the risks associated with ART. Instead, ART brochures and books highlight the hundreds of healthy babies that have been born using IVF. The models of choice offered by ART promote neither anti-authoritarian social and political values, nor a liberation of women from their biology. Rather, they reify cultural values of compulsory motherhood, and represent an intensified control of women's bodies. In this context, the notion of choice is appropriated to promote corporate economic interests rather than personal autonomy.

REPRODUCTION AND FEMINIST UTOPIAN THOUGHT

Understandably, feminist analyses or critiques of reprotech are rarely mentioned in mainstream ART literature. Feminist responses to assisted reproduction are too complex to be summarized here. However, contradictory strands of utopian feminist thinking regarding reproduction and maternity are well illustrated by two very different texts: the first, the extraordinary feminist utopian novel *Herland* (1915), written by the prominent socialist feminist Charlotte Perkins Gilman during the height of the first wave of feminist suffrage struggle; the second, *The Dialectic of Sex* (1969), by Shulamith Firestone, a fiery socialist feminist tract that inspired women during the second wave of feminism.

Gilman's *Herland* presents a country populated solely by women. Over the course of several thousand years they have created a rational, stable, peaceful, prosperous economy and social order, including voluntary eugenic reproductive practices, based on exalting the social principle of Motherhood. The grand task of Herlanders is "making people" in every sense of the word. There is no individual ownership of children. All the women act as nurturing and social mothers to all the children, who are all girls. There is no sexual intercourse and no "sex feeling." To solve problems of population control each adult woman is allowed to bear only one child. When born, this child, who is engendered by the intense inner desire and preparation of the mother-to-be, becomes part of the community, not part of a nuclear family. In *Herland*, women can only get pregnant because of their great desire for a child. For the good of the community, some women voluntarily defer or forgo motherhood, satisfying their desire for it by tending the communities' babies. In *Herland*, hundreds of years of rational, diligent attention to the problems of weeding out undesirable characteristics and choosing good ones by voluntary eugenics have paid off in a population that is strong, healthy, beautiful, and multi-talented.

Gilman was simultaneously a radical socialist feminist and a believer in "positive eugenics." Her writings call for women to be liberated from the biological burdens of compulsory reproduction, motherhood, and domestic work. Gilman believed in "female values" of co-operation rather than competition, sharing skills and property, and the labor of raising children. Though she welcomes technology to liberate women from backbreaking labor, in *Herland*, Gilman solves the problems of fertility and reproduction with social engineering and the development of a strangely mythic reproductive biology— a kind of parthenogenesis, like that practiced by creation goddesses. In her utopia, reproductive self-repression for the good of the community takes the place of autonomy as the solution to overcoming the constraints of biology and sexual reproduction.

In *The Dialectic of Sex*, on the other hand, Shulamith Firestone is adamant that technology, and technology alone, will provide human mastery of matter, and free women from the tyranny of biology: "The biological family unit has always oppressed women and children, but now, for the first time in history, technology has created real preconditions for overthrowing these oppressive 'natural' conditions, along with their cultural reinforcements."[5] Only women's technological control of their biology will change the patriarchal balance of power. Firestone was writing in the late 1960s, a time when research on reproductive technologies was developing rapidly. Astoundingly, by the mid '80s, many of the reproductive techniques she anticipated were already in place. Firestone speculates that the invention of an artificial womb will solve the vexing problem that women are still the sole bearers of children; pending this invention, she suggests that women pay other women to be surrogate mothers. Concluding her feminist socialist analysis of the biological and material causes of women's oppression, Firestone calls for a feminist revolution based on the creation of a humanly controlled ecological balance using cybernetic feedback systems and artificial reproductive technologies. Today, though the technologically based systems she advocated are highly developed, the feminist "revolution" is bogged down in conflicted debates about the impact and consequences for women of the purportedly liberating new technologies. In different ways, both Gilman and Firestone pin their utopian dreams on women freeing themselves from traditional (heterosexual) and 'natural' biological reproductive processes. However, neither Gilman's eugenicism nor Firestone's techno-utopianism (which is also racist) is defensible, since both depend on repressive or rationalized bodily and social processes, anathema to the goals of feminist autonomy.

INDIVIDUAL DESIRE AND REPRODUCTION
IN LATE CAPITALISM

From the mid-1960s onward, women's liberation, widening use of the birth control pill and availability of abortion, began to give large numbers of women the experience of separating sex from reproduction. Feminist health and abortion services supported a politics of female autonomy and helped to change women's attitudes toward childbearing and motherhood. Books like Adrienne Rich's *Of Woman Born* and Nancy Chodorow's *The Reproduction of Mothering* provided generative theoretical studies of female ambivalence toward societies' constructions of reproductive functions and the institution of compulsory maternity. Crucially, they questioned and challenged the assumption that the desire to bear children is a natural and innate one common to all women.

The following three decades saw significant changes in women's reproductive patterns and choices. Many women began to defer childbearing to pursue higher education and careers. Many opted for single lifestyles, child-free marriages, lesbian relationships with or without children, or experimented with collective household and child-sharing arrangements. The entrepreneurs of new repro-tech took advantage of these new cultural and social patterns. Deferring childbearing lowered women's fertility rates, and ART was ready to step into the breach with techniques of ovarian hormone stimulation, IVF procedures, and egg donation. During this time new definitions of infertility were established by medical authorities, and "infertiles" supporting a growing medical industry of infertility demanded that it be recognized as a disease or disability whose treatment should be covered by insurance. (At present, infertility treatments and ART are financed almost entirely by the private monies of mostly middle-class and affluent users, who often mortgage houses, sell stocks, or raise bank loans to pay for treatments.) Fertility doctors have supported this move; for example, the American Society of Reproductive Medicine (ASRM) and RESOLVE (an infertility support group) have joined in endorsing the Fair Access to Infertility Treatment and Hope (FAITH) Senate Act that calls for insurance to pay for up to four IVF treatment cycles and promises "minimal impact on the cost of health insurance."[6] While such legislation may seem like a progressive

move to make ART widely accessible to all economic classes, it still won't benefit the millions of Americans who have no health insurance at all.

American commodity desire is immediate, and is fed by the belief that science can provide technological solutions for every biological problem. The still
highly experimental technologies of assisted reprotech have a low success rate
and their long-term safety and biological and genetic risks have not begun to be
adequately assessed or studied. But ART is being driven by the twin engines of
manipulated consumer desire for new technologies and the enormous profits to
be made from the infertility business. At the macro level of politics, the function of reproduction in late capital is to produce compliant workers and successful consumers to serve and feed a global commodities economy. Corporate
biotech entrepreneurs must find ways to divert reproductive desire and autonomy to serve market imperatives to control and patent genes, germ lines,
and life processes. Rationalized and optimized methods of new eugenic reproduction are represented as being far more efficient than the random chance
method of sexual intercourse, because they can be technologically controlled,
and promise improved human characteristics and successful offspring. Even
though the success rate of ART is still very low (between 15 and 22.5 percent of
IVF cycles result in take-home babies), its spectacle is one of scientific authority and control. The ideology and practice of new eugenic principles that is part
of the macro discourse of ART has been masked by the micro discourse of individual choice. Many sperm banks, for example, accept only certain categories of
donors—Nobel Prize winners, successful professionals, heterosexuals, athletes
—and all require extensive genetic, medical, and racial background profiling.
Preferred and highly paid egg donors must generally be young, intelligent,
college educated, from selected ethnic and racial backgrounds, healthy, good-
looking, and able to pass a battery of psychological tests.

RADICAL IDEAS AND NORMALIZED/
NATURALIZED PROCESSES

In order to be territorialized by capital, radical ideas and processes must be
normalized/naturalized in everyday life, and their dangers rewritten as bene-

fits. This is done through literature, art, and mass media representations. Religious indoctrination works this way, as does political propaganda. Science too relies on these instruments to make it appear rational, humanistic, and necessary, rather than outlandish and threatening. In the consumer culture of late capital, public acceptance of formerly frightening or taboo scientific ideas is managed through carefully orchestrated propaganda campaigns that domesticate the previously unthinkable with promissory rhetorics of "improvement" and "choice," and with seductively aestheticized images of scientific processes, products, and services.

The often extreme, biotechnological procedures of ART have been naturalized in this way within a few short years. Starting with the birth of Louise Brown, the first IVF baby, in Britain in 1978, the new reproductive technologies were at first both sensationalized and glorified in the media, often by the use of apocalyptic language, or by dire warnings about the monstrous experiments scientists were conducting in their labs. These media reports played on the fears and fantasies of people worried about becoming guinea pigs in an authoritarian scheme to remake humankind. The media revisited all the classic archetypes and eugenic myths from *Frankenstein* to *Brave New World*. The icon of the baby in the bottle *in vitro* [literally, in the glass] was replaced with pictures of doctors mixing gametes in petri dishes, and hundreds of frozen embryos crammed into cryotanks.[7]

To counter much of the negative publicity and push their business, ART doctors and entrepreneurs entered the battle of representation, writing their own books and launching Web sites that present reassuring images, human interest stories, and descriptions of ART in matter-of-fact and easily assimilated ways. For example, detailed diagrams of the interior of the female pelvis and reproductive organs are often shown with a vision machine or surgical instrument in place. These cyborgian images help normalize the idea of technological intervention into the reproductive body. The literature is usually directed at the white, educated, middle-class, professional couple or career single; it is reassuringly scientific (i.e., it gives assurances that ART is cutting-edge medicine, not stitching together corpses), affirmative, and upbeat. It represents

ART as an exciting creative venture any couple could undertake with their doctor.

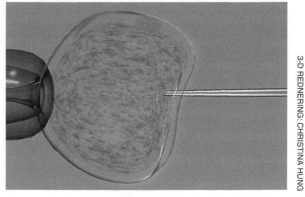

Intra Cytoplasmic Sperm Injection (ICSI).

ART literature also paints a picture of how clients can integrate these processes into their everyday lives (i.e., "Our clinics open early and close late so you can come in for your tests every day"), and systems that help them work out payment plans. Crucially, this literature pitches its utopian and promissory rhetoric in the non-sensationalized, calmly authoritative voice of the expert: "I helped to create the United States' first pregnancy produced from a frozen embryo."[8] Disguised as consumer advice, this approach benefits capital and reinforces scientific authority.

Consumer persuasion also works by aestheticizing scientific processes. An iconic representation of ART that has been circulated widely is a colorized microphotograph of intra cytoplasmic sperm injection (ICSI), a delicately precise micro manipulation process in which a single carefully screened, washed, and capacitated sperm is inserted through the zona pellucida of a selected egg by means of a hollow glass needle. This is an image of willful creation every bit as compelling as Michelangelo's iconic Sistine Chapel image of God creating Adam. It is simultaneously the ultimate image of scientific control and triumph, and a secular visualization of miraculous creation. Most viewers have no scientific understanding of the precise biotechnological process this image demonstrates, but the ideological reading is clear: technological control over life processes. Further, it is an image of eugenic choice that brings one superior egg and one fit sperm together in a technologically mediated act of fertilization. Without needing to spell it out directly, the ICSI image has become an unparalleled poster child for the new eugenic processes of genetic screening and manipulation. Such consumer-friendly representations have been effective in helping to naturalize the often frightening and extreme processes of ART in everyday life.

The abstract beauty of the aestheticized scientific ICSI image is made possible by sophisticated new visualization instruments including sonography, hysteroscopy, laparoscopy, microphotography, tunneling microscopy, PET scans, and MRI. After all, the breakthrough step of being able to "see" the fetus in the womb opened the way for it to become a strategic icon in the abortion battles. Both ART and abortion foreground the fetus or take-home baby, not the mother or the woman. Since the fetus icon was contested territory already claimed by anti-abortion crusaders, ART adopted the image of the radiant (usually white) biotech baby, the child of choice. After all, what ART was promising was a live baby, not just an unformed fetus. (Hard statistics of ART success are measured in "take-home-babies," not pregnancies.) These iconic baby pictures have helped to domesticate strange and threatening technologies that were previously unthinkable.

CONCLUSION: NEW CYBERFEMINIST PRACTICES

The micro and macro politics of the public discourses of ART are conflicted; currently the forces of market capitalism have won the field with the consumer-friendly appropriated rhetoric of choice. Consequently, this rhetoric is too compromised to be useful to feminists any longer. Instead, new critical practices and language must be introduced to address changed political and cultural conditions. Corporate research in assisted reprotech is still advancing rapidly, and increasingly there are contestatory interests at stake. Meanwhile, growing bodies of feminist cultural theory and literature, as well as new media practices and artworks, play with concepts of the posthuman cyborg body and the recombinations of women and machines. The 1980s saw strong feminist activism, both in the U.S. and internationally by groups such as Feminist International Network of Resistance to Reproductive and Genetic Engineering (FINRRAGE), founded in 1984, that critiqued and opposed new reprotech using many classic feminist arguments and tactics. But there is still a wide gap between liberal and radical feminist theory, activism, and practice in the domains of biotech and ART. In her groundbreaking article, "A Manifesto for Cyborgs," Donna

Haraway suggests it is of utmost importance that feminist politics address the social relations of science and technology. This would seem to be a productive strategy for cyberfeminist artists working with biotech issues.

The challenge for feminist activists/artists is to create practices that counter and subvert corporate biotech's increasing ability to control the female body and reproductive processes by means of advanced technologies. Recent repro-tech controversies, such as women growing embryos to be harvested for fetal stem cell research, suggest the urgent need for new ways to assess the threats to women's bodily sovereignty posed by rapid naturalization and deployment of such corporate-driven technologies. Since most women do not understand many of the complex implications and consequences of reprotech, it is necessary that feminists begin to generate autonomous (free from state, corporate, or entrepreneurial control) cross-cultural, decentralized, biomedical sex and reproduction education projects trans-nationally. In her book *Women as Wombs*, radical feminist Janice Raymond cautions that science has become overly focused on developing techniques employing lucrative high-end technologies. Raymond calls for a new feminist reproductive and sexual science that doesn't hinge solely on often risky, high-tech approaches that are financially unavailable to most women anyway.[9] Such a science could recombine diverse sources of knowledge to create new sexual and reproductive options that take into account women's differing economic, social, and political conditions and desires. New feminist reproductive science would have to devise flexible information and distribution mechanisms, perhaps based on a combination of electronic networking and embodied, performative practices. As the autonomous method of menstrual extraction practiced by lay people (bypassing the medical authority system) proved, new approaches to reproductive science can enlist feminist activists from diverse backgrounds to act as trained, non-specialist practitioners teaching methods that foster principles of autonomy and individual and social well-being. Feminists should lead the critique of the ways in which intensified biotechnological intervention is increasingly offered as the solution to every problem from infertility to world hunger.

subRosa has begun to activate a resistant cultural practice based on the goals discussed above. Initially, we focused on aspects of ART that have largely been silenced in public discourse. We hope to disrupt the current "choice" discourse of ART; to initiate an interventionist debate and practice among diverse non-specialist audiences; and to further probe and expose biotechnology's far-reaching repercussions for women's health and bodily autonomy worldwide. Our projects to date: 1) "Does She or Doesn't She" (poster), "SmartMom"(website), and "Vulva De/Reconstructa" (video) expose gender differences in ART practices and highlight the effects of high-tech body invasion on women's health and autonomy. 2) "Expo EmmaGenics" (performance and website) and "The Economies of ART" (article) question and challenge the ways in which market forces drive the research, development and deployment of reprotech's products and services through an analysis of the economies of ART; and 3) "Sex and Gender Education in the Biotech Century," (performance, workbook, and web site) interrogates the intersecting ideologies and practices that serve to normalize and naturalize ART, exposing their historical connections to eugenics and colonial ideologies.[10] ★

This essay was originally published in German in *Kunstforum International*, January–March 2002, Germany.

1   For a bibliography on women and biotech, see Appendix.

2   John A. Robertson, *Children of Choice: Freedom and the New Reproductive Technologies* (New Jersey: Princeton University Press, 1994), p. 235.

3   Advertisement appearing in the New York Times Magazine, July 21, 2000. p. 42.

4   For a discussion of "new eugenic consciousness" see Critical Art Ensemble, *Flesh Machine: Cyborgs, Designer Babies and New Eugenic Consciousness* (New York: Autonomedia, 1998).

5   Shulamith Firestone, *The Dialectic of Sex: The Case for Feminist Revolution* (New York: William Morrow, 1970), p. 193.

6   See <http://www.resolve.org/RELEASE_FaithBill.htm>.

7   Susan M. Squier, *Babies in Bottles: Twentieth-Century Visions of Reproductive Technology* (New Brunswick: Rutgers University Press, 1994).

8   Marrs, Bloch, and Silverman, *Dr. Richard Marrs' Fertility Book* (New York: Dell Publishers, 1997), p. xiii.

9   Janice G. Raymond, *Women as Wombs: Reproductive Technologies and the Battle over Women's Freedom* (New York: HarperCollins, 1993).

10 For more information on subRosa's projects visit our web site: <http://www.cyberfeminism.net>.

Vulvas with a Difference

Faith Wilding

INTRODUCTION

An age-old problem has resurfaced—with a difference—in the biotech century. The problem: What does woman (sic) want? This question, once so exasperatedly asked by Freud—as a corollary to his finding that woman "represents a lack" (of a penis)—is once again being vigorously addressed in the practices of (mostly) male scientists and doctors with new biotechnological and medical processes at their disposal. Freud's formulation of the question presumes an essentially identical desire (for the penis) in all women regardless of age, race, sexual preference, education, economic status, or geographical residence. It also represents "woman" as essentially lacking (because she has been found "wanting?") and as problematic, mysterious, unknowable, and eternally unsatisfiable. Freud makes it clear that the problem—traditionally described by the term "hysteria"—is that women want sexual pleasure; they want to know how to have it, how to get it, and how to control and ensure the supply.

In Europe and the U.S., nineteenth and early twentieth-century responses to the problem of female "hysterical" anorgasmia and decreased or absent sexual pleasure often called for medical interventions that were sometimes quite drastic, including painful body binding, purging, bloodletting, nasty douches and bath regimes, confinement to bed, bland diets, and in worst cases, hysterectomy and/or clitoridectomy. Women experiencing "vaginal relaxation"[1] and vulvar and vaginal damage due to too frequent childbirth, inadequate medical knowledge of women's genital structures and functions, and the total ignorance of the mechanisms of the female orgasm, had nowhere to turn except to their doctors, because the traditions of women healers and midwives with experience and knowledge of women's bodies had long since eroded in the moralized and rationalized body practices of the Enlightenment.

A valuable light is cast on age-old treatments of female disturbances by Dr. Rachel Maines.[2] She documents that an effective treatment for hysterical women since the Greeks had been "pelvic massage"—sometimes performed by male doctors, but more often by female midwives—to relieve women of the sexual tensions, pelvic edema, and nervous depressions brought on by the lack of orgasmic release in marital penetrative coitus. Maines chronicles the invention of the vibrator—originally designed to relieve doctors of the tedium of hand manipulation of women's genitals (pelvic massage)—and its fairly rapid adoption as a tool of "personal care" in private households; and shows that this technological solution to the "problem" of women's complicated sexual needs contributed to letting (male) lovers and husbands off the hook in terms of learning to satisfy their partner's sexual desires. At the same time the vibrator supported the centrality of penetrative coitus climaxing in male orgasm as the dominant form of heterosexual practice.

Meanwhile, in many north African countries such as Kenya, the Sudan, Ethiopia, Somalia, Mali, Egypt, and Chad (as well as in many parts of the Middle East, such as Saudi Arabia, Iraq, and Yemen, as well as large parts of Indonesia, and to a lesser extent in other parts of the world), varying forms of female circumcision and female genital mutilation (FGM) have been practiced for centuries by both Muslims and Christians. While there are deep and complex reasons for the origin and perpetuation of these practices, nearly all African and Western researchers who have studied them—as well as the evidence of extensive testimony from women on whom these operations have been practiced—agree that most of these procedures are extremely painful and dangerous to a woman's health; they usually destroy women's sexual pleasure, and are performed to "purify" and control women's sexuality.[3] Thus, though there seems to be no social construction of female hysteria in these countries, it is significant that the circumcision practices have the effect of controlling and curtailing women's sexual pleasure, which must somehow seem a threat to social order and masculine power. And although they are often compared, female genital circumcision can in no way be equated with the circumcision of men, even though some circumcised men do report diminished sexual sensation due to the loss of their foreskins. It is also important to note that in the past decade or so in the U.S., there has been a fairly vocal revolt against the almost universally adopted medical (and sometimes religious) practice of routine male circumcision right after birth.

THE BIOTECH SOLUTION

> You don't have to fly to LA or NY to get the hottest trend in the world of cosmetic surgery—labiaplasty and vaginal tightening, also known as a "designer vagina." —WEB SITE

Currently, biotechnologies and new microsurgical medical technologies (MedTech) are being used to pioneer new flesh technologies. MedTech is being used by doctors to address the Freudian "lack" directly by re-engineering the body of the woman rather than by treating her psyche. Consider, for example, this website text describing "Vaginal Rejuvenation through Designer Laser Vaginoplasty: Designer Laser Vaginoplasty is the aesthetic surgical enhancement of vulval structures, such as the labia minora, labia majora and mons pubis."[4] Texts on these websites make clear that what is lacking or inadequate is the woman's body and the structure of her sexual organs—not medical knowledge and sexual practices.

Though many men still complain that they cannot find the clitoris, recent research into the structures of the clitoris and vulva have revealed an astonishing new terrain of erectile tissue and nerve networks which show that the size of the clitoris is much bigger than previously depicted in medical literature. Part of the problem of the invisibility of the clitoris (the dark continent) is that the ancient methods of comparative anatomical studies of male and female genitalia still permeate scientific and medical literature and practice. In a recent article, Dr. Helen E. O'Connell and colleagues pointed out that even the nomenclature for the female genital parts is consistently incorrect: "We investigated the anatomical relationship between the urethra and the surrounding erectile tissue, and reviewed the appropriateness of the current nomenclature used to describe this anatomy.... A series of detailed dissections suggests that current anatomical descriptions of female human urethral and genital anatomy are inaccurate."[5]

Girls and women in the U.S. are routinely taught to call their external sexual organs "vagina" (as in the current Off-Broadway show, "Vagina Monologues"), rather than "vulva." The vagina is not the homologous organ to the penis, and the incorrect nomenclature perpetuates the invisibility and unmentionability of the female sexual (orgasmic) organs—the vulva and clitoris. The subversive '70s feminist use of the term "cunt" (as in "cunt art") was a direct response to this problem of naming.

However, now that vast amounts of money can be made from new microsurgical and biotechnological medical interventions, some scientists/doctors (in the U.S. and Canada) have decided to educate themselves about the "problems" of women so they can fix them once and for all in the postmodern (post-hysterical) way—through medical and biotechnology:

> To date there has been no such interest (as that dedicated to the correction of male impotence), let alone research, in vaginal relaxation and its detrimental effects on sexual gratification.... The obstetrician and gynecologist is looked upon as the champion of female health care.... Your doctor is a scientist. His [sic] knowledge is based upon this science (the science of obstetrical and gynecological specialty). This science is founded upon research, bio statistics, established facts [sic], theories, and postulates. If there is none of this science pertaining to vaginal relaxation and sexual gratification then it doesn't exist. It won't exist until we look for it. Therefore, let it begin now![6]

And so the scientist/doctors are off and running. Purely elective vulvar/vaginal surgeries that are done for "aesthetic reasons only" can cost between $2,000 and $3,500 for a fairly simple "plumping" (liposculpture) of the outer lips of the mons, using fat suctioned from the inner thighs. Or, you may be advised to employ labiaplasty to shorten and symmetricalize those dangerous, dangly vulvar lips that might interfere with horseback riding, wearing pants, or be painfully drawn inside during intercourse. ("Labiaplasty is a reduction of the labia minora, the flaps of skin which form the lips of a woman's genitalia and cover the clitoris and vaginal opening.") Or, for women from certain "ethnic" groups: "When a woman marries and consummates the marriage she must bleed to prove virginity to her partner... since in this day and age (due to exercise, and physical activity) the hymen is rarely intact... (some) women do request a hymen repair."[7] It is no surprise that this latter sentence is the only mention of "ethnic" groups or practices that I found in the websites and online literature from vaginal rejuvenation clinics. I found no mention of the practices of female genital mutilation (FGM), or the connection between the new MedTech surgical practices and FGM, though these doctors must surely be aware of it. The new vulvar and vaginal surgical technologies would be put to much better use in helping women seeking reconstruction and healing of sexual organs mutilated and damaged by FGM practices, than in making unnecessary "aesthetic" interventions on perfectly healthy women.

TECHNOLOGIES WITH A DIFFERENCE

"Women are multi-orgasmic.... From this factual data, laser vaginal rejuvenation was designed in order to *enhance sexual gratification for women who, for whatever reason, lack an overall optimum architectural integrity of the vagina.*" [author's emphasis]

For most affluent (white) Western women accustomed to rejuvenating their looks by plastic surgery, the re-engineering and aesthetic enhancement of the vulva is a so-called "elective" procedure, and seems to represent a voluntary consumer excess not that much different from a nose or breast job—although the term "voluntary" is questionable here, considering the disciplinary pressures of Western beauty standards.

By contrast, for non-Western women, female genital alteration, including many forms of female circumcision and infibulation, is generally a mandatory cultural ritual or procedure usually practiced on women by women. With globalization and increased East to West migration, women from societies still practicing various forms of female circumcision sometimes seek these services from qualified obstetricians/gynecologists in modern hospitals. Such is the

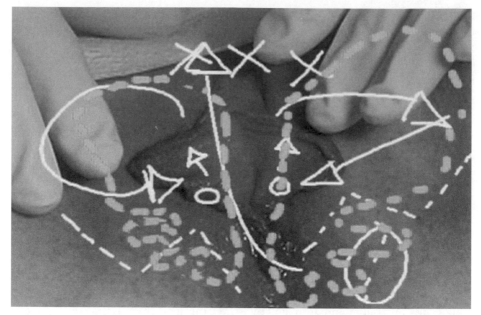

Still from "Vulva De/Re Constructa" video, by subRosa.

compelling nature of this cultural custom, however, that many mothers are still sending their daughters back to their countries of origin for these ritual procedures, where they may be performed by the traditional female circumcisers, usually operating with rusty tools and no anesthetics or disinfectants. Despite years of organizing against Female Genital Mutilation practices on the part of many Africans and Westerners—resulting in legal bans of the practices in some countries like Guinea, Niger, and Sudan—the bans are no match for the compelling cultural rituals. In many parts of Egypt, for example, though hospitals had been forbidden to perform clitoridectomies, "the procedure was now carried out in barber shops and similar, non-official places... and led to an increase of complications."[8]

The paradoxical situation then is that women from quite different economic, social/cultural backgrounds and geographical origins are undergoing vulvar surgery and alterations for completely different reasons—and with differing results—all of which however have their roots in patriarchal gender practices. The (Western) aesthetic vulvar surgery is claimed (by doctors and patients) to enhance sexual enjoyment for the woman, although there are no medically persuasive reasons or proofs given for this. In actuality there is a likelihood that nerves and sensitive tissues are being damaged, and that erectile tissue—which is far more extensive than is depicted in standard medical and anatomy texts—is being reduced and replaced by nerveless scar tissue. So even though in these operations the clitoris is not excised (although it sometimes is "repositioned") there is loss and disturbance of sensitive tissues, and hence probably also of subtle and deep sensation.[9] Undaunted by the contradictions, the aesthetic surgeon can win three times: S/he treats the high-income Western spenders who are seeking *"enhanced sexual gratification"* through genital surgery; s/he can treat the women forced by their cultural traditions to alter their genitals *with the result of controlling and curtailing or destroying female sexual pleasure*; and s/he can reconstruct the deformities and traumas caused by botched circumcision operations.

Nowhere in the online or other literature from the aesthetic "rejuvenation" clinics which practice this new surgery is there any mention of other ways of treating "vaginal relaxation," or of helping women achieve more sexual pleasure by other than medicalized means. Nowhere is it mentioned that during second-wave feminism, for example, women gathered to teach each other about their sexual organs and bodies: how to have orgasms, how to give themselves and other women pleasure, how to teach men to give women pleasure. Nowhere are vibrators, dildos, Kegel exercises, counseling, sensual massage, pleasurable body practices, or other (non-medical) self-help practices mentioned. The literature works by seduction, promising scientifically enhanced sexual pleasure and improved performance. It insists that women are (and ought to be) multiorgasmic and if this isn't happening for you something may be wrong with your body, and you should hasten to the nearest surgeon for the medicalized, technological fix. To cap it off, there is no awareness in the literature of the explicitly heterosexual assumptions of this type of surgery, and of the way in which it reinforces the idea of female lack.

Neither do we see any discussion about the problematic of Western doctors making it possible for non-Western women (and men) to perpetuate their harmful and painful "customs" by using "safe" and "modern" Western technologies. This would seem to be an important medical ethics discussion. Although laws have been passed in the U.S. forbidding female circumcision practices, doctors are increasingly being called upon to do these operations, or to repair botched genital jobs on women who come to emergency rooms. It seems that many Western feminists have been too reluctant to participate fully in this discussion for reasons of false race consciousness, and lack of understanding how related it is to issues raised by the new flesh technologies now pervading Western culture.

(ANTI) AESTHETICS OF THE VULVA

> Aesthetic surgery of the female external genitalia has been neglected by physicians. However, awareness of female genital aesthetics has increased owing to increased media attention, both from magazines and video. Women may feel self-conscious about the appearance of their labia majora (outer lips) or, more commonly, labia minora (inner lips). The aging female may dislike the descent of her pubic hair and the labia and desire re-elevation to its previous location. Very few physicians are concerned with the appearance of the female external genitalia. *A relative complacency exists that frustrates many women.*"[10] [author's emphasis]

Surely one of the strangest aspects of the new female genital surgery are physicians' website texts (such as the one cited above) that sound rather self-conscious, and seem to be included for purposes of self-justification (or perhaps to pre-empt people wondering why a self-respecting doctor would get into the vulva re-engineering business). An examination of some of the terms used in these texts (for example, "elective vaginal enhancement," "female genital aesthetics," "vaginal rejuvenation," or "optimal architectural integrity of the vagina") imply that there is an implicit set of desirable traits or aesthetic standards for the female genitals—and according to the doctors, "lack" is now operable. These implicit aesthetics for female genitalia need to be made explicit, and a subversive (anti) aesthetic suggested in their place.

What aesthetics of the vulva are revealed in an examination of these Web pages and of other mass-circulation images? The passage quoted above states that "awareness of female genital aesthetics has increased owing to media attention, both from magazines and video." One can only assume that what is being referred to here are features on "Designer Vaginas" in such magazines as *Cosmopolitan*, but probably not the increased media coverage and feminist activism regarding banning female genital mutilation. Referring to the terms found on the websites of aesthetic surgeons, it seems clear that in the plastic surgery profession at least, female genitals are seen as lacking in youthful resilience and appearance, tightness, architectural integrity, symmetry, dainty labia size, tasteful hair distribution, and plumpness. A template of the ideal vulva emerges: The tight, small, pulsing, plump, juicy, glistening, pearly pink, virginal-yet-hot cunt found in pornography, art, or erotic literature. As can be seen on the website *before* and *after* pictures of labia reduction operations, vulvas are surgically reconstructed to look very much like wounds. The crinkly, "redundant" labia—which shield the exquisitely sensitive clitoris from too harsh an approach and too direct a touch, and which form a moist, protective surface of rubbing and touching flesh that engorges with pulsing blood during sexual arousal—are drastically reduced. The entire vulva *becomes* a slit, a gash, a hole, a wound, an orifice just right for penetrating male entry and direct access to the vagina. Here lack becomes enhancement through diminishment—a peculiar logic indeed. The glowing testimonies of enhanced women that appear on the web pages speak only in the most vague terms of the wonderful new lives that this operation has given them.

Advanced digital visualization technologies are currently giving new insights into heretofore invisible and unexplored territories of the interior body (see the citation from the work of Dr. Helen O'Connell above). Seizing upon these technologies, scientists and plastic surgeons are leaping into the breach to claim and redesign the newly discovered territories—much as the conquistadores and colonists did in the newly discovered Americas. (In this connection, one wonders how, and whether, the sexual proclivities of different colonial cultures [Dutch, French, Portuguese, British, etc.] were influenced by the differing aesthetics which seem to govern the various styles of African female circumcision?)

Because language and naming construct the medico/scientific perception and treatment of the body—as well as clarifying the phenomenological experiences of the body—women need to inform themselves about the new scientific discoveries of vulvar and clitoral structures, and feminists should insist that scientists and doctors be educated in the feminist research about female desire, biology, pleasure and sexuality. Only then will their eyes be fully opened to the possible implications of the newly discovered erectile and pleasure structures.

Many consumers, it seems, are all too willing to leave behind enjoyment of organically varying bodies, and are looking to technology and science to give them new ways of creating ideals for the new technologized body, regardless of what they may have to sacrifice and suffer by doing so. The existing medico/scientific aesthetic for female genitals seems to have been affected only in some respects by the cunt-celebrating 1970s, the feminist-*jouissance*-theory '80s, and the bad-grrl '90s. The *jouissance* and libidinal excess pursued by many feminists as a path to autonomy and power, is being replaced in public discourse by the consumer spectacle of the cyborg porn babe, whose predatory surface is adorned by every well-worn sign of coded sexuality that the market will bear.

An (anti) aesthetic of the vulva might posit first of all that looks and surface are not the important thing when it comes to vulvas. Instead, sensation and feeling, and the excitation of deep structures are pre-eminent. Perhaps our scopophilic culture desires to establish once and for all a visual "proof" of the female orgasm so it can be compared to that of the male? Could it be that a dangerous precedent was set in the early 1970s, when Masters and Johnson, the avowed champions of the female orgasm and of the multi-orgasmic prowess of women, began to measure and chart female orgasms in the lab? Eye opening as this information was in so many ways, it doubled the efforts to quantify, measure, and represent the female orgasm, this time by medical charts and graphs, rather than by psychological or poetic terminology. Masters and Johnson are still invoked by the new pleasure surgeons, who, under the banner of championing female orgasmic capability and entitlement, wield their knives in order to give women the optimal vulva/vagina for enhanced sexual satisfaction, for better sex through surgery.

Can feminists counteract these entrenched views and disseminate a new (anti) aesthetic of the vulva? How can we counter the medicalized or pornographic images of vulvas that are usually the only ones offered for public view? Feminist artists tried to reclaim the cunt as a powerful pleasure source in the early '70s; and the vulva as a sign of sexual contention and gender construction has made many appearances in the art of the '80s and '90s. In everyday life, men, lesbians, and doctors see many more vulvas than most heterosexual women ever do. There are few possibilities for women to see other women's vulvas in a pleasurable, convivial, or desiring environment. Most women probably have not even thought twice about the looks of their vulvas (many haven't dared look), but this new worry is being created (in post-hysterical terms) by the existence and deployment of new flesh technologies. Subversive tactics that critique the commercial and cultural coercion and potential physical danger of such operations are called for. Why not have parties where women can examine, compare, and explore the myriad different forms of vulvas? Why not set up spa days (paid for by medical insurance) in which women teach themselves and their sexual partners about female sexuality and desire. Let's educate children in the proper nomenclature and sexual and pleasure functions of the female genital organs. Above all, let's call for resistance to the unquestioned technological "solutions" to issues that have profound psychological, emotional, cultural, and even political origins and histories. Let us not obliterate the vulva as we now know it—before we do know it! ★

This essay was originally published in German in *SexPolitik*, ed. by Doris Guth and Elizabeth von Samsonow. (Vienna: Turia + Kant, 2001).

1   Vaginal relaxation is "the loss of the optimum structural architecture of the vagina...the vaginal muscles become flaccid with poor tone, strength, and support." According to statistics, 30 million American women suffer from this. Just think of that marketing possibility!

2   Rachel P. Maines, *The Technology of Orgasm: Hysteria, the Vibrator, and Women's Sexual Satisfaction* (Baltimore and London: The Johns Hopkins University Press, 1999).

3   "Types of Female Genital Mutilation: Circumcision or Sunna: Removal of the prepuce or hood of the clitoris, with the body of the clitoris remaining intact. Excision or Clitoridectomy: Removal of the clitoris and all or part of the labia minora. Intermediate: Removal of the clitoris, all or part of the labia minora, and sometimes part of the labia majora. Infibulation or Pharaonic: Removal of the clitoris, the labia minora and much of the labia majora. The remaining sides of the vulva are stitched together to close up the vagina, except for a small opening, which is preserved with slivers of wood or matchsticks." Alice Walker and Pratibha Parmar, *Warrior Marks: Female Genital Mutilation and the Sexual Blinding of Women* (New York: Harcourt, Brace & Co. 1993), p. 367.

4   Laser Vaginal Rejuvenation Center: <http://www.drmatlock.com>.

5   Dr. Helen O'Connell et al, "Anatomical Relationships between Urethra and Clitoris," <http://www.wwilkins.com/urology/0022-53476-98abs.html#page1892>.

6 Op. cit., Laser Vaginal Rejuvenation Center.

7 Op. cit., Laser Vaginal Rejuvenation Center.

8 Arnold Groh, *Manual for the New Strategy against Female Genital Mutilation*,
   p. 2. Pamphlet reporting the meetings of the United Nations Working Group on
   Indigenous Populations in Geneva, July 26–30, 1999.

9 This loss of sensation is comparable to that documented for circumcised men, who
   often report diminished sexual sensation because of the loss of the foreskin, which
   is richly endowed with blood vessels and nerves.

10 <http://www.altermd.com/female/index.html>

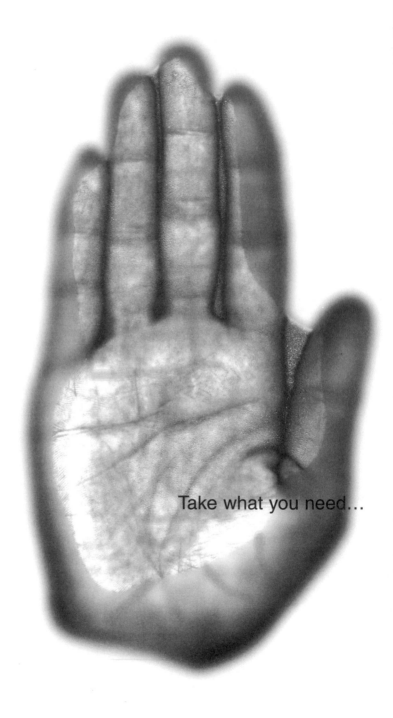

Take what you need…

Take a 10 minute rest: lie down with this book resting on your

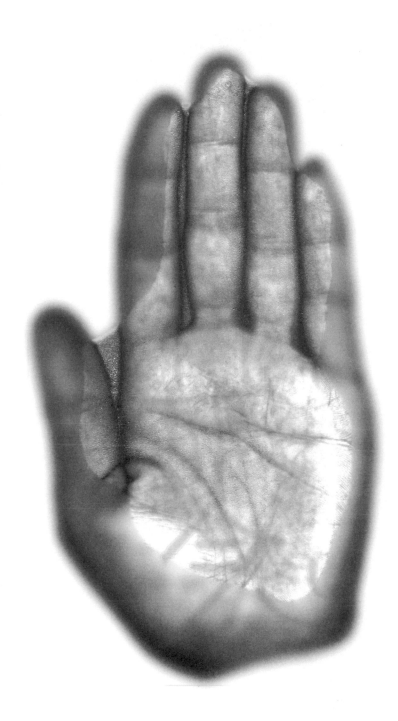

face, chest or stomach. Make sure it is open to this page.

A Summary History of Eugenic Theories and Practices in the United States

Compiled by Emily de Araujo and Lucia Sommer

The term 'eugenics' was conceived by Sir Francis Galton (Charles Darwin's cousin and the inventor of composite photography) in the 19th century. Eugenic practice includes the systematic elimination of so-called 'undesirable' biological traits and the use of selective breeding to 'improve' the characteristics of an organism or species.[1] One branch of eugenics held that the rich and powerful were genetically superior to the poor, and that whites were in general superior to other races. Such a philosophy has provided convenient justification for a system of structuring inequities.

1904 Steel magnate Andrew Carnegie establishes a center for the study of "hybridized peoples," where researchers seek to understand the "idleness, the inconstancy...and...inadequate intelligence" of "racial mixtures."[2]

1906 The American Breeders Association (ABA) forms a Committee on Eugenics. Their purpose is to investigate and report on heredity, emphasizing the value of "superior blood" and the menace of "inferior blood."

1907–WWI Sixteen states adopt sterilization laws for "socially inadequate biological varieties"—i.e., criminals and the mentally ill.[3]

1910s The wealthy Harriman family establishes the first Eugenics Record Office in Cold Springs Harbor, NY, in 1910, and the Kellogg family, the Race Betterment Foundation in 1913. Subsequent societies spring up throughout the U.S. during the teens.

1914 A report made to the ABA states that "Society must look upon germ plasm as belonging to society and not solely to the individual who carries it."[4]

1919 Margaret Sanger, a leader of the birth control movement, moves to the political right, declaring "More children from the fit and less from the unfit— that is the chief issue of birth control." Her *Birth Control Review* begins to publish eugenicist arguments. By 1932 she is calling for the sterilization or segregation by sex of "the whole dysgenic population."[5]

1924 House of Representatives passes a law effectively restricting all immigration by Southern Europeans (who were considered non-white, or 'degenerate') to the United States.

1925 German officials write to state governments in the United States for information on sterilization laws. A leading advocate of eugenics in Germany at the time remarks, "What we racial hygienists promote is not at all new or unheard of. In a cultural nation of the first order, the United States of America, that which we strive toward was introduced long ago. It is all so clear and simple."[6]

1928 Seventy five percent of all colleges and universities offer courses on eugenics. A professor at Harvard University teaches that "the solution to crime is the extirpation of the physically, mentally, and morally unfit or (if that seems too harsh) their complete segregation in a socially aseptic environment."

1930s Eugenicist Frederick Osborn, director of the Carnegie Institute, argues that the public will never accept eugenics as top-down militarized directive; rather, eugenic consciousness would develop as an emergent property within the population as the capitalist economy increased in complexity. Once a specific set of social structures (consumer economy and the nuclear family) developed to a point of dominance, eugenic activity would cease to be seen as a monstrous activity, and instead become a taken-for-granted part of everyday life.[7] Beginning in the Great Depression, the Genetics Society of America maintains an unresolved debate whether or not to formally condemn the Third Reich's policies.

1931 Thirty states adopt sterilization laws, and tens of thousands of American citizens undergo non-consensual sterilization.

Post WWII While the Nazi atrocities do much to discredit this brand of eugenics in the United States, it has never completely disappeared. Some of its arguments will resurface in the 1950s in the population control movement.

Racism continues to infect the birth control movement. In 1939, the American Birth Control Federation designs a "Negro Project," whose aim is to control the "breeding" of Blacks in the South.

1942 Sanger's Birth Control Federation changes its name to Planned Parenthood. While "these organizations did perform the very valuable role of making contraception more available and accessible...at the same time...they shifted the focus away from women's rights, embraced eugenicist and elitist views of the poor, and adopted a limited, top-down approach to services."[8]

1960 Beginning of second wave eugenics in the United States. Unlike the first wave of eugenics, which had a conspiratorial aura about it, the new eugenics are (as Owen predicted) emerging as voluntary, driven by the dominance of consumer economy and the nuclear family in late capitalist culture.

1970s–90s The number of articles in the popular print media that attribute genetic causes to complex social and economic phenomena increases dramatically. In the six-year period from 1976 to 1982, *The Reader's Guide to Periodical Literature* displays a 231 percent increase in the number of articles attempting to demonstrate a genetic basis for crime, mental illness, intelligence, and alcoholism. Between 1983 and 1988, the number of articles attributing a genetic basis for crime quadruples in frequency over the previous decade. As Troy Duster points out, the explosion in such claims in both the popular and scientific literature came not from those working at the vanguard of molecular genetics or biochemistry, as one might expect. Instead, the major data source for the resurgent eugenicist claims was "a heavy reliance on Scandinavian institutional registries dating back to the early part of the century."[9]

1980s Sperm banks that select donors according to intelligence, looks and success are founded. One of these sperm banks prohibits artists from being donors. [One scientist] founds a sperm bank exclusively for Nobel Prize winners. In this explicitly eugenicist project, only women who were members of MENSA could receive the sperm.

1990s At least one college coed with "desirable traits" has sold her eggs for $50,000.

A spate of books such as *The Bell Curve* reintroduces earlier eugenicists' arguments about the genetic basis of social inequality. This argument is only the most extreme variation, symptomatic of the ideological geneticism being accelerated by the new bio-technologies.

1999 A website devoted to the sale of the eggs of supermodels promising "beauty to the highest bidder" asks $10,000 to $150,000 per egg. Its owner declares, "This is Darwin's 'Natural Selection' at its very best...this 'Celebrity Culture' that we have created does better economically than any other civilization in history..."

Rather than being forcefully imposed, these new eugenic mechanisms reflect the ideological values of the social formation in which the rationalized reproductive process occurs, where 'quality of life = economic performance' and human value is determined by a person's economic success. As Owen predicted, eugenic ideology, if not practice, is rapidly being naturalized.

Under the guise of optimizing reproduction—and "improving" human beings—today's reproductive technologies are being implemented without a critical discussion of their latent eugenic content. ★

---

1   Jeremy Rifkin, *The Biotech Century: Harnessing the Gene and Remaking the World* (New York: Jeremy P. Tarcher, 1998), p. 116.

2   Betsy Hartmann, *Reproductive Rights and Wrongs: The Global Politics of Population Control* (Boston: South End Press, 1995), p. 98.

3   Jeremy Rifkin, *The Biotech Century: Harnessing the Gene and Remaking the World* (New York: Jeremy P. Tarcher, 1998), p. 126.

4, 5, 6 Ibid.

7   Critical Art Ensemble, *Flesh Machine: Cyborgs, Designer Babies and New Eugenic Consciousness* (New York: Autonomedia, 1998), Chapter 6.

8   Betsy Hartmann, *Reproductive Rights and Wrongs* (Boston: South End Press, 1995), p. 98.

9   Troy Duster, "The Prism of Heritability and the Sociology of Knowledge," Laura Nader, ed., *Naked Science* (New York: Routledge, 1996), p. 119–120.

The *Cyborg Mommy* User's Manual

To: Mother
From: Cyborg Mommy (pattie)
Subject: Job Description
Cc:
Bcc:

Computer programmers and technology executives are some of the most sought after and well paid white collar workers in this country. Desired skills include the ability to keep up with a quickly changing work environment, creating bodies of knowledge, managing flows of information and machines, constant innovation, and creativity. It goes without saying that the world of technology is mostly populated by men. The job description of Mother also includes the ability to keep up with a quickly changing work environment, creating bodies of knowledge, managing flows of information and machines, constant innovation, and creativity, yet, this position is unpaid, and for many, undesirable. Obviously, most Mothers are women.

As machines and bodies increasingly become fused, Cyborg Theory celebrates, criticizes, and condemns the process. The machine/body relationship is at once liberating and oppressing. While movies and fiction depict the Cyborg as a futuristic superhuman or techno-logical monster, I propose that it is *actually* your average Mother and Housewife that are among the first so-called Cyborgs. The machine has extended the body of the mother for centuries as she tended the stove, cranked the washer, peddled the sewing machine, and vacuumed the house, but she hardly exists in discussions of technological culture, except as a con-suming unit for manufacturing and advertising or in the case of reproductive technologies—the body that carries the baby. There has been little or no discussion about the postpartum technologizing of the mother and child. With microchips embedded in everything from toys and greeting cards to thermometers and baby monitors, increasingly, the mother/child relationship is mediated, complicated and enhanced by machines. We are encouraged to feed our infants information as if we were storing data on a hard drive with a push to begin "programming" their brains in utero. What is a cyborg mother to do?

Here's to the recognition of the Cyborg Mommy— the Cyborg as oppressed and the Cyborg as liberated.

PATTIE BELLE HASTINGS

The cyborg is a kind of disassembled and reassembled, postmodern collective and personal self. This is the self feminists must recode.
—Donna Haraway

Mother taught me everything I know.

Glossary

(OR Everything I Know About Computers I Learned From Mother)

agent A software program that performs a service, such as alerting the user of something that needs to be done on a certain day; or monitoring incoming data and giving an alert when a message has arrived; or searching for information on electronic networks. An intelligent agent is enabled to make decisions about the information it finds.

Mother operated as the intelligent agent for all of the members of the family. Among the plethora of services provided by our personal agent she found art lessons for me, tutors for my little sister, colleges for all of us, and home care nurses for my grandmother. This of course meant she had little or no time for herself, her interests, and had no agent of her own. The selflessness of the intelligent agent is both a gift and a curse.

avatar A pictorial representation of a participant in a three-dimensional chat environment. The avatar is chosen by the user and may look like a bird, a fish or some other colorful character.

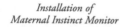

*Installation of
Maternal Instinct Monitor*

Mother had many avatars of all genders—Santa Claus, the Easter Bunny, and the Tooth Fairy, to name a few. She was so adept at these personas that it was years before we figured out it was her.

background task A task that runs on its own while the user interacts with the computer on another (foreground) task; for example, some computers can run a printer in background while the user edits text or reads other files.

There was always something going on in the background with a family of five children. It might be laundry hanging on the line, homework, music practice, or something cooking, but you could be sure that more than one thing was happening at any given time. This requires a constant juggling of background and foreground activities making for a scattered sense of self and a surreal compression or expansion of time. The extreme toll it takes on body and mind showed up in Mother as a deep and recurrent depression.

batch processing Processing a group of documents or files all at once. In batch processing, the user gives the computer a job, for example, printing letters to everyone on a mailing list, and waits for the whole job to be done.

Mother taught me to do laundry when I had enough like colors to make a full load. If I needed my gym suit or something for the next day it might be hand washed by itself (transaction processing.)

cache A temporary storage area for frequently-accessed or recently-accessed data. Having certain data stored in cache speeds up the operation of the computer. A cache hit (accessing data from a cache) takes much less time than retrieving information from the main memory.

There were always caches of lunch snacks, certain foods, small gift items, and school supplies hidden around the house in strategic locations so that they could not be accessed by unauthorized individuals. Mother had her own well-hidden private caches of candy bars for her sugar addiction.

computer A programmable electronic machine that performs mathematical and logical operations and assembles, stores, correlates and processes information.

We expect as much or more from the Mother as we do from the computer and yet we condemn the Mother that breaks down under the pressure. If the computer breaks down, we upgrade the hardware, software or memory. In other words, we provide what it needs to function reliably. There is no parallel of provision for the Mother.

debug To fix problems in hardware or software.

Homework, toys, sewing, friendships, arguments...need I say more? Mother even debugged the dog. Literally. Of course, that left her no time to deal with her own problems, such as a husband with an alcohol problem, feelings of isolation and despair, lack of romance, and no time to pursue her own interests or even figure out what those might be.

Easter egg A secret message hidden somewhere in a program, that can be revealed by entering some unusual combination of commands, such as pulling down a menu while holding the command and shift keys. Computer users can stumble upon Easter eggs by accident, or hear about them through rumors. The messages can be jokes, political statements, music, or pictures; often they are credits for the developers of the software.

A candy egg or soft-boiled egg that is hidden in the house or yard for "hunting" during the Easter holiday season.

Post-Human Sex Toy

The child who collects the most eggs or finds the golden egg wins a prize.

elegant Simple, graceful, yet effective; demonstrating the highest efficiency and economy of design. For example, in mathematics, an elegant proof; in computer programming, an elegant program.

Father was a Mason and Mother was an Eastern Star. On the nights that she went to these events she wore an evening gown, perfume and red lipstick. I thought she was the most beautiful and elegant creature that walked the earth, even though I did not want her to leave me behind with the baby sitter.

fault tolerance The ability of a system to keep working in the event of hardware or software faults. Fault tolerance is usually achieved by duplicating key components of the system.

Mother always had a back-up plan for the important goings on in the family, whether it be a spare car, working around weather, or surprise guests. There was never a standstill in the family machine. It kept on cranking— come what may.

guiltware Freeware or shareware that has a message attached which attempts to make the user feel guilty until making some kind of payment.

Parents are some of the best at enlisting guilt and Mother was no exception. It sometimes worked for getting rooms cleaned, the trash taken out (see **delete**), and other assorted chores. As I got older it was used for life decisions, keeping in touch, and coming home for the holidays.

help Explanations, available on the computer screen, about the various icons and tools and how to use the computer. Many programs have help menus that explain all their capabilities.

Life questions, homework questions, "how to" questions, if Mother didn't know the answer she would find it or someone who did.

ill-behaved Programs called ill-behaved are designed to bypass normal operating system functions, which may result in better performance but makes the program less

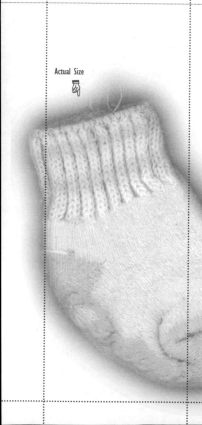

Actual Size

portable and more likely to be restricted to specific hardware. (See **well-behaved**.)

This type of action restricted you to the house. As simple as that. If you couldn't behave, you couldn't leave the house. We weren't badly behaved as kids, but managing a car full of five children was such a chore that we just didn't go out that much. The only restaurant that we ever went to was a Chinese place owned by a friend of Father's. I guess they figured friends would be more forgiving if we misbehaved or became unruly.

iteration The process of running a series of instructions over and over until some condition is satisfied. Or, one repetition of the series.

ABCs, shoe tying, flashcards, spelling tests, music practice, multiplication tables… Over and over and over, until we got it right.

JAM Just A Minute. (Chat Expression)

An expression used daily in order to reach a stopping point in the task at hand before responding to a call. JAM was used frequently by all members of the family and often used as a stalling factor. Mother would also use it in conversation to stop a train of thought as in disbelief or outrage. "Just a minute there young lady!"

knowledge base A database of knowledge about a subject; used in artificial intelligence. The knowledge base for an expert system (a computer system that solves problems) comes partly from human experience and partly from the computer's experience in solving problems.

I still consult Mother the Database about cooking, cleaning, child raising, marital relationships, and so on. And believe it or not, sometimes my knowledge base is of value to her.

LIFO Last In First Out. A method of storage in which the data stored last will be retrieved first.

LIFO is best demonstrated by lunch boxes and overnight bags. Mother would put the lunch items in the box in the reverse order of consumption, so that the first thing to come out of the box or bag was the sandwich. This also helped to prevent mushy bread (especially in the case of peanut butter and jelly—there's nothing worse than a soggy purple sandwich). When packing a bag for an overnight with a friend the last to go in were the pajamas and toothbrush, because they would be the first items needed.

machine A device consisting of fixed and moving parts that modifies mechanical energy and transmits it into a more useful form. A system or device that performs or assists in the performance of a human task.

The incorporation of machines into the household goes back thousands of years. A day in the life of a Mother requires interaction with a number of technological devices; vacuum cleaners, garbage disposals, washers, dryers, microwaves, automobiles, telephones, answering machines, TVs, VCRs, computers, calculators, cameras, blenders, and food processors, to name just a few.

multiprocessing Using two or more processors in the same computer, or two or more computers connected together, to execute more than one program or instruction at the same time.

Field trips always required multiprocessors. Several Mothers would volunteer their time to assist in the oversight of the class outside of the school grounds. This prevented unruly bus rides and losing children at museums or historic sites.

multitasking Running more than one program at a time. When a machine has this capability it is easy to switch between programs without having to quit, or to copy material from a file in one program to a file in another.

Mother could switch between tasks, demands, and thinking at notice. In fact, she never had the luxury of concentrating on one thing at a time. Everyone said that there was never a dull moment in our house, which also means that there was never any peace, rest, quiet or time to be with oneself. The idea that Mother might get away for some time alone or to vacation was unfathomable.

nag screen A screen displayed in a shareware program that reminds the user to register and pay the fee. It usually appears when the program is opened or closed.

The look on Mother's face when you didn't do what you were supposed to or you did what you weren't supposed to—no words necessary. (See **error message**)

off load To remove data from a computer and put it on another computer or storage medium.

Out of season clothes were uploaded from the closets to the attic until needed along with holiday decorations and old toys.

overwrite To write over data that is already on a disk; for example, when updating a file.

Permission for a thing, an act, or an event was overwritten due to behavioral changes or in the case of trying to go around Mother and get permission from Father. Approval or permission from Father was easily and often overwritten.

packet switching A technology for sending packets of information over a network. Data is broken up into packets for transmission. All the data packets related to a message may not take the same route to get to their destination; they are reassembled once they have arrived.

Adjusting Maternal Sensors in cyborg model MFAY2K

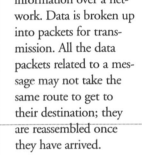

A common process for quilting, where individual members of a sewing circle constructed a block or section of fabric at home. Patterns and fabric were distributed, members sewed at individual locations and then met to assemble the blocks into a single quilt.

parallel processing Using more than one computer at the same time to solve a problem, or using more than one processor working simultaneously within the same computer.

A technique used for bake sales. Each Mother would bake a pie, cake, brownies, or cookies, then congregate at the designated location and sell the goodies to raise money for school or church activities.

quantifier One that quantifies; in mathematics or logic, a prefixed operator that states for which values of a variable a formula is true.

Mother was the quantifier for stating which values were true. We often disagreed with her, but we did use her basic formulas for developing our own value sets.

random access A way of storing and retrieving information in which all information locations are immediately available. For example, on a music CD any song can be selected and played randomly.

"Mother, have you seen my...?" She knew the location of everything at all time and was constantly besieged by six people always searching for something.

remote login Logging in to a remote computer by a program based on Telnet, to access files, etc.

Logging in by phone was required if you were to be late from a date or upon arrival and departure from activities or events.

save To store a file on a disk or other storage medium. When a file is being edited, the changes are only in temporary memory (RAM), and will be lost when the power is shut off. To keep the changes in permanent memory, the file must be saved. If there is a power failure or crash, all data not saved will be lost.

Family photos, report cards, art works, cherished books, awards...Mother saved it all for the time she would pass it on to us as mementos of precious memories. She also saved a lot of junk. Every nook and cranny of the house was filled with stuff. She said that Father was a pack rat, but the truth is that she was just as bad.

task management In a multitasking environment, the part of the operating system that controls the running of tasks within the computer, coordinating resources when several tasks are running at the same time.

Just think of Mother as the part of the family that simultaneously controlled the execution of tasks and the coordination of resources. The Control Center. And, boy, could she be controlling...

user-friendly Easy to learn and use, especially for people who are not experts. This term is most often used to describe software.

Perfect Specimen

The Mother-to-child interface is implemented from birth. Ours was user-friendly with an infectious laugh and a sense of humor. This is not the case with all Graphical Mother Interfaces.

virus A program that infects a computer by attaching itself to another program, and propagating itself when that program is executed. A computer can become infected by files downloaded over a network, or by the installation of new software or floppy disks that are infected with virus- es. Some viruses are only pranks, and perform harmless actions like displaying a screen with a joke message on it. Others can destroy files or wipe out a hard drive.

If one of us got it we all got it. Nothing much could be done about it except for taking us to the doctor and nurs- ing us back to health. But who took care of Mother? Illness became a method for Mother to check out of the system. She wasn't able to give herself the time or care that she needed, so taking to bed was the only way for her to escape the demands, isolation, and drudgery of life as a housewife and mother.

volatile memory Memory that loses its content when the power is shut off. The main memory (Random Access Memory or RAM) of the computer is volatile memory. Any changes made to files must be saved to disk before the power is turned off or they will be lost.

We called it forgiveness—forgetting all the bad choices, hurtful behavior, and mistakes. We put Mother through various kinds of hell and she forgave and forgot it all. I have yet to forgive myself for some of it.

well-behaved Acting in accordance with standards; software is said to be well-behaved if it uses the operating system in the expected way for such tasks as screen display, key- board input, disk input/output, etc. (See **ill-behaved**)

Simply, what we were expected to be.

XOXOXO Kisses and hugs. (Chat Expression)

No explanation necessary.

YAFIYGI You Asked For It, You Got It. Refers to user inter- faces which are not WYSIWYG (What You See Is What You Get). With YAFIYGI, the file on the screen may show text and code, but does not show what the printed out copy will look like.

A term usually associated with disappointment in a much requested new toy or food product. Closely related to BCWYWF (Be Careful What You Wish For—you just might get it.)

Modern Reproduction Tools

ZZZ Also known as sleep. This occurs when the screen dims on a computer monitor in order to save energy and preserve the integrity of its image capabilities; or in the case of laptop computers, sleep mode conserves battery power.

Sleep. The process by which the brain and body are rejuvenated and energy is restored. Also known as something of which a Mother never gets enough.

So You Wanna Be A Cyborg Mommy? Queer Identity and the New Reproductive Technologies

Tania Kupczak

I remember the first time I fell in love with a cyborg. I was eight years old and, of course, she wasn't really a cyborg. However, Juno, the plastic woman of Amazon proportions, was human enough for my sensibilities and she set my neurons a-snapping. It was on a second-grade field trip to the Health Museum that I discovered her in all her electric glory. An *überfrau* model of human anatomy, she spun slowly on a pedestal, her insides pulsing and even speaking. Suddenly it sickened me to imagine my own interior to be dark and slimy instead of blessed with blinking lights. I knew then that Juno was the kind of woman for me.

At the time I did not know—though I might have guessed—that at the turn of the twenty-first century, I would place myself in close context to Juno. Although I am still 99.8 percent biological, I believe the omnipresence of technological intervention in daily life implies conscription into the ranks of cyborg status. As women and men of a computerized society, we have long passed the critical juncture of accepting or rejecting cyborg identity. We are deeply embedded in a culture that often does not offer us alternatives to technologically mediated reality. In her oft-cited "A Cyborg Manifesto,"[1] Donna Haraway asserts that "the cyborg is a creature in a post-gender world." Gender identity remains, however, a large thorn in the side of those who wish to transcend the systematic categorization of the techno-science culture.

Reproduction is a particularly potent jumping-off place for a search for identity. Haraway's utopian cyborg does not validate heterosexual sex as reproductively necessary, thereby widening the scope of fecund events to include those that are technologically mediated. The innovations in assisted reproductive technologies (ART) are a useful avenue for people who cannot or do not wish to create kinship in the biologically ordained way. It is through ART that queer identity has been linked to reproductive desires. Finally, those women and men who wish to build alternative kinship models have the available tools to do so outside the dominant societal structure of family. The terms "gay" and "family" are no longer mutually exclusive.

The search for a queer identity within the clinical research designed for heterosexual, middle-class, white infertile couples requires subversive attitudes and actions. There is a necessity of conscious language in order to validate experiences that fall outside the status quo and which begin to re-write the syntax of family make-up. Kinship is a fluid term, and while historically it has specified blood relations, it does not necessarily limit itself to this category. Rayna Rapp writes, "When we assume male-headed, nuclear families to be central units of kinship, and all alternative patterns to be extensions or exceptions, we accept an aspect of cultural hegemony instead of studying it."[2] I would add the necessity of actively questioning it as well.

This is precisely the argument for the use of ART by gays and lesbians who wish to parent. Although financial determinants still play a large role in access to services, the rhetoric of familial relationship has already been changed by the dominant group of ART users. The ART encourage reproduction through "cyborgification" and can, therefore, be more easily appropriated by lesbian and gay families wishing to have children. The physical body is the locus where the ART are engaged. The context of their placement is dependent upon a long history of what Haraway refers to as the "informatics of domination." This system of networks replaces the old mode of hierarchical domination with an information system which cannot be coded as natural. It is, however, no less threatening.

Our perception of reality is filtered through the lens of technology. A controlled environment and control of the environment are primary societal desires. The unwavering faith mainstream society places in our computer-generated reality is clearly connected to the instances of technological intervention in pregnancy and birth. A woman undergoing an ultrasound is encouraged by the technician to bond with her fetus through the image on the monitor. Because she sees the fetus on the screen, everything is supposed to be okay. Her knowledge of her body is supplanted by the reality of the present technology.

We have been ushered into unquestioned acceptance of a specific kind of information, technological data, which is presented as absolute truth. Recent feminist theorists, such as Sandra Harding and Emily Martin, have finally broken through the rhetoric of technological complacency. Their work has disproved the concept of science as value-free, and more importantly, questioned it as a useful methodology. Harding writes, "though scientific methods are selected, we are told, exactly in order to eliminate all social values from inquiry, they are actually operationalized to eliminate those values that differ within whatever gets to count as the community of scientists."[3]

The compulsory cyborg citizenship of the twenty-first century offers choices in representation and realization, if only we know how to see them. The postmodern notion of cyborg is radically different from its original form in science fiction. No longer simply a physical being with mechanical and biological parts, the cyborg has become the representative, even a metaphor, of a spectrum of technologically mediated identities and lifestyle choices. The notion of a genderless cyborg seems to be coupled in popular culture with the over-sexualized robot, which is usually female, but does not carry the equipment for sexual intercourse. Takashi Murakami's sculpture *Hiropon*, which is Japanese slang for heroin, depicts such a cyborg, naked, lacking genitals, and spurting copious amounts of breast milk. She is a fantasy, able to nurture without the threat of reproductive capacity. Sharply in contrast with the buxom abundance of this figure, the familiar C3PO of "Star Wars" fame prefers friendship with other robots, and has been given a slight British accent to seem intelligent, or perhaps, prudish. Neither the androgynous cyborg nor its feminine *doppel-gänger* present biological reproduction as a strategy for fecundity. Technology now offers a variety of options for offspring through cloning, self-replication, and ART.

It is within these cyborg identities, which are touted as superior to biological existence, that we can begin to construct alternatives to the informatics of domination. By its very existence as flesh/machine, the cyborg is a hybrid creature. It exists in many realms, not all of which are benign. This allows for conscious creation of syntax and action in many avenues of technological progress. The ART are particularly relevant in the delineation of new approaches to kinship models. Our society's trust in science and technology has allowed those couples who are infertile to seek an alternative which is touted to be superior to the act of sexual intercourse in assuring offspring.

The development of ART has led to a less stable definition of filial relationships. Language is one of the main issues of confusion regarding offspring produced through ART. Those who consider themselves "other," be it for racial, sexual, or economic reasons, can use this confusion to create new paradigms of language for identification as kin. For example, the abbreviation 'AI' commonly stands for "artificial insemination," but is referenced as "alternative insemination" by almost all queer parents. Because ART were developed for white heterosexual couples with infertility issues, the need for different kinship models has required new definitions of "family" to be accepted. It has, in effect, been normalized to indicate a whole range of actual relationships.

For example, in her essay "Quit Sniveling, Cryobaby…"[4] Charis Cussin uses the terms "opaque" and "transparent" to indicate the relationships to a developing fetus. An egg donor may be excluded, i.e., transparent, from the pregnancy of a woman whose own eggs are damaged. Likewise, the egg donor might be seen as the "real mother," i.e., opaque, if she is paying to have her eggs gestated in another woman's uterus. The contextual meaning of the terms speaks to the nature of the new cyborg family.

Before the development of ART, queer families consisted primarily of children from previous heterosexual unions, and those conceived through sexual intercourse. Today, however, these methods seem distasteful compared with the technological options. There are increasing numbers of donor banks that cater to queer families, many of which will ship sperm in liquid nitrogen right to your home. Also, agencies exist which put gay men into contact with willing surrogate mothers, help with non-traditional adoptions (i.e., not a married heterosexual couple), and find sperm donors of specific sexual preference, ethnic background, or educational level.

While many lesbian moms rely on male friends as co-parents, legal control of a child's well-being is often the reason lesbians choose anonymous sperm donors. As Kath Weston describes in her book *Families We Choose*, AIDS also plays an important role in ART choices in the last two decades. Many queer people, specifically women seeking donors, are comforted by pre-tested sperm-bank material. The uncertainty of HIV status prohibits both men and women from making use of sperm that does not come from a bank. Most see the sperm as merely a tool toward a specific goal, e.g., conception, and very rarely refer back to the man who once produced the genetic material. When known-donor sperm is used, however, most queer women prefer a gay or bisexual man, perhaps because he is already outside the informatics of domination in terms of normative heterosexual reproductive relations.

Access to information and services is often the root of distress for queer families wishing to use ART to create a family. There is a clear lack of support for people outside the status quo who wish to parent. Gay and lesbian couples or individuals who want to have children must often circumvent the existing system in order to have their wishes fulfilled. For example, many gay men seek out surrogate mothers through private means, because mainstream agencies refuse to put them in contact with such women. However, according to documented interviews, many surrogate mothers are quite willing to perform their services for gay men, already having placed themselves outside the biologically reproductive norm.

Most queer parenting books[5] spend a number of chapters discussing the role assignments of parents and various support people. Because of the biological improbability of an accidental pregnancy, there is a certain luxury of pre-conception planning. This allows each person involved in the family to have a clear idea of her/his role in the child's life. For example, a lesbian couple might invite a close friend to provide a "male role model" for their child, but be clear about the limits of his authority in parenting. Unlike a father who has biological ties to the child, the women can be in full control of the male's presence in the family organization.

The definition of family roles by queer parents is as individual as the families themselves. Studies have shown, however, that although a small child might have a variety of people in her/his life, there is rarely any confusion among them. In the same way that most children have no trouble differentiating between their sets of grandparents, so most do not have difficulty with the concept of two mothers, two fathers, or some other combination of care-takers. In reality, most children in America today do not grow up in a household with two biological parents of opposite sex either.

Problems arise for queer families with kinship creation because although the ART are hidden measures, the family will "look abnormal." Adoption, although not a technological intervention, is often denied to queer parents, and those approaching an agency often do so as single parents. Because of a queer family's visibility as "other," there are huge challenges in surmounting the societal construction of the nuclear family norm. Under the best of circumstances, use of ART by queer families positively undermines the dominant construction of kinship.

The importance of financial accountability, i.e., payment for services, is at the forefront in determination of kinship structures. Families are becoming amalgamations of technological and organic elements, and informed choice is centrally relevant. Legally binding agreements, which attempt to protect non-biological relationships, are commonplace among queer families who have made a commitment to co-parenting. While no law exists to date that will guarantee a non-biological parent rights to a child, second-parent adoption has become a reasonable measure of security for a queer family. Unfortunately, a court of law can still deny the validity of the agreement. The desire to be recognized as a "normal" family has been the source of contention in the queer community. As with marriage rights, some people do not feel that buying into the heterosexual status quo is the answer.

Thankfully, within the queer community there is more acceptance now of individuals who wish to parent. Contemporary queer theory does not discredit gays and lesbians who want children. They are no longer accused of wanting to imitate the "hetero breeders." In her personal memoirs, feminist Cherríe Moraga writes "I know that blood quantum does not determine parenthood any more than it determines culture. Still, I know blood matters. It just doesn't matter more than love."[6] In part, is it due to the ART, which make it possible to use the words "gay" and "family" together to make a "gay family." It is encouraging to know support systems are being placed for queer families. There are a number of useful publications, periodicals and web sites, such as *Gay Parent* magazine, *Alternative Families* magazine and <http://www.gayparenting.com>. There is room, in this cyborg society, to accept all sorts of people who wish to create families outside the prescribed suburban picket fence reality.

More than any other type of identity, that of the human as a flesh/machine amalgamation is the most truthful to our twenty-first century existence. The reasons for living in a border region between biology and technology are many, and the outcome likewise unwritten. Because it is only in the last few decades that such technologically mediated reality has been placed into our hands, it is difficult to predict its effects. The cyborg has no original language. It must be manufactured consciously, in the same way a queer family constructs kinship. It is located at an intersection of experiences, full of possibility and choice. While technology has been created by the informatics of domination, it no longer refers directly back to its patrilinear roots. Our conscription into the ranks of the cyborg allows us the creativity to defy nature. We are no longer simply biological creatures. Likewise, we are no longer bound by biological rhetoric. It is language which must be subverted in order to effect change.

Nearly twenty years after my first meeting with Juno, the beautiful plastic woman, I still remember the necessity I felt to understand her origin and purpose. Now I know that she was fabricated as a teacher, to laud the extent to which science has dissected the human body. However, the fact that I see something different in her, something much more subversive, betrays her creators. Juno has no male consort, no biological counterpart twirling next to her, and yet her gravid womb lights up with the potential for positive change. We can become like her, carrying our ideas of kinship to full term. It begins with acknowledging those people in our lives to whom we are not tied by blood, but who mean so much to our well being. It begins by consciously choosing our families, by calling ourselves new names, by appropriating patriarchal symbols and structures and rebuilding them to suit our own needs. It begins by supporting local agencies, either financially or emotionally, which help those outside the biologically reproductive norm gain access to ART and adoption services. It can even begin with something as simple as a word of encouragement to a friend who is considering single parenthood. The avenues are many, and the results are equally myriad, shimmering with a new generation of children who no longer are pressured by the constraints of the nuclear family structure.

When the museum finally relieves Juno of her pedestal duties, I want to put her in my front yard as a new kind of holy nativity, blinking and spinning, as a testimony to the possibility of the cyborg that cannot be predicted by science, and which resides in all of us as subversive intention and action. ★

1   Donna Haraway, *Simians, Cyborgs, and Women: The Reinvention of Nature.* (New York: Routledge, 1991).

2   Rayna Rapp, "Toward a Nuclear Freeze? The Gender Politics of Euro-American Kinship Analysis." In J.F. Collier and S.J. Yanagisako, eds., *Gender and Kinship: Essays Toward a Unified Analysis* (Stanford: Stanford University Press, 1987), p. 129.

3   Sandra Harding, *Whose Science? Whose Knowledge? Thinking from Women's Lives.* (Ithaca: Cornell University Press, 1991), p. 41.

4   Charis Cussin, "Quit Sniveling, Cryobaby..." Robbie Davis-Floyd and Joseph Dumit, eds., *Cyborg Babies: From Techno-sex to Techno-tots* (New York: Routledge, 1998).

5   An excellent source is D. Merilee Clunis and G. Dorsey Green, *The Lesbian Parenting Handbook: A Guide to Creating Families and Raising Children* (Seattle: Seal Press, 1995).

6   Cherríe Moraga, *Waiting in the Wings: Portrait of a Queer Motherhood* (Ithaca: Firebrand, 1997).

Inside Infertility

Amelia Jones

I write this essay as a feminist and advocate of critical thought who cannot attain the proper critical distance from my experience: I am still inside infertility and will no doubt always be held in its grip, though the force of this grip may lessen over time. I am a married, white, economically and educationally privileged, heterosexual woman from a large nuclear family (I have five siblings) who has found herself caught in the throes of the most normative kinds of desire for children in the face of extended difficulties with infertility. Although, on a rational level, I am well acquainted with the huge ethical, social, and individual problems connected to the discourse of infertility and the industry it has spawned (and I will attempt, with the help of a few feminist theorists, to point to some of these problems here), in relation to infertility, I cannot even begin to keep my emotions from subverting my critical awareness.

Although, of course, women and men from all classes experience infertility problems, the discourse of fertility and the way it is experienced and handled is clearly class, sex, and gender differentiated; and as with everything in our culture, class inevitably brings with it certain racial and ethnic connotations. I am, in fact, the perfect customer for the infertility market: I have the economic means and connections to pursue advanced medical intervention, and am deeply invested both in recreating my own childhood experience of a house filled with people (though smart enough to wish for only two children!), and in controlling the basic parameters of my life. By and large, the industry of infertility is clearly geared towards the upper classes, and women take on far more of the emotional and physical burden of infertility. In my experience, too, it is almost always assumed within mainstream discourses of infertility that the person undergoing fertility treatments is one-half of a heterosexual couple.

I now have two spectacular children, a boy born in 1993, and girl born in 1999. Before each pregnancy, I underwent assorted infertility treatments including two hysterosalpingograms, several cycles of fertility drugs, and the preplanning for an *in vitro* procedure; my husband had an operation for a varicocele, and I had a laparoscopy to clear my fallopian tubes. However, while it seems as if my body was being medically manipulated for years, I spent only a few months actually on fertility drugs or undergoing procedures. The rest of the six or so years of trying to conceive a child (roughly two the first time, four the second) were spent in mental anguish and seemingly endless cycles of waiting until a next step could be taken. This essay, then, is mostly about the emotional aspects of suffering infertility problems—from the inside.

...

I spent these six years dealing with my own little mourning after my period would come, then a day or two raking myself over the coals as to why it didn't work this time. Then there would be another week interrogating my desire to have a biological child. By then, it would be ovulation time again and my hopes would slowly start to rise from the depths of my conviction that it was never going to work. Then the two weeks of waiting and treating my body like a fragile vessel—trying not to exercise too much, work too hard, have negative thoughts, you name it—all under the guise of pretending I had control over whether I got pregnant or not, followed by the crushing disappointment again. The worst aspect of this disappointment was the feeling of what a fool I'd been even to imagine I might get pregnant, and the self-chastisement for wanting to have a biological child in the first place. I had a political conviction that adopting would be a better choice in terms of world population and giving a needy infant a home.

I spent the years of suffering infertility, then, feeling like I was at war with my body. Having conceived our son about a year after my husband's operation, we mistakenly thought our problem had been solved. Unfortunately, it wasn't that simple and we launched into another period of infertility treatment while trying to conceive a second child. In our second bout with treatment our excellent (and expensive) private fertility doctor advised—since we knew we could conceive and carry a pregnancy to term (i.e., we already had once)—that I go through several cycles of fertility drugs to see if this would promote conception. It was at this point I tried a few cycles of Clomid and one of Fertinex. In spite of the doctor's claims of the innocuousness of these hormones, I walked around feeling like a balloon pumped full of dangerous gases, ready to explode and spew poisonous fumes.

This feeling of danger was borne out by the fact that, shortly after the Fertinex cycle, I began to have panic attacks for the first time in my life. While I am predisposed to panic (it probably would have happened anyway at some point), I'm sure the hormone surges triggered these initial attacks. Among other things, this seemed like an antithetical state of being in which to promote conception. Drugging yourself in the attempt to conceive a child feels like a contradiction in terms.

After I started having panic attacks I took a hiatus from the fertility drugs—as it turns out, forever. The next strategy was for me to go through a laparoscopy to see if either of my tubes were blocked (one had been blocked before my first pregnancy). This had to be postponed because of my panic attacks but eventually, about four months later, I went through the operation and the doctor said it was successful; she had opened one of the tubes completely and partially cleared the other. Again, the cycle of hope was renewed. My husband and I waited expectantly (at first) and then with increasing impatience as one, two, three...then six months went by with no pregnancy.

After this wait, we were urged by the doctor to try to become subjects in a study, which would allow us to obtain one free *in vitro* cycle (running upwards of $10,000 on the open market), so it seemed worth a shot, so to speak. Although I had severe ethical reservations about this process (which involves putting out a huge amount of money and emotional energy for a procedure that is often not successful and begins to call into question how much intervention one is willing to undergo to achieve pregnancy), we launched into the process of qualifying for the study. Finally, results would be assured...or so it seemed.

That's the endless lure of fertility treatments: Each process has its own kind of promise. But no process can guarantee conception and a full-term pregnan-cy. In fact, an *in vitro* cycle only has a 10 to 40 percent likelihood of success (depending on whom you ask, and who and what age the patient is). At any rate, we were dropped as potential subjects when it became clear I had to stay on my panic medication. (What a recipe for disaster for a victim of panic disorder and infertility—making the possibility of conception contingent on being well, which is precisely the kind of pressure and perfectionist thinking that causes people to have panic attacks in the first place!)

At this point, for the first time, my husband was willing at least to talk about adoption. We felt strongly that pursuing *in vitro* outside the study was the wrong thing to do, given the fact that we would be putting out a huge amount of cash that would not ensure our having a baby at the end. Ethically, it would make more sense to use this money towards adoption, knowing that we could make a difference for a baby who needed a home, especially since we were lucky enough to have already had one biological child (odd term, biological child, as if adopted children are produced in factories…). At the same time, as my husband was fond of pointing out, adoption—which these days basically amounts to purchasing an infant, the laws against this notwithstanding—raises its own host of complex and unpleasant ethical dilemmas.

Leaning towards adoption, I was also reluctant to submit my body to the pun-ishment of more hormone treatments. However, my husband wanted to try fertility drugs for a few more cycles. By way of a compromise, I agreed to do this if he would then agree to adopt if it didn't work. By that time, nine months had gone by since the laparoscopy. The month we were planning to try the drugs again, I awaited the morning of my period in order to begin calculating when to take the drugs (one becomes hyper-aware of the different phases of one's monthly cycle when going through infertility treatments); a day past the onset of my expected period, I half-heartedly took a pregnancy test, assuming I would face the usual disappointment and feeling foolish for even hoping enough to waste the test. Surprise! It had happened again. Just like the first time—when, after two years of trying, we had conceived our son at the very last possible moment before further intervention. So here I am, the mother of two—panic disorder and all—experiencing the miraculous fact of these two children every day. One of the best legacies of having suffered from infertility is the feeling of total, overwhelming gratitude that one experiences in relation to the mere existence of one's children; one of the worst (which is closely related), is the feeling that one isn't allowed to be a flawed parent or to be ambivalent about parenting since it is the long-desired outcome of infertility procedures.

···

More than the infertility treatments I went through, which were minimal compared to those that other women experience, the pain of infertility for me was largely due to the emotional circumstances surrounding this state of being.

I'm sure I'm not alone here: During infertility one's entire identity becomes wrapped up in it such that one experiences oneself, before anything else (professor, partner, parent, etc.), as *infertile*. Both times I went through the process of trying to conceive, I walked around feeling barren, a nineteenth-century word, but one that, in its evocation of vast plains of dead soil, sums up my feeling of inadequacy as an infertile woman better than any more clinical postmodern term. Seeing other women or men with babies would drive me crazy because I was barren; walking past a preschool would feel like a personal insult because I was barren; catching a moment of "Sesame Street" on someone else's television set would fill me with despair because I was barren. And this was equally true when I already had one child, strangely enough.

Certainly my feelings of failure had something to do with societal norms, the expectation that a woman will be a mother and, in my case, that she will be a mother of a household full of children (well, at least two, given that I have a busy career). But this is almost a truism at this point and not very revealing. I think the real issue is that of how we conceive of ourselves, and is linked to the way in which we deeply internalize certain ideas about what we want to be. It's not the external pressures that are the hardest to bear—I'm rather good at bucking those—it's the pressures that have been so thoroughly internalized they are part of who we are, and, of course, the way in which each of us internalizes norms and societal pressures is unique.

This is the power of ideology, for better or worse: As Louis Althusser and others have theorized, its most insidious effects come from the fact that it structures us internally, defining our desires and wants. Among other things, my bouts with infertility made me confront the fact that I have always imagined myself as a certain kind of woman, merging incompatible roles: One who is both my mother (super-competent, multi-tasking, nurturing many souls other than her own) and my father (professionally successful, enjoying his children mostly from a distance, funny and self-absorbed, as one has to be to a certain extent in order to get academic work done). If I had not had to question over and over again my desire to have children (that is, if I had been able to conceive and bear them easily), I would not have gone to such depths of self-questioning, interrogating these impossible dual desires. Ultimately, I cannot answer whether my desire for not only one but two children is purely social and ideological or partly biological (linked to our culture's current romance with genes[1] or to some drive to replicate the self). I can only say it is bone-deep, and at this point I can't separate the two forces since they are so deeply interwoven in my psyche.

In patriarchal capitalist societies, the whole notion of infertility is itself constructed in relation to some fantasy of perfect virility (for men) or maternal wholeness (for women); as Sylvia Tubert has noted, *the mother* is the model proposed to women to identify with, and to organize her Ego Ideal around, and it is difficult for [her] to find a place as a desiring subject in a patriarchal culture if [she doesn't]"[2] (hence my great respect for women who, knowing they do not want to be mothers, refuse the role). Even many women who are aware of these pressures are still entirely prey to the promise of bodily restoration (correcting the broken body) that fertility procedures seem to offer. We find ourselves caught in a morass of contradictions and ambivalences: Wanting to be both *women* (mothers, like our mothers) and *men* (controlling the means by which motherhood takes place and in my case also combining it with a high-powered career).

The paradox of infertility is that infertile people who pursue fertility treatments feel simultaneously empowered by this act and completely objectified by the science enlisted to help. Reproductive technologies promise to remedy the split in the self (between the desire for children and the body's recalcitrant refusal). But simultaneously, they are instrumentalizing technologies; submitting our bodies to them as separable objects that can be mechanically or chemically "fixed," we infertile people are alienated "from the bodily experiences of reproduction."[3] There is enormous pain compacted into this paradox, which gives a false sense of empowerment over something that ultimately can't be controlled and, paradoxically, gives this promise of control through the instrumentalization and domination of the body as an object that is broken and can be fixed. One is led, or leads oneself, to believe that one's state of mind, on the one hand, is irrelevant and, on the other, can deeply affect one's chances of conceiving. Thus, when I got pregnant the unassisted way both times, I felt as if I had suddenly done something *right* to make this happen. The other side of this is that I felt guilty, as if I had personally failed, when I didn't conceive.

Every month of being actively infertile (actively trying and failing to conceive), I blamed myself for having been in too negative a frame of mind to achieve a pregnancy. Somehow, the unfortunate guilt of the working mother became conflated with my sense of defeat so that the failure to become pregnant seemed a consequence of the fact that I work. Endless magazine stories and anecdotal input from friends and strangers warning the reader just to slow down and relax in order to achieve pregnancy reinforced these feelings. Again, the ideological dimensions of infertility discourse become clear: If a working class woman were having trouble conceiving, I doubt she would be chastised for, or would accuse herself of, the career-woman "syndromes" supposedly causing her infertility, though she might be blamed or blame herself in other ways that I wouldn't know about.

The experience of infertility thus produces the paradoxical feeling of being both alienated from one's body, which one submits to doctors so they can fix its barrenness; and too close to it, as if every thought can somehow influence its fertility status. I believe that this is only true for women.

I think men feel equally frustrated over infertility but in a different way. While male impotence is a major societal and individual concern, tapping into anxieties about male sexual prowess, there is no discourse of male barrenness, no discussion of men's incapacity to father children. Men can feel frustrated because they are distanced from much infertility treatment and can't do something to make it work out; often they come into conflict with the woman's tendency, even if both are eager to have a child, to push more to take action. There is no question that women still feel (are made to feel?) responsible for conception not occurring, even in cases, such as mine, where the male partner has a diagnosed problem as well. This has to do, again, with broad societal notions of woman-as-mother and men as incidental to conception, notions that are, again, internalized so that most women feel that conception and care for the child are primarily our responsibility. Women are the vessels, women are responsible: This is the conjunction that the fertility business primarily plays on.

...

Facing one's desires is an excruciatingly painful but productive part of infertility. It feels so deeply unfair, in the same way that early death or chronic disease seems unfair, that many people get pregnant at the drop of a hat and never have to confront how or why or whether they want to have biological children. (Whether they want to get pregnant or not is another story.) Those of us who have been through infertility are forced to confront and work through this desire over and over again if the infertility period lasts a long time. This can create enormous self-consciousness about being a parent and overly controlling tendencies during the process and once the desired child arrives. The control issue is profound from the very beginning of infertility and gets to the roots of our complex attitudes towards bodily health. On the one hand, we want to surrender ourselves to a highly technologized medical industry (cure me! make me pregnant!), defining our medical problem as purely biological rather than an inextricable and complex mixture of psyche and body. On the other hand, we live in a culture of control: Discourses of self-help and natural healing imply that if we just get the right attitude we can cure ourselves of cancer, get pregnant, or solve whatever medical problem we think we have.

This conflicting set of desires conditions the infertile subject. Infertility produces a body that becomes out there, someone else's to manipulate into submission. And yet we experience every moment of this manipulation inside.

Infertility makes tracks on our bodies and minds. We are conditioned by it just as our desires direct its course. (For example, the technologies developed to ensure ideal physical or mental traits in the selling of designer eggs are born out of our desires as much as the medical profession's marketing.) The crucial issue, perhaps, is for us to understand the way in which these desires and the technologies that supposedly fulfill them but also partially construct them are co-constituted. There is no way to determine which causes which, as Donna Haraway has so eloquently put it, objectivity—the objectification of the infertile body, in this case—"is less about realism than it is about intersubjectivity."[4]

If we allow our bodies to be instrumentalized as purely reproductive sites rather than asserted as aspects of ourselves in a fully intersubjective relationship with the doctors we turn to for help, we are allowing our physical body to be separated from our emotional/mental self in the most dangerous process of commodifying human life. This is a process that ultimately leads to the horrors of such cases as the recent suit brought by a divorcee in order to claim possession of embryos developed from donor eggs fertilized by her ex-husband's sperm. Those who have infertility problems must recognize at every step our participation in this commodification and continually work to keep our bodies fully attached to our minds.

The process of undergoing infertility treatments must be a thoughtful one. The embryo is an embryo, not a person or a child, much less a thing to be bartered or sold, in spite of what anti-choice advocates would argue. Children don't belong to adults the way cars or books do. The trick—which I certainly failed in sustaining—is to go as far as we are comfortable going with infertility treatments while, one would hope in a productive rather than self-chastising way, interrogating all the way through our burning desire to deliver and raise only "biological" children. Throughout the process we must continue to be skeptical of medical interventions and their promise of hopes fulfilled as well as our own urges to look to them as miracle cures for our own feelings of inadequacy.

The infertile person, the one "inside" infertility, must sort through these dilemmas on his or her own while also, ideally, sharing stories with others and generating and/or participating in a more public discourse about the experience of infertility. Too much of infertility is experienced in a vacuum by women afraid to expose our own thwarted desires or too wounded to speak out in an empowered and empowering way. Those of us who have experienced infertility will always be "inside" it but, when the immediate pain subsides, we might focus on the fact that being inside infertility has its virtues, if one can use this inside view to cast a different light on the desires that produce and are produced by infertility discourse in the first place. ★

---

1   Valerie Hartouni, *Cultural Conceptions: On Reproductive Technologies + the Remaking of Life* (London and Minneapolis: University of Minnesota Press, 1997), p. 9.

2   See Silvia Tubert, "How IVF Exploits the Wish to Be a Mother: A Psychoanalysts Account," trans. Barbara MacShane, *Genders* 14 (Fall 1992), p. 41.

3   Helen E. Longino. "Knowledge, Bodies, and Values: Reproductive Technologies and the Privilege of Partial Perspectives," *Technology and the Politics of Knowledge*, eds., Andrew Feenberg and Alastair Hanna (Bloomington and Indianapolis: Indiana University Press, 1995), p. 208.

4   Donna Haraway, "Fetus: The Virtual Speculum in the New World Order," *Modest_Witness@Second_Millenium.FemaleManC_ Meets_ OncoMouse* (New York and London: Routledge, 1997), p. 199.

Sex and Gender Education in the Biotech Century

A subRosa Performance

The audience-participatory performance, "Sex and Gender Education in the Biotech Century," gives a digital twist to the use of traditional low-tech classroom methods and teaching aids (such as filmstrips, slide shows, workbook projects, vocabulary tests, model building, and role-playing), in order to inspire critical thinking about the relationship of Assisted Reproductive Technologies (ART) to sexuality, reproduction, and gender. The show includes segments on "How to Have a Baby with the New Reprotech," "What is the Human Genome Project?" "Recombinant Genetics and Genetic Engineering," and "Applied Social Genetics (Social Eugenics)." Participants are involved in a full range of learning activities, and the show ends in a "mixer" during which participants attempt to match up with a genetically ideal mate to create a perfect baby. (This performance was commissioned for "Digital Secrets," Arizona State University, Tempe, AZ, 2000; and performed a second time at St. Mary's College of Maryland, 2002.)

Following are excerpts from subRosa's *Sex and Gender Ed in the Biotech Century Workbook*, and pictures of both performances.

Morena Subterra addresses class.

A New Creation in the Biotech Century

"Every major economic and social revolution in history has been accompanied by a new explanation of the creation of life and the workings of nature. The new concept of nature is always the most important strand of the matrix that makes up any new social order. In each instance, the new cosmology serves to justify the rightness and inevitability of the new way human beings are organizing their world by suggesting that nature itself is organized along similar lines."
(J. Rifkin, The Biotech Century, p.196.)

SEX and GENDER in the BIOTECH CENTURY

The mysteries of the creation of matter, of nature, of what life is, and of the processes of human reproduction have preoccupied scientists, philosophers, artists, writers, theologians—and children—since human culture began. The new bio-technologies, genetic and medical human engineering, as well as social, cultural, racial, gender, and economic factors fueled by global exchanges and mixings, have the potential for producing "new humans," new subjectivities, new relations among bodies, and new answers to ancient questions about life and being human. Sexuality and gender construction are at the heart of (Western) discussions of human identity and subject formation. To date, there has not been much research about the effects the new bio-technologies may have on our conceptions of sex and gender, and on subject formation. These questions are the basis of **subRosa's** speculations, research, and experiments. Our topics include: Sexuality and gender now (new representations of the sexual organs, new conceptions of anatomy and human biology, queer sexuality, multicultural constructions of sexuality and gender); Reproductive technology (Assisted Reproductive Technologies including IVF, cloning, fertility and infertility); Genetics and genetic engineering of plants, animals and humans; mutation and the Human Genome Project; Applied Social Genetics (Eugenics, gene pool mixing, hybrid families, finding your ideal genetic mate, designing "perfect" babies). "The story of creation is being retold. This time around, nature is cast in the image of the computer and the language of physics, chemistry, mathematics, and the information sciences."
(J. Rifkin, The Biotech Century, p. 211)

3

Sex and Gender Ed web site.

Recombinant Sexuality and Gender

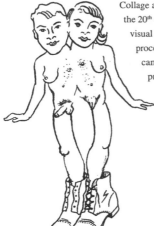

Collage and Montage were the groundbreaking aesthetic modes of the 20th Century in film, radio, advertising and publicity images, visual art, literature, poetry, architecture and photography. These processes which rely on recombination of elements, also became the basis of most image and text producing software programs on computers and in electronic media.

In the Biotech Century DNA splicing and recombination, and digitized morphing, 3-D modeling and animation software programs, present new imaging possibilities and new EMBODIED flesh possibilities. DNA splicing across species boundaries can cause organisms to EXPRESS recombined characteristics in REAL BODIES. Among the myriad new possibilities which this technology will spawn, let us consider 3 suggestions of how to extend "normal" sexual and gender binaries of male/female, hetero/homo, couple/single, to a range of embodied libidinal expressions.

For example: the palm of the hand could be genetically programmed to grow erectile tissue, thus making shaking or holding hands an orgasmic experience. Hi-fives, applause, and political glad handing will truly come into their own!!

Similarly clitoral tissues could be grown in inner elbows so that linking arms with someone can cause an orgasm. Just imagine the joy and skyhigh morale of a group of protesters with linked arms!

Provocative is also the idea of intrapersonal brain sex in which the neurons of one person's brain could fire genetically programmed receptors in another person's brain just by thinking about them, and cause instant orgasm in the other. A whole room full of people could be stimulated and reduced to useless bliss at the same time. Imagine!!!

21

Lecture at Sex and Gender Education Show.

Ten Ways to Enhance Yourself Genetically

1. Triple your income.

2. Move to a gated community in a first-world country.

3. Invest in your children. Send them to a major research university.

4. Have children only by Assisted Reproductive Technologies.

5. For women wanting "natural" children: Have sex with many different men during ovulation to ensure that the best sperm wins. For men desiring "natural" children: Impregnate as many women as possible in order to ensure continuation of your genetic line.

6. Practice parental eugenics and eugenic sacrifice when necessary. When making babies with Assisted Reproductive Technologies choose genetic traits in donor eggs and sperm which will enhance your genetic germ line in a few generations. For example:

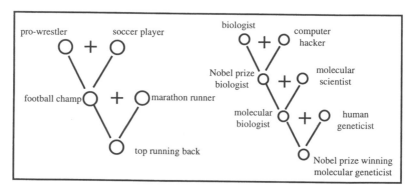

7. Practice pre-implantation genetic diagnosis through embryo biopsy, and employ selective reduction after embryo implantation.

8. Take advantage of all new medical procedures based on genetic therapy, for example, somatic gene therapy.

9. Invest in new biotechnology and genetic research stocks.

10. Eat genetically modified foods.

15

Filling out Workbooks.

Applied Social Genetics / Eugenics

Monsters
Hybrids
Mestizos
Cyborgs
Freaks
Androids
Mulattos
Goddesses
Recombinants
Teratomas
Dwarfs
Aliens
Martians
Witches
Zombies
Mutants
Conjoined
Twins
Ghosts
Artifical Life
Mermaids
Replicants
Centaurs
Giants
Freaks

Why are we so fascinated and terrified by the impure, mixed creatures which exist in real life and have populated our imaginations, dreams, myths, stories, and art since human culture began? Uncertainty and the unknown can now be banished. **Applied Social Genetics** or **New Social Eugenics** is a rationalized procedure for making babies based solely on the parents' pragmatic selection of physical attributes and desirable genetic traits. This circumvents the old style, patently race and class based eugenic practices that negatively sought to get rid of certain ethnic, racial, and economic groups, and replaces them with fully scientific and genetically based choices for producing the best offspring possible.

22

Looking for ideal Genetic Matches.

A Modest Proposal for the Biotech Century

It is time to celebrate that humanity is now in the position to solve one of its most pressing and tragic problems--that of infant mortality and the birth of unwanted and "unfit" children, including:

    *the missing babies of the favela carried away by diarrhea
    *girl-babies smothered at birth or aborted
    *US crack babies which do not thrive
    *fetuses aborted for whatever reason
    *AIDS babies all over the world
    *famine babies, war babies, poor babies, congenitally malformed, diseased, and damaged
     babies—the list is endless.

Advanced Reprotechnology and genetic modification of plants, animals, and humans, coupled with nationally and globally enforced new eugenic practices and applied social eugenics (including parental eugenics, eugenic sacrifice, genotype mating and fiscal eugenics) is the rational, efficient, humane and technologically feasible way of over-coming age-old problems which ravage even the most advanced nations. No longer will there be illegitimate children, poor people having too many children, or infant mortality due to bad heredity, poverty, and economic and social deprivation. No longer will there be genetically unfit babies due to perpetuation of defective genetic lines. Moreover, a globally planned and enforced eugenic policy will get rid of the problems of overpopulation or unbalanced population once and for all. And then The Four Horsemen of the Apocalypse–Famine, War, Ruin and Death will ride no more.

Think about it:

No More Dead Babies

No More Ghost Babies

No More Little Angels

No More Reproductive Waste

No More Missing Offspring

No More Abortions

No More Unwanted Children

What You Can Do: Organize local eugenic education groups and begin to lobby your local, state, and federal governments to form a Federal Eugenics Administration which will pass legislation to positively enforce new eugenic practices nationally and internationally. Practice new eugenics yourself and encourage your family and friends to do so also.

27

A successful match!

TimelineS:
Production/Reproduction
and Children-as-Commodities
in the United States

Lucia Sommer

I n writing a 'timeline,' or summary history, about children we were aware of the dangers of both terms. A timeline reproduces the notion of a singular, seamless and consensual history, while we are interested in revealing the cracks, seizures, and weak points of all such pretenses of a legitimating telos. But, for purposes of a text, there is a need for limits; a need to de/lineate a beginning and an end. So we rashly mobilize these contradictions and produce a history that does not claim to be singular or complete, but that seeks interruptions, intersections, deviations, and radical breaks.

The notion of childhood is equally fraught with difficulties. In the West, prior to the 17th century, it did not exist. Only when the industrial take-off had begun to create capital accumulation, did the sons and daughters of the newly wealthy classes enjoy leisure time that allowed an ideology of childhood to emerge.

The 1989 United Nations Convention on the Rights of the Child was the most widely and rapidly ratified human rights treaty in history. Among the rights of the child under international law are: "The right to life, survival and development... The right from birth to an identity... The right to freedom of expression...thought, conscience and religion... Access to information and material from a diversity of national and international sources... Protection from physical or mental violence, injury or abuse, neglect or negligent treatment, maltreatment or exploitation... The right to the highest attainable standard of health...social security... A standard of living adequate for the child's physical, mental, spiritual, moral and social development... Education... And the right to use his or her own language." Wilhelm Reich was persecuted for arguing for children's sexual rights. Postcolonial writers like Gayatri Spivak have cautioned against the importation of context-specific notions of right into contexts where their application could do more harm than good. For example, in the case of child labor: Without fighting for and ensuring an adequate compensation for adult workers, child labor will remain a necessity of survival.

Some Lines

The revolution in Assisted Reproductive Technologies (ART) is being accompanied by the rise of new eugenic consciousness as its ideological component. One symptom of this is the reprotech industry's aggressive marketing, which encourages potential parents to believe that complex traits such as intelligence and talent are genetically transmitted, and to select these traits for their children by buying a "donor's" eggs or sperm. In the new eugenic consciousness promoted by the reprotech industry, success = economic dominance, and traits such as beauty and intelligence are deemed valuable because they represent cultural capital. Tellingly, while it is equally unlikely that traits such as kindness, empathy, altruism, and psychological difference are inheritable, these qualities are rarely mentioned as desirable. Perhaps more dangerously, the overwhelming geneticism of this cultural moment overrides all discussion of the political causes of many complex social problems (see "A Summary History of Eugenic Theories and Practices in the United States" in this book).

Among subRosa's many questions: What is the relationship between the current "pricelessness" of the (middle-class) child in dominant discourse, and h/er mundane market value as a collection of genetic raw material? What happens to the reprogenetic child who costs h/er parents $50,000 for a single egg donation cycle, yet does not exhibit the desired and "selected" traits? Or, on the other side of the flesh commodity tracks, what happens to the children of the working poor whose suffering is seen as increasingly irrelevant in this brave new

I. Slave Children, Kentucky, 19th C.

world? Such questions have prompted subRosa to examine the history of children's relation to the commodity in the U.S. As it turns out, the commodification of children is nothing new, but simply part of an unending chain of equivalencies produced under the logic of capital.

The early American economy was based in large part on the labor of enslaved Africans, including children. Statistics give us a hint of the brutality of this system which tore apart families and communities. Of 32 slaves who died on a North Carolina plantation between 1850 and 1855, nine died before the age of five. Yet African-American collective child-rearing practices, in which all adults were responsible for all children fostered life-affirming forms of solidarity and resistance.[1]

In turn-of-the-century U.S., the near-starvation wages of workers made child labor a necessity (as it remains in much of the world today). Parents falsified documents so that children as young as six could work in coal mines and

II. Victim of Industrial Accident, c. 1900.

III. Child Textile Worker, c. 1900.

IV. Amputee Newspaperboy,
age 8, Austin, TX, c. 1900

other industries. Countless numbers died under the dangerous conditions. When children could not keep up with the pace of production, they frequently lost limbs, which meant the loss of work and further destitution. Some children continued to work with false limbs or without.

The boys who worked in the coal mine breakers worked 18-hour plus days sorting coal. Forbidden to wear gloves or use backrests, which would slow down their rate of production, they were frequently beaten by the bosses. Like all workers under capitalism—early and late—children had only their labor power to sell in order to survive. By 1908, one in four mine-workers in the U.S. was a boy aged 7-16.

Children resisted intolerable conditions by striking, running en masse out of the breaker. Because the mill owners depended on their labor power, such collective action could bring a factory to a standstill. (Sometimes desperate par-

V. Breaker Boys Sorting Coal, West Virginia, c. 1900.

ents were forced to join the bosses in whipping the children back into the mines.) Child mine workers played a crucial role in organizing strikes for better working condi-

VI. Children from Lawrence, Mass, striking in NYC, 1912.

tions, the eight-hour day, and safety, and frequently staged school strikes. These actions eventually helped force the improvement of working conditions and the recognition of worker's rights. Because workers fought and died for higher wages and safer conditions, families could survive without children's labor, and child labor laws were passed.

Native American children suffered because of racism and because of their different relationship to the means of production. As Ward Churchill has pointed out, the genocide of Native Americans was and is tied to their existence on land which was capital to the Europeans.[2] The forced removal of First

VII. Boys at Pierre Indian School, Pierre, SD, c. 1900.

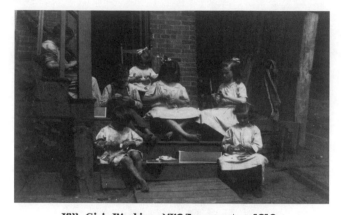

VIII. Girls Working, NYC Tenement, c. 1910.

Nations children to boarding schools—where thousands of them died—served a twofold purpose within the mandate of imperialist expansion: to attempt to exploit the children as labor and to remove them from the land-as-capital. When Native American children refused to assimilate this logic, they were killed. While sympathetic to the Native Americans, Edward Sheriff Curtis and other European photographers were seemingly unable to see collective resistance, rendering their subjects instead as tragic, solitary, stoic martyrs. However, children played important roles in many of the uprisings against the Europeans.

Hauling water made up a large part of the labor of women and girls in turn-of-the-century industrializing cities, as it does for a majority of women/girls in the world today. As Lisa Frank has noted about Pittsburgh, "The massive industries situated at the river's banks both increased a woman's need for water and competed with it," since men working in those industries often drank thirty to forty glasses of water a day, and the mills' production lowered the water pressure so that water had to be hauled from further down the hill as the day wore on. Often this water was grossly contaminated. Yet while big steel laid streetcar tracks and pipe for the commuting bourgeoisie, it wouldn't send pipe to working-class neighborhoods. The labor of women and female children in reproducing and maintaining the working class—though bound tightly to the industrial revolution—was not recognized as 'industrial.' It represented mere use-value within a system increasingly based on exchange-value—the appropriated and abstracted value of a worker's labor. Thus "women's [and children's] work—their very industrial work—was performed under conditions which left them farther behind."[3]

IX. **Lewis Carroll's Alice Liddell as a beggar, 1859.**

Children have historically been simultaneously eroticized and desexualized. Their sexuality—when captured as spectacle—is fetishized, yet rendered invisible under the sign of "innocence" when it is a question of knowledge of their own bodies. On the cusp of the 21st century, it is still extremely difficult for children and adolescents to receive information on sexuality or birth control; girls are still not told they have a clitoris even if they receive cursory sex education; standard anatomy textbooks such as *Gray's Anatomy* are inaccurate regarding the female reproductive system; and homosexuality is silenced although its affirmation could prevent many teen suicides. While our culture's obsession with the child sex taboo (a function of industrial economy where the age of adulthood is increased by the increasing division of labor) renders it more seductive, the power relations and naturalized familial structures that encourage sexual abuse of children are rarely discussed. In Carroll's photograph, even poverty is fetishized.

The children of farmers and sharecroppers are heirs to a system which has pitted industrial workers against rural; slave labor against "free"; and first world against colonized nations, in a race to the bottom. In the U.S., "race" is the investment the ruling class makes

X. **Girl, Gee's Bend, Alabama, 1938.**

in the conditions of its own reproduction, where racism is an obstacle to work-ing-class solidarity. "It was only because 'race' consciousness superceded class-consciousness that the continental plantation bourgeoisie was able to achieve and maintain the social control necessary for proceeding with capital accumu-lation on the basis of chattel bond-labor."[4] The WPA documentary photograph-

XI. Children demonstrating against segregation, Birmingham, Alabama, 1963.

ic aesthetic, like its 19th century counterpart, favors images of solitary, tragic individuals rather than images of resistance.

What if, as Irigaray has asked about women, the commodities "refused to go to market"? If, as the French feminists have argued, woman is a commodity exchanged by men, who only gains access to the Symbolic (the social) through the birth of a male child, how does this work differently—given differences of race and class? What of the children themselves? If they "refused"? Elementary and high school students played critical roles in the Civil Rights movement. These students demonstrating against segregation took part in the SCLC's campaign to fill the city's jails with protesters. On May 2, 1963, more than nine hundred Birmingham schoolchildren went to jail.

Under pancapitalism, "globalization" means that elite institutions like the World Trade Organization erase borders for multinational corporations, who are free to search out the cheapest labor, while creating and maintaining

XII. Children, Peru, 1965.

borders against the world's poor, who are not free to search for better wages. The World Bank and the International Monetary Fund's Structural Adjustment Policies intensify the impoverishment of the world's majority by making privatization, austere social budgets, and market deregulation conditions of loans to the world's poorest countries. In the current conjuncture, effective global means of resistance to counter this hegemony have yet to be realized, although cross-border labor organizing is an important strategy. The trade in human cargo—whether of bonded labor, immigrants in search of work, or human organs—now represents one of the largest and fastest-growing sectors of international trade.

In global pancapitalism, U.S. policy ensures that workers in the U.S. must

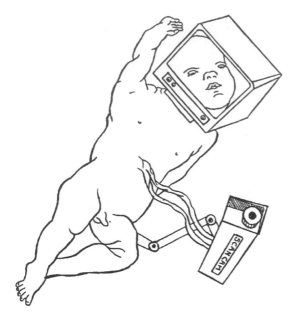

XIII. Reprogenetic Baby, 2000.

compete for the lowest wages with workers—including children—in the neo- colonized nations of the South. It brutally (and often covertly) maintains the totalitarian regimes and the borders that make this super-exploitation possible. Adolescents fought against the U.S.-trained death-squads in El Salvador and Nicaragua in the 1980s and '90s.

In the recent intensification of the international division of labor, women and female children are "the true surplus army of labor in the current conjuncture. In their case, patriarchal social relations contribute to their production as the new focus of super-exploitation."[5] Girls from formerly colonized nations enter the sex industry in the hope of escaping poverty, where often they can travel across heavily policed "first-world" borders only as slaves.

The conditions of intense competition and alienation of pancapitalism require the elimination of unproductive desires and nonrational behaviors other than those directed toward consumption. Currently this is accomplished in part through the use of mood stabilizers and antidepressant drugs. The explosion in diagnoses and pharmacological treatment of medicalized conditions such as Attention Deficit Hyperactivity Disorder (ADHD) among school-age children has led many critics, including doctors, to question whether this phenomenon is in fact a symptom of the increasing streamlining and commodification of education. Increasing demands for children to sit still, follow rules, and carry out routinized tasks in preparation for taking their place as technocratic or service workers in the labor force, may be to blame. Biotechnology and Assisted Reproductive Technologies now hold out the dystopian 'promise' of producing bodies predisposed to normative behaviors, and eliminating or reducing the unproductive and nonrational at the genetic level.

How will children of the Biotech Century resist the ideological values associated with the new hyper-rationalized reproductive process, in which human value is determined by a person's economic worth and the human body is "raw material" for the production of profit?

XIV. Twin Boys, Apache (Bear Clan), at Intertribal Dance Competition, c. 2000.

OTHER LINES

To attempt to say anything by way of a timeline is only a beginning. There was a need for limits, a need to de/lineate a beginning and an end. In first limiting our examination of the commodifiation of children to the U.S. we found that it was impossible not to break those boundaries. Given the reality of the global economy, the lives of children in the U.S. cannot be meaningfully separated from the lives of those across borders. There are inevitably other lines and narratives that would criss-cross and interrupt this one. ★

1 Howard Zinn, *A People's History of the United States 1492–Present* (New York: Harper Collins, 1995), pp. 168-173.

2 See Ward Churchill, *A Little Matter of Genocide: Holocaust and Denial in the Americas, 1492 to the Present* (San Francisco: City Lights Books, 1997).

3 Lisa Frank,"Women's History Month," in *Working Ideas: Newsletter of the Pittsburgh Labor Party*, March, 1999.

4 Theodore W. Allen, *The Invention of the White Race: The Origin of Racial Oppression in Anglo-America* (New York: Verso, 1997), p. 240.

5 Gayatri Chakravorty Spivak, *In Other Worlds* (London: Methuen, 1987), p. 167.

6 Critical Art Ensemble, "Buying Time for the Flesh Machine: Pharmacology and Social Order," *Flesh Machine: Cyborgs, Designer Babies, and New Eugenic*

Consciousness (New York: Autonomedia, 1998).

I– **X** Images from the Library of Congress, Prints and Photographs Division.

XI Photographer unknown, *Out of Many: A History of the American People*, Faraghar, John Mack, Mari Jo Buhle, Daniel Czitrom, Susan S. Armitage eds., (New Jersey: Prentice Hall, 1997).

XII Photograph by Arthur Domike.

XIII subRosa, 2000.

XIV Photograph by Lelan Strongbow.

Research!
Action!
Embodiment!
Conviviality!

RESEARCH!
ACTION!
EMBODIMENT!
CONVIVIALITY!

subRosa manifestation

S ubRosa's name honors feminist pioneers in art, activism, labor, politics, and science: Rosa Bonheur, Rosa Luxemburg, Rosie the Riveter, Rosa Parks, Rosalind Franklin.

subRosa is a reproducible cyberfeminist cell of cultural researchers committed to combining art, activism, and politics to explore and critique the intersections of digital information and biotechnologies on women's bodies, lives, and work.

subRosa produces art events, activist campaigns and projects, contestations, publications, media interventions, and public forums that address aspects of technology, gender, and difference; feminism and global capital; new bio and medical technologies and women's health; and the changed conditions of production and reproduction for women in the integrated circuit.

subRosa practices a situational embodied feminist politics nourished by conviviality, becoming autonomous, and the desire for affirmative alliances and coalitions.

Let a million subRosas bloom

subRosa SELF-ORGANIZING TIPS:

Start a subRosa cell! subRosa cells organize around local/global biomedical, biotechnological, and environmental developments, and their effects on women's sexuality, reproductive health, and living/working conditions. The cells act autonomously and can also activate an international network of feminist support, information, and action through the Internet. subRosa cells reproduce and mutate according to local conditions, needs, and desires.

Use the subRosa logo! subRosa invites you to use its logo and name to create solidarity, connection, confusion, and multiplicity. subRosa opposes proprietary authorship, ownership, and copyright, and encourages collaboration, difference, gift economy, *detournement*, and collective invention.

Connect to subRosa! subRosa works situationally within given localities, and it communicates, manifests, and connects globally. Each new subRosa cell becomes part of an emergent subRosa organism. Since there is no centralized bureaucracy, agenda, office, or fixed membership, there is no telling where this self-organization may lead. Contact subRosa at *subrosa@cyberfeminism.net* or see our web-site <http://www.cyberfeminism.net>.

A BRIEF BIOGRAPHY OF subRosa:

October 1998: a loosely organized cyberfeminist study group emerges from Faith Wilding's fellowship at the STUDIO for Creative Inquiry, Carnegie Mellon, and begins to research intersections of digital information and biotechnologies; genetics; cultural theory about the body; and feminist and postcolonial theory and practice.

March 1999: The first subRosa cell is formed and prints an organizing flyer (text above) that is distributed both nationally and internationally through

the mail, and in local schools, clinics, and public spaces in Pittsburgh. The first version of the subRosa Web site is launched in time for The Next Five Minutes Tactical Media festival in Amsterdam. subRosa's first "cellular muTations" performance (leafleting and education action) also takes place at the Next Five Minutes.

April 1999: Publication and distribution of first issue of *@Second Opinion*, a broadside on Women, Health, and Biotechnology. Presentation of two public panels on Women, Health, and Biotechnology, at Carlow College, Pittsburgh.

June 1999: subRosa dispenses leaflets and lemonade at Race for the Cure

breast cancer research benefit in Pittsburgh. That summer collective members are trained in Web page and video production, and electronic design and layout. Research/Discussion group continues meeting.

August 1999: Expansion and re-launch of subRosa website on Artswire.

Fall 1999: Launch of SmartMom, a web project, detourning the technology of the Smart T-shirt (developed for remote battlefield medicine by the U.S. military) to the uses of pregnancy surveillance and assisted reproduction technologies.

September 1999: Publication and distribution of second issue

of *@Second Opinion* in poster format, "Does She or Doesn't She: Cheaper by the Dozen," a performance and informational text about egg donation addressed to university co-eds.

Winter 2000: subRosa presents lectures at various symposia and festivals in Europe and the U.S. Work begins on Sex and Gender in the Biotech Century project.

March 2000: "Vulva De/ReConstructa," a video on the subject of aesthetic surgery of the vulva is exhibited at "Die Verletzte Diva" exhibition, Taxispalais, Innsbruck, Austria, and screened in Los Angeles, and Baltimore.

August 2000: subRosa presents its projects in the Open Space of the Internationale Frauen Universität (IFU) at Expo 2000, Hannover, Germany. That same month, it also exhibits "Knowing Bodies," a performative multimedia show in the "Fusion: Artists in a Research Environment" exhibition at the Regina Miller Gallery, Carnegie Mellon, Pittsburgh.

October 2000: subRosa stages an intervention on a panel about artists and biotechnology at the Performative Sites Conference, Penn State University, State College, PA.

November 2000: Presentation of commissioned performance, "Sex and

Gender Ed in the Biotech Century" at the Digital Secrets Think-Tank sponsored by the Institute for Studies in the Arts, Arizona State University, Tempe, AZ.

February 2001: subRosa panel

presentations at the Women's Caucus for Art, and the College Art Association in Chicago.

March 2001: Presentation of commissioned performance, "Expo EmmaGenics," a biotech trade show, at the Intermediale Festival, and participation on a cyberfeminism panel at the Seventh International Performance Studies Conference, Mainz, Germany.

April 2001: subRosa pilots a participatory research residency for "Knowing Bodies," an on-going project on biotechnology and women's health care, sponsored by St. Norbert's Art and Cultural Center, Winnipeg, Canada.

June 2001: subRosa presents current projects at the International Sculpture Conference, Pittsburgh.

Fall 2001: subRosa presents its projects at "female takeover," Ars Electronica Festival, Linz, Austria; at Welcome to the Revolution symposium, Zurich, Switzerland; at Techniques of Cyberfeminism, Thealit, Universität Bremen, Bremen, Germany; and at Very Cyberfeminist International conference, Hamburg, Germany.

March 2002: subRosa participates in the Women's Studies Colloquium: "Hardware, Software, Wetware, and Women," at St. Mary's College, Maryland; and performs "Sex and Gender Ed in the Biotech Century."

April 2002: subRosa is invited to perform "U.S. Grade AAA Premium Eggs" in the Student Union at Ohio State University, Bowling Green.

Making Babies the American Girl® Way

Terri Kapsalis

W hat catches my attention is the look in the girl's eyes, combined with the doll clutched to her 10-year-old belly. All in all, it is a normal enough sight: a suburban family out for a day of shopping on Chicago's Magnificent Mile. But the girl has the look of one possessed. She leads the parade and is clearly the focus of the day's outing. I pass them and turn a corner, only to come upon yet another girl, a few years younger, cradling a doll whose blonde locks seem clipped from her own. The girl and her doll wear identical blue jumpers. A camera dangles from her mother's wrist. They are headed in the same direction as the group I had passed, and this girl, like the other, has the dazed look of a pilgrim too long on the road. I cross the street: another girl, same scenario. She, too, carries a doll, not unlike the other two dolls, but with a different hair color to match her owner's.

> **American Girl Photo Op**
>
> *Claire Pentecost*

Has some kind of odd convention come to town? Or are they all bound for a Jerry Springer shoot somewhere nearby: "Girls with doll disorders and the families who support them?" This girl's mother points to a store across the street, and her daughter's body seems to rise a foot off the sidewalk, her inflated smile giving her a helium-lift. There it is. Girl Xanadu. Taj McDoll, a.k.a. American Girl Place.

There had been American Girl dolls long before this singular boutique

opened in 1998. A coworker at a women's health clinic first showed me a catalog nearly a decade ago, bringing me up to speed on the latest rage among pre-pubescent girls. Another coworker chimed in, regarding her daughter's favorites. They complained about the steep prices and sheer number of collectibles, but as good liberals, they commended the dolls' diversity. Finally, a doll company was being responsive to ethnic differences by offering Asian, Latina, and other dolls of color.

We discussed these new-fangled poppets in the staff room that doubles as the storage area for tanks of frozen sperm. (These tanks, bearing an unfortunate resemblance to two-foot tall circumcised Caucasian penises, arrive via Fed Ex from sperm banks around the country. The tanks stand in front of the copy machine, awaiting summonses from pre-ovulatory alternative insemination clients.) We often use the tanks as makeshift stools and did so that day while paging through the glossy American Girl catalog. A stack of sperm donor catalogs rested nearby.

Pleasant Rowland founded the Pleasant Company in 1986, announcing start-up with a catalog offering dolls and books. She sold the company to Mattel in 1998, for $700,000,000. Earnings grow from year to year, with the American Girl catalog roping in more than two-thirds of the income. The first 60 or so pages of the American Girl catalog are dedicated to the American Girls Collection, a line of dolls who come complete with a name and a personal history, accessories and storybooks. There's the 1854 pioneer girl, Kirsten, whose family immigrated from Sweden. There's former slave girl Addy whose family escaped to the North. There's Samantha, a Victorian orphan of means, and Josefina, "an Hispanic girl of heart and hope." Their lives are further sketched in picture books, telling tales of school, summertime and birthdays. Each book, naturally, is paid

(by the consumer) advertising for the outfits and accessories featured within. You can buy them all, from Kirsten's summer dress with straw hat to Josefina's pet baby goat, Sombrita.

These American Girl dolls are a new breed. They're neither pudgy, round babies nor busty Barbies. They're post-potty trained, pre-adolescent girls, closer in proportion and size to a life-size infant than a foot-long Barbie. When you make a purchase from the American Girl collection, you're not just buying a doll, you're buying a plausible life history. Juan Garcia, a history professor at the University of Arizona, is quoted in the catalog as vouching for the authenticity of the "Hispanic" doll: "The books and products that accompany Josefina richly capture and recreate a significant time, place, and heritage in New Mexican history that young people seldom learn about." Such knowledge does not come cheaply. Josefina's New Mexican Table & Chairs are $75, her Feast Day Finery is $22, and her Heirloom Accessories are $12. As Josefina's complete collection runs $925, only a few youngsters will have the opportunity to get that whole story.

The catalog is extensive, with at least eight pages dedicated to each of the six dolls in the collection. Every outfit, piece of furniture, and accessory is described, complete with teasers about the school, summer, and birthday narratives found in the accompanying books. Rather than arriving as a blank slate, each doll comes pre-endowed and packaged with *a la carte* personal milestones and memories.

That's not the end of it. Girls can purchase their own outfits to match their dolls'. Under the caption "Dress Like Your Doll," a young, apparently Latina girl is pictured modeling the same camisa, petticoat, skirt, and rebozo that Josefina wears on the opposite page. A black girl stands beside doll Addy, in a matching striped pink dress. A light-skinned brunette girl in a white nightie is pictured holding light-skinned brunette Samantha in a white nightie. The catalog encourages girls to pick dolls that look like them, selecting skin, hair, and eye color as close as possible to their own. Choosing a true look-alike, the girl can then step into the doll's elaborate narrative, fully outfitted.

...

When I started working in the alternative insemination program at a women's health center in Chicago nearly a decade ago, it was my job to make sure we had up-to-date sperm bank catalogs and donor profiles. Donor catalogs are composed of profiles that provide the information a consumer uses to choose a donor. All donors, who don't actually "donate" but are in fact paid for their semen, are anonymous, identified only by alpha-numeric codes.

Begun nearly 25 years ago—when "unmarried" women were often refused access to insemination, or made to undergo a battery of psychological tests to prove they'd make "fit mothers," our program was and is solely for lesbians and other women without male partners. In the early 1990s, donor profiles were mainly straightforward, focusing on what was termed "physical characteristics": blood type, height, weight, eye color, ethnicity, religion, and personal and family medical history. (I'd never thought of religion as a "physical characteristic," but it was always there on the list, as if fundamental to a consumer's decision.) You'd know, for example, that donor F645 was English and Portugese, an atheist with A-positive blood, brown hair, hazel eyes, a fair complexion, six-foot, one-inch tall and 160 pounds. Some banks included what was deemed "personal information" such as hobbies and talents. These items always struck me as funny, but I supposed the extra information that F645 was interested in "sports and game theory" was provided to whet a prospective consumer's

interest. I couldn't imagine that consumers might entertain the idea that such characteristics were genetic and therefore heritable.

Since the mid-1990s many banks have expanded these profiles. Some now include essays written by donors. Printed either in a script-like font, or hand-written, they present a donor's response to questions like: Why do you want to be a sperm donor? If we could pass on a message to the recipients of your semen, what would that message be? Where would you like to travel and why? What is your ultimate ambition or goal in life?

Some banks have expanded "personal information" to include math skills, mechanical ability, athletic ability, favorite sport, musical talent, foreign languages, artistic ability, and favorite foods, color, type of music, or pets. Some include SAT scores and GPAs.

Such information has a price. Xytex, a sperm bank based in Georgia, offers short profiles that include basic information and brief medical histories. The first five are free; after that, each costs $2. Long donor profiles that include personal essays and supplemental information cost $10 each. Xytex was the first sperm bank to provide photographs of their donors. Introduced in 1994, PhotoFiles™ include short and long profiles as well as three 4x6-inch photos of the donor: $35 each. In 1996, Xytex started offering BabyFiles™ which contain the same written information as PhotoFiles™ but in place of current photos of the donor, 8x10-inch reproductions of donors' baby pictures. Xytex explains that "BabyFiles™ are helpful for those who have concerns about how their baby might look."

In 1997, Xytex introduced VideoFiles™ which they claim to be "the most comprehensive donor information packages available anywhere! They are videotaped interviews of select donors, and not only provide you with a glimpse of the donor's appearance, but they reveal the donor's personality as well." A steal at $100.

Xytex also keeps what may be considered the ultimate file on donors by permanently preserving "donor cells that can be used as a complete chemical record of genetics." The program is aptly titled Patriarch Genetic Tracking. According to Xytex, this genetic archive is maintained in case future progeny ever "need" such genetic information. What defines need is left open at this point and will certainly shift over time, as will, undoubtedly, the consumer cost of access to such information.

Some banks now have an assisted donor matching service. At Fairfax Cryobank in Virginia, a prospective consumer can send two photos (front and side views) of the person to be matched, along with a list of important characteristics to be met, and a staff member will suggest a donor match. Although none of the clients of the program where I work have used a formal matching service, many of our single clients self-select donors to "match" themselves, and clients with female partners often choose a donor that may resemble their partner.

For a fee, California Cryobank provides audiotaped interviews with many donors. Fairfax Cryobank, based in Virginia, hopes to lure customers with long profiles which include the donor's "personality type" as dictated by the Keirsey Temperament Sorter. Fairfax is the first bank I know of to start an

exclusive, higher-priced, sperm line, listed separately from other donors. Named "Fairfax Doctorate," this line includes semen from donors who have completed or are completing doctoral degrees. This new sperm line follows in the footsteps of the famed Repository for Germinal Choice, a bank run by outspoken eugenicist Robert Graham, who claims to "improve humankind by gradually increasing the proportion of advantageous genes in the human gene pool," by featuring donors with genius-level IQs. Fairfax Cryobank supports Graham's vision by asserting that sperm from men with doctorates is more valuable (and therefore more costly) than rank-and-file sperm.

This trend among banks to provide more and more information is part of a marketing strategy which assumes that more information about donors leads to increased sales. But it is also a kind of false advertising that leads consumers to believe that they get what they pay for. Nowhere in the catalog are there warnings stating: "Your child may not turn out the way you think." The consumer shops not just for an exponential number of DNA dollops with flagellae, but for a personal history, personal interests, wishes and dreams. A postgraduate degree, a "personality type," a cute baby picture and a personal essay are just some of the new spermatic accessories.

This seductive marketing strategy, combined with a social climate rife with bio-deterministic ideas that genes are the basis for future behavior, can cause the sperm consumer to forget that she is purchasing a spot of DNA which can combine with her own in myriad configurations and that a future baby will be subject to any number of transformational environmental and social factors. Instead, she may believe—traveling backward in centuries, ideologically—that she is purchasing a homunculus, a mini-human to be implanted

into her uterus and emerge fully accessorized, and who, once grown, will play the guitar, like dogs, and be an intuitive, thoughtful extrovert with a Ph.D. in math.

Sperm banks that pursue such marketing strategies do not discourage consumers from believing that they are purchasing completely transmittable traits, and that they can, therefore, style their future child to their liking. To the contrary, designer babies are just what new reproductive pioneers promise. Genetic testing already allows the consumer to determine whether individual embryos created using egg and sperm prior to *in vitro* fertilization have a predisposition for genetic conditions such as Down's syndrome. Simply eliminate the ones that do and implant the ones that don't. With this kind of pre-implantation testing, any genetic trait could theoretically be selected for or against before birth. With the claim that genes have been identified that cause such traits as obesity and homosexuality, how long will it be before you can order up a thin, heterosexual baby with good spatial skills, eliminating the risk of a fat, dyslexic lesbian? This is reproduction reminiscent of Starbucks, where the consumer designs a baby as she might a beverage, selecting from a long list of specifications. Making a baby the old way will be as outmoded as ordering coffee with cream and sugar, instead of a "grande, skinny latte with a double shot."

...

Many of the clients I see in the insemination program become thoroughly exhausted by the arduous and stressful process of choosing sperm. Some become almost obsessed with choosing the right donor. They may feel they're not provided enough information. One client couldn't understand why she knew that a donor had a tenor voice, but not whether he'd ever been to jail. Another joked that what she really wanted to know was if her donor was good at Scrabble. As one said, "It's a lot different than choosing a new car."

But American Girl customers, soon to be of reproductive age, will be just the kind of shoppers ready to meet the challenge. They're already familiar with the basic process, as matching doll traits isn't so different from matching donor traits. The consumer pays for a narrative—whether Xytex's VideoFile™ or Addy's birthday storybook—which in turn advertises and sells more product. American Girl aficionados are primed for the kind of expensive, detail-oriented shopping necessary to buy a baby in an age of reproductive technologies.

After all, what are dolls but instruments for simulating mothering? Traditionally, fussing over dolls is practice for future motherhood. You can care for, burp and diaper them, and truck them around. And the selection process has grown ever more complex. Long gone are the days when all baby dolls looked pretty much the same. At most, you could choose one with eyes that could shut, or one with a little pee hole. Otherwise they were almost entirely white and fair.

Back then, having babies was fairly straightforward as well, at least if you were married and heterosexual. Either you could, or you couldn't. Now, if you can't due to infertility or lack of access to gametes, as long as you have the money to pay for it, there are options, namely a variety of expensive reproductive technologies.

And so it goes with shopping for dolls in the age of the American Girl. Choosing the right doll, with her attendant characteristics, history, and accessories, is the first part of the mothering simulation, a pre-echo of the experience of shopping for a sperm or egg, and of designing a real baby. The American Girl line provides girls with the skills to be good future consumers in the reproductive technologies market.

As that market grows and changes, American Girl appears to be ahead of the curve. Consider the American Girl Today line of 20 dolls without distinguishing dress or accompanying stories. They have variegated skin tones, hair and eye colors. Not unlike sperm donors, these dolls are identified by ordering codes rather than given names. "GT 20D" has light skin, blonde hair, and gray eyes. "GT 18A" has dark skin, textured black hair, and light brown eyes. "GT 4D" appears to have almond-shaped—or generic Asian—eyes.

These American Girls don't come with their own histories. The idea here is that the consumer makes this doll into whomever she pleases. The catalog reads, "She's an American Girl like you! Her adventures are your adventures. Her dreams are your dreams. This is her moment in history, and your moment, too." Whereas the original American Girl Collection asks the buyer to step into Addy's nightie or Samantha's tea dress—girl imitates doll—the American Girl Today line enacts a reversal: Doll imitates girl. Each customer is encouraged to pick her match from the 20-doll line-up. Including four blondes, one Asian, and two "dark skin" dolls, these dolls presumably mirror American Girl's sales demographics rather than any other population of America's real girls. In much the same way, sperm banks supply semen from some donors of color, but offer far more choices when it comes to white donors. Thus "consumer demand" is a reflection of the new eugenics where supply does not mirror actual world demographics.

As with the purchased genetic material, these coded American Girl Today dolls are the raw material onto which the consumer can then impose her own dreams and activities, thanks to accessories galore including a mini-Macintosh computer, soccer gear, or an American Girl horse and riding outfit. The doll is not endowed with some historical narrative, she is there to receive the consuming girl's life story, whether actual or imagined.

The ordering code for each American Girl Today doll begins with GT. I assume this stands for "Girl Today," but is it by uncanny coincidence that these two letters are also codes for two of the four chemical bases of DNA, guanine and thymine? Does American Girl take us from the phenotypic and the display of simple surfaces to the genotypic and the marketing of not altogether

PHOTO: CLAIRE PENTECOST

decipherable codes? Girls are asked to pick a doll that looks like themselves and identify her based on an ordering code. Have we arrived at a time when ordering codes and genetic codes are one and the same?

The American Girl Today line forecasts the future, when cloning will be the new frontier of reproductive technologies. The My Twinn™ dolls, available by mail order, already take this leap forward. Mail in a girl's photo, a personal profile form, a hair sample, and $128.95, and in four weeks you will receive a "poseable" doll with that girl's individual facial features, including matching eyes, skin, and hair. Not unlike American Girl, matching doll and girl outfits and accessories are available for purchase. The Twinn (note the doubling of the "n") label refers to an identical or near-identical genetic make up. Here, the twinning occurs at the phenotypic level, but in an age of genetic obsession, will the genotypic be far behind? My Twinn™ undoubtedly uses the girl's hair sample in order to match texture and color, but this very hair sample could be used by scientists to extract DNA for a not altogether different purpose.

Although cloning is currently a risky process, some have proposed it as an ideal option for consumers who have tried older sperm-and-egg reproductive processes to no avail. And with cloning, theoretically at least, there are no genetic surprises: You know exactly what code you're ordering. Ever since physicist and cattle breeder Richard Seed announced in 1998 that he would begin cloning humans within 90 days, a growing number of scientists and civilians seem to share his particular fantasy of eternal genetic life. There's a long line forming of potential clone consumers—those who want to duplicate a favorite pet, a dying child, Elvis, or themselves.

...

Back on the Magnificent Mile, I follow the dazed girls, their dolls, and families into American Girl Place. Inside, consumers wander around, nearly hushed, as if at a museum. Girls stand transfixed in front of glass cases, eyeing the accessories they've seen in the catalogs. After passing display after display of the historical dolls, I happen upon the glass case containing all 20 American Girl Today dolls, with their GT ordering numbers, lined up like little soldiers ready for some kind of odd battle, dressed in identical red vinyl jumpers and plaid tights. Transfixed as any of my younger sisters, I realize that the new reproductive technology industry has a lot to learn from American Girl's marketing strategies. While the sperm and egg banks Internet and catalog sales soar, and fertility clinics haul in the big out-of-pocket medical bucks, perhaps they, too, should consider opening a boutique of their own.

As I step onto the escalator, I see that American Girl Place has a cafe where girls can have tea with their dolls. Why couldn't a fertility corporation—call it American Baby Place—have a cafe where a customer could take tea with an egg or sperm donor? I see a marquee advertising American Girl Place's $25-a-ticket live musical, written and performed by real American girls. Perhaps an American Baby Place could offer the "American Clones Revue," a live musical written and performed by clones and their DNA doubles, where one could chat with the cast after the show, and where droves of dreamy-eyed consumers, having packed up their American Girl collections years before, could line up, money in hand, eager to order a clone of their very own. ★

Happy Endings: Engagements with Women Artists in Singapore

Irina Aristarkhova

I have good news for you: we still deliver miracles,[1] after all...

After the comfortable, transparent and always-already anti-Western, anti-men or generally oppositional rhetoric that has over-determined our practices and discourses;

After unrestrained quotations that mimic without subversion or local appropriation fashionable Anglo-American and French poststructuralist and postcolonial figures;

After being consumed by antipathy towards anything not 'ours,' that is negated or embraced in accordance with the logic of sameness;

After being taught how to compete with each other under a "phallic" sun without respect for female genealogy, continually denying feminist history and the radical creativity of our fellow-women;

After being left without feminist education, theory, ethics and aesthetics as part of our curriculum, and still not teaching it when we have an opportunity;

After "cutting off the tree branch on which we sit" by reproducing jealousy, ignorance and disrespect towards other women's achievements;

After having no positive articulations of/for the word "woman" and for women in our lives;

After having no mediators for professional long-term and short-term relationships that would still leave a space between us to breathe and to create in all our radical otherness among ourselves;

After all that has stood between you and me.

As you may have noticed by the preceding statements, I am by no means unaware of the obstacles that surround us and surely cannot be blamed for being "too optimistic" about doing feminism in, so-called, "non-Western contexts." It is exactly this measured caution that leads me to consider the enactment of any complex and fruitful professional relationships between us as an engendering of miracles, where we co-evolve a new language, new art and new writing, that many other women can partake of (and happily, they do—sometimes acknowledging us, sometimes not).

Here I would like to share with you two of my constructive and happy engagements with women artists in Singapore, presented in the collaborative form in which they developed.[2]

AN ART OF COLLABORATION: AMANDA HENG

Amanda Heng is arguably the most well-known and persistent *feminist* artist in Singapore who in the course of many years has tried to introduce a critical feminist agenda into the Singapore art scene. Though I had heard about her and had seen her art works before, we first met at the symposium on feminist art

that my colleagues and I organized at an art institution in Singapore. The symposium itself was a result of a graduate workshop and an exhibition on feminist art entitled "A Self of One's Own" that I conceived and curated in 1999.[3] Amanda Heng's serious commitment to collaboration among women of different perspectives and views was clearly evident even in this first encounter. For Amanda Heng, to be a feminist means "to be aware that women are still in the position of being dominated by gender stereotypes,"

Amanda Heng: "Let's Walk," performance, 1999.

and to be aware of "a patriarchal construct that functions to limit our experiences, expressions and expectations of the lives we live." It means "a conviction to express women's oppression, to investigate, explain and analyze the causes and consequences and to seek new possibilities, strategies and relationships for liberation of women's personal and political life." She admits to having been radically transformed by feminism. She says, "Feminism has made very important contributions to contemporary cultural discourses by proposing alternative points of view to phallocentric thinking. It has been basic and fundamental to my discovery of myself as a female person. It gave me confidence to accept myself as I am and helped me realize that my lived experience as a woman in my own terms is important and valid. I find feminist thought liberating because of its diversity, vitality and its refusal to stop changing and growing with time. More importantly, it permits each and every woman to think through her own thoughts and set herself free."

For me, to be a feminist means to learn about women's cultural histories and celebrate women's creativity around the world, in order to try and reverse the language of oppression into a language of fecundity and inspiration. The persistence of the image of women as an oppressed group (though I do not deny the existence of sexist oppression and discrimination on a day-to-day basis) seems to me complicitous with a perpetuation of masochistic trends within women's culture that adds to their anger and unhappiness. Alternatively, I believe, the challenge lies in the following questions: How to invent and introduce alternatives, embodied and embedded in our everyday life, that would provide women with building material, both theoretical, aesthetic and psychic, to materialize happier ways of being a woman, relating to women and to men? And here our collaboration is essential.[4]

Amanda Heng persistently addresses issues of the social and cultural position of women in her works and her artistic practice that draws from a strong sense of the history of women in Singapore, particularly colored by the experiences of the women in her own geneaology. She says,

> For my grandmother's and mother's generation who came to Singapore from China in the 1920s and '30s, women had only one life, that is to serve their husbands, have children, look after their households and work as unpaid laborers for family businesses. In that generation women worked their whole lives without pay. Their only hope for better lives was their children. Many Chinese women looked for life-long security and became *amahs* or maids in rich or British families. They lived and worked as a member of the families until they were too old to work, and then they would return to China before they died. Salaries were sent back to China to support their families. Some remained single throughout their whole lives, and others depended on their luck to get married in Singapore or China, usually becoming second or third wives or mistresses because of their low status.

The postcolonial period in Singapore's history saw an unprecedented rise in social and economic developments that radically changed the lives of women here. While acknowledging the real changes in women's lives, Amanda has struggled in her art to point to some of the contradictions within these newly acquired social positions. For example, she notes that the developments in the lives of women in Singapore have been enabled by a displacement of their traditional roles and tasks to some other economically underprivileged women from Southeast Asia:

> The educated middle class became the dominant workforce in businesses, industries and technologies. Women enjoyed equal opportunities for education and employment not because the government respected the rights of women here but because it recognized that they could not afford to ignore half of the much-needed female work-

force for economic development. Women have gained financial independence and have more choices in life generally. Today women are seeking not just economic independence but also personal meaning, satisfaction and identity from their work. Women are also expected to fulfill their social responsibilities in the reproduction of population to replace the fast graying population. Women found themselves in a difficult position to take on multiple roles. In many families, household chores and child-raising tasks are now relegated to cheap domestic help imported from countries of different cultural backgrounds. These domestic helpers from Indonesia, the Philippines, Sri Lanka, Myanmar & Pakistan are not provided life-long security, like my grandmother's generation; they work on a contract basis under very strict rules and regulations for little money. Globalization and the new economy have changed the relationship between employers and employees and projected exciting prospects in life for all, but the welfare and the fate of these workers in the domestic arena have remained unchanged.

There are women from all over Asia working as live-in maids in local and expatriate families in Singapore, and the very important question of how and in what ways a community of women artists can address and reflect on such issues is rarely discussed. Amanda Heng is one of those very few artists who questions the exploitative attitudes in relations among women, thus exposing the complicity between economic structures and patriarchal structures. Her current work in progress focuses on presenting some of her views on the situation of domestic maids in Singapore. Her works—predominantly performances, installations and videos—have always sought to engage the wider community, thus following a long feminist tradition of political engagement and its focus on raising public awareness. Many of her previous works have sought to bring critical attention to various aspects of women's lives and experiences. It is noteworthy that Amanda Heng has established a name for herself in the international art scene, having shown across Europe and Asia, and undertakes as many projects overseas as she does locally.

In the Singaporean art scene, where many seem to have a skeptical or, at best, cautious attitude toward feminism, I found Amanda Heng to be the only one who throughout the years has consciously taken a stance both as a woman artist and a feminist, and refuses to give up on opening doors for collaboration. It created numerous problems for her in terms of funding, relations with other women artists, with men artists, and with the mainstream art world in Singapore as well—a not-unfamiliar picture to many. However, it is her commitment to holding herself open to collaboration, to difficult questions of art theory and contemporary art practice, to society and its problems, and to welcoming differences between us, that have made her into one of the most active and critical artists in Singapore.

Judging from my other experiences both in Singapore and Russia, I can affirm that the most welcoming and engaging of artists are those creative women who have thought, learned, and worked through their relation to a heterogeneous feminist heritage, and/or who are still searching and ready for highly complex theoretical and aesthetic negotiations. Margaret Tan Ai Hua, another woman artist from Singapore strongly committed to a feminist agenda says: "The fact that the term 'feminist art' or 'feminism' was coined in the West does not mean that we in the East should reject/oppose it. Of course there was also consciousness among our foremothers here, and, in fact, the concerns might be the same as their Western counterparts: the role of women in a patriarchal system and the need to question such an allocation. I have no problems with the terms and I see the squabbles of East versus West, who became aware first, etc., a waste of time and energy. Patriarchal views and practices are still so predominant both here and elsewhere in the world, we should be more focused on empowering each other, to make a change in the system and ourselves."

Margaret Tan here seems to be responding to dominant oppositional attitudes toward both men and Western feminism that one often hears expressed in forums that address the position of women in Singapore. There are clear similarities in this aspect to my experiences in Russia, where very often our feminist discussions do not extend beyond criticizing men or social constructions that make women into sexual objects, and Western feminism for being "too Western and too wealthy" to be applicable to women in Russia. However, those given the privilege to speak during such occasions rarely reflect on their own complicity in perpetuating hierarchical attitudes towards women around them, especially when it comes to class, ethnic or religious differences.

Such anti-men or anti-Western rhetorics often serve as claims to truth in our cultures, or as ethical justification, which in fact, works against the critical re-valuation and re-working of alternatives to the hierarchical (and hence, still phallocentric) frameworks within which women in positions of power (teaching, inviting, curating, distributing) speak and act.

Amanda Heng has been teaching art students a workshop on "Collabora-tion." Collaboration, a wel-coming of differences, is especially strategic for women artists: Learning how to respect and expect each other's otherness, to safeguard borders of cre-

A Women Artists' Registry meeting.

ativity of one self, to leave a space for the creativity of the other. The question of collaboration and coming together without draining each other of energy and inspiration has been central to feminist debates for decades. Amanda Heng's conviction that it is only in being "together" with all our differences that we can leave a permanent, long-term impact, and her willingness to engender diverse collaborations has been crucial for our professional contact, and more impor-tantly, for seeing a miracle of embodied new collaborations of women artists in Singapore who often do not share the same frames of reference.

As an example of Amanda Heng's ideas of collaboration it is useful to men-tion one of her latest projects which is also symptomatic of her long-term engagement with the history of women's art. With the help of other women artists, she organized a "Women Artists' Registry" that primarily targets Sing-apore and potentially other South-East Asian countries. The meetings she organized in her art studio to launch the Registry were the first coming togeth-er of many prominent women artists practicing in Singapore, who came despite their differences of opinion and cultural experiences. Some of the artists, like Amanda herself, share a feminist agenda with awareness of their position, while others expressly refused the feminist label or agenda. The Registry interestingly gives the space and opportunity to negotiate these differences without having one dominant point of view. Amanda's work on this Registry stirred some controversy among certain men artists working in Singapore who suddenly discovered that they were in fact, male artists and not artists, in general, anymore! Because of Amanda Heng's international recognition and associations, this Registry promises to serve as an important point for documentation and institutionalization of the thus-far ignored contributions of women's art in South-East Asia.

On a few occasions Amanda Heng voiced an argument that I deeply share: Unless we, in our own local contexts, create a theoretical web which is both aware of international heritage even while radically localizing and historicizing it, women in non-Western countries will be left without "A Self of One's Own." And to this end, the issue of collaboration is crucial, but it has to work both ways: There must be a *you* there, a committed *you*, a you-she with desire for an ethically inflected relationship of sharing, for our collaboration to happen. However, this last point is extremely complex. Women have been historically habituated to situations where they learn of necessity to form personal networks of survival which are rather inimical to open-ended professional inter-subjective relations with fellow men and women alike. The groups that result from such emotionally effected ties often lull them into complacent states of feeling comfortable and safe, sometimes to the very exclusion of other dimensions that are always necessary for creating new spaces and languages. We are still often left with bitterness and grim questions as a result of our failed attempts to collaborate (by failure I mean jealousy, plagiarism, disrespect, stagnation, emotional distress, instead of feelings of growth, fulfillment, happiness and movement). Maybe we must learn how to be *separate*, to have *borders* that leave some air for those who would like to share this air with us, respecting their borders too. And the notion of woman that we engender by happy collaborations changes together with those localized strategies of feminism that women artists like Amanda Heng create, together with others. It is exactly this notion of "woman" that I will try to engage in the pages that follow.

ART MADE BY A FEMINIST: SARASWATI GRAMICH

A radical change in the notion of woman and our re-appropriation of that notion and others is at the core of my fruitful engagement with the work of Saraswati Gramich. She is a lecturer and a practicing artist, currently residing in Singapore. Her view on being a feminist is closely tied to her art. It means, she says, to challenge a number of discourses: The hermetic view of scientific inquiry as it was challenged by Donna Haraway, when she suggested that objectivity means 'situated knowledge,' instead of transcendence of all limits and splitting of subject and object. Luce Irigaray who envisages "a culture of difference" between men and women, and opening up a space that allows creativity and mutual inspiration.

Saraswati Gramich's art is concerned with the issues of order and chaos and their aesthetic embodiments, and she researches extensively questions of the history of science, chaos theory and general issues in contemporary art. She says that she tries to question "the definition of objectivity in scientific methods" and "the binary logic in Western tradition, such as good/bad, order/anti-order as chaos. Also questioning what is good/strong art and bad/weak art, men's art/women's art, etc. Traditionally, these have been regarded as oppo-

© SARASWATI GRAMICH

Sarasawti Gramich, "Self-Organization," Installation, 1999.

sites. But, chaos theory, and feminist philosophies, have re-evaluated these views radically. Chaos theory explains that not-order is also a possibility, distinct from, and valued differently than anti-order. It explains that chaos may either lead to order (through a self-organizing system), or it may have deep structures of order encoded within it. In both cases, its relation to order is more complex than traditional Western oppositions have allowed."

The important question that Saraswati Gramich's work challenges us with is why the notion of woman artist or "woman's issues" cannot be redefined to be wider than, not just inclusive of, humanity at large. Why could it not be two humanities, at least two? For only by having at least two, can we have some kind of encounter. Otherwise, we fool ourselves about meeting each other; if we are all the same and thus can be dissolved by one there is no possibility of encountering some/any other. The issue here is of creating a space for general and transcendental dimensions of female genre (not resting on such fashionable and still reactionary notions like 'excess,' 'subtext,' or 'remainder'), a thinking about woman-kind that is not restricted to a masculine human, but rather transcendental also, though different from it. Having its own relation with spatial and temporal dimensions of generality and particularity of the female being, as proposed by feminist philosopher Luce Irigaray. Thus I see the radicality of the works of Saraswati Gramich in her awareness of the necessity to create alternatives to masculinized notions of chaos, order, space and time, and even implying a different approach to the questions of transcendence or God. However, her positioning of herself as a feminist tends to provoke questions about how her art can be related to the question of gender difference if it is embodied in supposedly gender neutral installations and paintings, that seem to have nothing to do with "women's issues."

When considering the question of the definition of feminism, and especially feminist art, it is important to stress that it is more productive, as art theorist Selma Kraft suggested, to work out a *feminist definition of art* instead of a definition of feminist art. I think feminism seeks to identify, reflect, and act upon the social, cultural and political conditions of women's lives, where even the category of "woman" is not taken for granted. Let me explain why we cannot take the category "woman" for granted by deliberating on the label, "woman artist." Let us start with the comment of one student about works exhibited in "A Self of One's Own" that responded to the theme 'space.' This student felt uncomfortable about Saraswati Gramich's installation being there, because he said it does not seem to "look like lady's work," but rather like... and he hesitated for a moment. I then completed his sentence by asking "men's work?" He was obviously not happy with this definition. After trying to find a way to describe the work, he said: "It looked to me not like a woman's work, but rather 'normal.'" I am not sure how much "normal" also meant "neutral" for him, but his unreserved sincerity provides us with a useful introduction into the conditions under which women artists find themselves.

Normality and gender-neutrality of men's art is taken for granted. When men produce works with reference to space, spirituality, the universe, human existence, or sexuality, their gender does not seem to be an obvious part of the creation process. Until recently our art history had practically no references to women's art, making it gender-blind. Women artists were so invisible that female students often did not even ask themselves what had already been done by women artists before them: It was simply not there. And given the prejudicial exhibition and curatorial practices of the past, many aspiring women artists had very little chance of coming across works by critical women artists. Thus, the masculinity of the artist disappeared as an incidental element of art making. However, what made the student who commented on "lady's art" feel uncomfortable about calling men's art "normal" is exactly what demands the widening of the notion of woman, such that it necessarily includes interests in space, spirituality, or the universe. Saraswati Gramich's work displayed in a feminist art exhibition nudged one to question the gender neutrality of men's art that hides itself behind notions of "human" and "normal." By making works on space, and on order and chaos belong to feminist art, Saraswati forces the notion of "woman" to be wider than our presently narrow notion of "human." With this gesture she teases the man out of the 'human.'

Responses to feminist art are often expressed through the insecurities and anxieties of the mainstream art establishment that suddenly finds itself guilty of having represented mainly men artists as if they represented all of humanity. I will exemplify my point on another level. When we discuss issues of ethnic difference, we seem to agree that European art cannot pretend to represent world art, and that Western artists should not pretend to be cultural-ly neutral, devoid of a particular cultural and historical background. Their relation to spirituality, body, space, and time might be specific to their training and upbringing but that, of course, does not mean it is not valuable. However, in the case of sexual difference, many still insist that gender does not matter in issues like space and time or order and chaos. Moreover, the surprise in seeing Saraswati's work in relation to feminism can be read in at least two different ways. First, that feminism can only be about those things that the category of "man" cannot be: Giving birth, PMS, etc. and, thus, the category of woman is reduced to that which is "not-man," depriving her of an identity of her own. As a result, if she takes on issues of space and time, she must stop being a woman, she must switch herself off and become an 'artist,' that is, try to become or mimic the art of men, since feminism has nothing to do with space and time!

Second, such a reading is uninformed by the fundamental nature of this primordial opposition between male/female in our cultures. "Order" in major philosophies and religions around the world has been associated with the so-called "male principle" while chaos has been labeled 'female'. Many other oppositions and combinations have a direct relation to such reasoning: Mind/body, purity/impurity, good/evil, reason/instinct, etc. Feminist interven-tions into such oppositional categories are meant to redefine the way we think about ourselves and the world around us. This project seems to be much more complex than stereotypical notions of feminist art and women's issues, and one of the reasons I see it as radical. However, it is necessary to stress that this project is in tune with contemporary philosophy and art. This project is also part of an attempt to think outside the comfortable split of people into white and non-white, or civilized and non-civilized. Constructing a self of one's own for a woman is a long path, since the very category of "woman" has been so restricted, but it is worth it, and there is an urgency for it.

Saraswati's work also has been sexualized and dismissed as "too beautiful" by some critics and artists. Her insistence on aesthetic qualities and balanced attention to the material and compositional sensibilities often go against the grain of what is considered a strong artistic statement in contemporary art, both by "riot girls" and "bad boys" in the art world. She says: "Many times my artworks are criticized as 'too beautiful.' One art critic said, 'Wonderful work. My only criticism is that the work is too beautiful. In the paintings and drawings there is an exquisite refinement particularly in color. This tends to undermine the work as it veers too close to the sensibilities of the fashion industry and décor.' It seems to me that the 'definition' of good art is still coded. Isn't beauty also a possibility?"

Thus *exquisite refinement* in the work of a woman artist, taken together with transcendental questions, is seen as disturbing and, hence, asking for immediate appropriation of it or resolution within some habitual and readily available framework like "too beautiful," "too sensitive," "not strong enough," that is, somehow and somewhat "too much." This unbearable nature of beauty and refinement in works supposedly not relating to a women's agenda is of particular interest to me in Saraswati Gramich's work, since I am trying to think of the inspiration and positive alternatives that we want to create in women's culture and for female-kind. The subtle sophistication and complexity can help to play at the border of both dangers: Of essentializing the woman artist and women's issues, on the one hand, and of draining away the positive energy associated with "angry art," on the other. Her art questions comfortable restrictive definitions of women's issues even for many women artists themselves who prefer to see such issues as outside of more general or "non-women's" questions of order and chaos, or space and time.

Even though it is not readily apparent in her works, Saraswati Gramich also reflects a strong concern for the immediate social condition of women in her home country, Indonesia. She writes that the main problem for women is a lack of information on sex education, including sexually transmitted disease, contraception and abortion: "Lack of information on sex education causes many young women to be abused sexually, sometimes clandestinely. Many young women are harassed on the street by individuals or groups of boys, and live in fear of violence. Women in Indonesia have no right to an abortion, even if the pregnancy is due to a "forced" sexual intercourse. Abortion is only legal if medical doctors state that the pregnancy endangers the mother or the child. This leads to a high incidence of infanticide by young mothers."

She also notes that in Indonesia, as in many parts of the developing (and one suspects even developed) world, there is a predominant tendency for women to undertake the responsibilities for family planning: "More women are taking precautions for contraception than men. This causes more women to have side effects due to the Pill or IUDs. I think there should be a negotiation between men and women in deciding who should be the one who takes the precaution." Again, I would stress that very often women participate in such silent practices of "following a tradition" even when social and cultural conditions have changed considerably and the notion of tradition itself is being questioned.

It brings us back to the notion of 'woman' and its restrictive definition that imprisons female identity, when such notions as motherhood or intimacy are taken to be natural, depriving them of their more enabling cultural and legal dimensions. Here, two points that Saraswati Gramich thinks especially important, are to be engaged together: On the one hand, she says, "in case of virginity, women in Indonesia will be regarded as immoral for losing it before marriage"; on the other, "celibacy is regarded as not-woman. A lot of gossip will be spreading and buzzing around her." Thus, actually virginity is not a cultural option, it cannot be chosen. Virginity is not considered as a woman's choice, but rather seen as a natural condition to be preserved as a gift for husbands, but not as a 'thing in itself.' The same goes for the Christian tradition: Virginity is for God–husband–father, and not a socially acknowledged choice of a woman herself— for herself, or for someone whom she chooses. This dimension of legal ownership of one's body and social status, especially in relation to husbands, is absent in Indonesian women's lives. Gramich writes that "As in a predominantly Muslim country, a lot of women have to accept it if their husbands have mistresses even without their consent (Muslim men are allowed to marry up to four wives, but only with the wife's consent). And as a wife, she still has an obligation to serve him. The perception of a good or civilized woman is someone nice, kind, loving, enjoys serving, good cook, pleasant, simple, not argumentative, will always support her husband from behind (in Indonesian: *Tut wuri handayani*)."

The relationship of a woman to her body is still largely outside legal and symbolic language, and remains so even in its translation into the language of new technologies[5] (for example, the notion of the *matrix*). Hence it is often appropriated for the use of the "community"—children, husbands, family, their welfare and their future—like in the abortion rights debates. The issue of her subjectivity and ethics is somehow dismissed by conflating all women's issues with the notion of the natural, meaning that they are given, and therefore cannot but be any other way. Unfortunately, even when addressed within and by women's art, there is a tendency to enact empowerment through some natural link with earth, moon, softness, and smallness—everything that is not-man, everything oppositional, with claims of "taking it back" from masculine patriarchal culture and its structures. I would argue differently, that there is a serious need to redraw the map of women's issues, and how women artists might address that, and feel comfortable precisely as women-artists with a wider notion of sexual difference. In many contemporary practices of women artists, I sense the creation of a new dimension and expansion of women's art as an embodied feminine universal, that is, interactive for both genders on the issues of technology, space, and human existence, exactly because it deals with it without collapsing sexual difference into (n)one, or into two opposites, thus allowing other differences to be acknowledged.

Saraswati Gramich, in place of the term 'feminist art,' prefers the expression "art done by a feminist." She says, "personally I would like to see an acknowledgement of *difference of interest* in dealing with the issue, exploration of ideas, possibilities, space for creativity, collaboration among women and/or men. It makes me understand my standing in my artwork, culture, condition of being a creative and productive human-woman, and my position relating to human beings (men and women). Being of mixed ethnicity (Eurasian), I don't identify myself as belonging to one specific culture/country, but as having mixed-cultural identity. My art questions the notion of chaos and order in space and time from this mixed-cultural upbringing, woman artist point of view, and visualizing an acknowledgement of difference in ideas, possibilities, and art-language. A feminist point of view has definitely empowered me."

Her last phrase is very simple, but it contains all the power that feminisms have been about. And if they fail it, if they make women and men oppositional to each other and among themselves, hating each other and desperate; if they do not bring *shared* happiness and confidence into women's lives; if they do not make us more respectful of each other's differences and listen to them, then it is time to redefine our position, since it is feminism that was born to deliver miracles into women's (and therefore also men's!) lives. We have certain responsibilities to the history and commitment of international feminisms, but at the same time, because of this history we have to re-learn our ethics and aesthetics.

Thinking of such historical responsibility, I have tried to highlight here two examples of my productive and happy engagements with women artists in Singapore: Through the art of collaborations, short-term and specific, benefiting from differences among us, and via a long-term investment into searching for new frameworks of women's creativity. ★

1　The notion of miracle draws on the possibilities open to us despite all that inhibits or frustrates them. Following the call of Luce Irigaray to learn how to be happy, I have renamed them here as an "engendering of miracles" using two main strategies: 1) effective collaboration, and 2) radical re-evaluation of the notion of "woman artist."

2　Of course there were, and are, many more women in Singapore with whom an atmosphere of mutual interest and respect was created, and I would like to express here to all of them my deepest gratitude, especially to my students and colleagues at work, and also to members of AWARE (Association of Women for Action and Research in Singapore).

3　The exhibition and symposium "A Self of One's Own" featured thirteen women artists and four scholars from nine countries. It was the result of a graduate workshop that I conducted in 1999 in Singapore. Currently, I am finishing work on a publication which documents and reflects on this event.

4　Amanda Heng has since clarified in a conversation that her position is multifaceted, and not merely oppositional, and this is indicated by her statements quoted above.

5　For examples of my cyberfeminist interventions see "Cyber-Jouissance: A Sketch of a Politics of Pleasure" at <http://www.heise.de/tp/english/pop/topic-33/4126/1.html>; and "Hosting the Other: Cyberfeminist Strategies for Net-Communities," in *Cyberfeminist International Reader*, Hamburg, 1999.

Cybernetic
Social Space

Nell Tenhaaf

E mpathy has been a topic in my recent practice, starting with the interactive video installation *UCBM (you could be me)* in 1999, and continuing into the photographic works of *The Empathy Sessions* in 2000. In *UCBM*, viewers experience a "test" of their adaptation to artificial empathy or intimacy. A speaking female, shown as a video projection, is an intensely self-absorbed and ironically controlling scientist persona. She is my surrogate in the setup and the visible face of a computer-driven exchange. In a set of questions directed to them by this persona, viewers consider their reaction to her, as well as to a sequence of small LCD images that mimic a web cam located in someone's private space.

UCBM uses a genetic algorithm (GA) as its method for assessing the viewer's "empathy factor." The GA takes a viewer's empathy score derived from their speed of approach to the video projection and from their answers to three questions via touch input, and calculates it as a set of "genes" that mutate and cross over to form "offspring." Viewers with adaptive offspring pass their genes into the gene pool that subsequent viewers interact with. In this way the recombinant computation of the GA links together a population of nine viewers before resetting. Each viewer is given feedback on how they did through voice, a light display, and a fitness chart.

The working definition for empathy that underlies both *UCBM* and *The Empathy Sessions* is something like this: It is a process of knowing through imagining the state of mind of the other. Both affect and physical signs are

involved in this process, and they are in balance with intellectual identification. The physical aspect can be characterized as an experiential resonance
with the other, based on reading body language or other material signals from
that person (or animal, or thing, for that matter). The physical aspects of interacting with *UCBM* include setting off motion sensors that are positioned in the

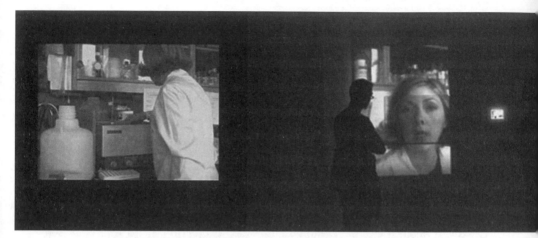

**Still and installation view from "UCBM (you could be me),"
interactive video installation, 1999.**

space, as well as touch response to the questions that are asked. Emotional
involvement is suggested in the tone of the questions. In *The Empathy Sessions*
affect is alluded to in the language of the titles: Fellow-feeling, Recognition,
Care, Esteem, Camaraderie, and Courtesy.

The notion of empathy in my work encompasses both human–human and
human–machine exchanges. I began to think about empathy as "cybernetic" in
human–machine exchanges, because of the important role the computer plays
in facilitating the interactive loops I set up. But this developed into a more
metaphorically resonant idea: that empathy is cybernetic even in strictly
human–human exchange because it emphasizes a two-way flow of relational
qualities with a lot of feedback signals built into the process. This perception
absorbs much that has been written about cybernetics in the past three or four
decades, especially its extension into social systems theory.[1] But it is surprisingly not at odds with the original definition. In Norbert Wiener's pioneering work of the 1940s, the theory of cybernetics is based on three key
insights: a) the idea of self-regulating systems that use feedback loops to

maintain their internal state; b) the idea of a kind of learning machine, or as Wiener put it, "an apparatus [that] assumes a specific structure or function on the basis of past experience;"[2] and c) the importance of information and communication as mechanisms of organization, both within a single entity and in the social realm.

The popular conception of cybernetics certainly leans away from the emotional realm and towards the structural and cognitive aspects of information flow, because of its origins in systems control and its intimate links with the development of computing. But it is interesting to probe further into why this is so, and what impact it has had. One could argue that most readings of Wiener's theory have carried the same language conventions and interpretive biases as are often applied in scientific thinking, conventions, and biases that are difficult to overturn. Evelyn Fox Keller has given us some cogent feminist analysis of this phenomenon in relation to the history of science. She has critiqued, for example, the idea that natural selection can be equated with competition by calling attention to a succession of erroneous assumptions that result from "reading cultural norms into natural law."[3] She outlines how the conventional idea of natural selection arose and became entrenched through language, such that competition came to cover "all possible circumstances of relative viability and reproductivity," even where the juxtaposition of organisms or species is not occurring in nature at all but "only in the biologist's own mind."[4]

The domain of cybernetics, and its broadly popularized extrapolation, cyberspace, have not been immune to interpretive bias. This is evident in the general sense of robotic or otherwise dehumanized interactions that tend to be associated with cyber-anything, as if the machine will invariably overpower the human, who is made frail precisely by h/er affective dimension. In a sense, the cybernetic modeling of social relations that is suggested in *UCBM* parallels the exposure of conventions embedded within scientific thought that has been key to feminist theories of science. *UCBM* establishes a relational exchange in which information is both objectively "out there" and, at the same time, subjectively activated in the viewer's imagination, where it sways her or his

**"Session #1–3, Fellow-feeling, 31/03/97" from "The Empathy Sessions," 2000,
light box (aluminum, LightJet transparency), 14 x 17 x 3½ in.**

emotional register. The scientist figure represents a provisional point of view, that is, she both embodies an objective data gatherer and stands in for the viewing subject who identifies with the work by choosing a path through it. Both the scientist and the viewer move back and forth between places of enunciation, acting conditionally as participant and as external observer. These features of interacting with *UCBM* contradict the traditional subject/object split of scientific enquiry, and also create a space for the affective aspects of an exchange that are usually written out of a scientific context.

In *The Empathy Sessions*, I extend the theme of empathy by taking stills from the image flow of *UCBM* in the form of close-ups of the lab coat that the scientist character wears. These become the setting for screen captures from CUSeeMe sessions that I participated in between March and December of 1997. (CUSeeMe is software that allows several people with cameras connected to their computers to see low resolution video of each other, accompanied by a chat window for verbal exchanges.) The lab coat detail carries the doubled

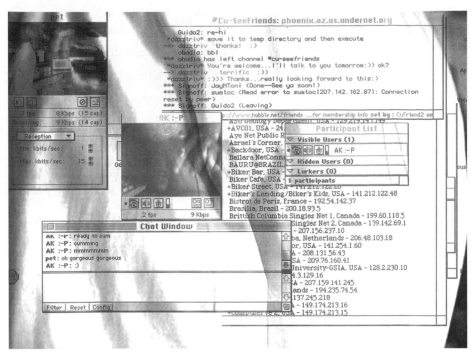

"Session #2–2, Care, 30/11/97" from "The Empathy Sessions," 2000,
C-print, 17 ³/₄ x 23 ⁵/₈ in.

signification that I associate with all clinical accoutrements because it suggests both coldness and care, or picking up on the description above, the ambivalence of the researcher who is both removed and involved. The CUSeeMe screen captures are mostly graphic portraits of masturbating men, which admittedly conveys a biased portrait of the sexualized content one finds on the Internet. It does predominate in the amateur porn to be found there, though. It is the content I was looking for in the CUSeeMe sites I chose to enter and snap pictures of because I wanted to directly address people's commonly-held and often contradictory beliefs about sex on the Net, for example, that it is deviant, distasteful, and dehumanizing in entirely new ways, but at the same time is nothing new.

There are, in fact, things that are new about the raw and most often solitary sexuality that is shown in *The Empathy Sessions*, and they are meant to suggest deviance from the norm. But this isn't located in the obvious voyeurism, in the coldness of the computer context, or in the "unwholesome" onanistic connotations that solo sex has for some people, eliciting everything from prurience to pity. How I deviate from the norm is that my on-line sex encounters have left me with a surprisingly strong sense of empathy toward the participants in this kind of vicarious sexual expression, and related to this, an unexpected impression that my intellectual response enriches the overall experience. The discovery of subtle subject/object reversals in these encounters, and the recognition of moving between participant and observer roles, strike me as potentially creative features of what Sean Cubitt calls "post-privacy culture."[5] Because there are real people interacting here, caught up in the ambiguity of distance and intimacy characteristic of on-line display exchanges, this is a zone that can help us appreciate how the integration of computer technology into so many facets of our communications is changing social relations. If contemporary culture is indeed becoming increasingly characterized by post-privacy, artificiality, and cybernetic human–machine interaction, it seems important to understand and nurture relational qualities like empathy that can apply to both familiar and new forms of exchange. ★

---

1   See R. Felix Geyer and Johannes van der Zouwen, eds., *Sociocybernetics:An Actor-oriented Social Systems Approach* (Leiden/Boston/London: Martinus Nijhoff Social Sciences Division, 1978), Vol. 1 and 2.

2   Norbert Wiener, *Cybernetics: or Control and Communication in the Animal and the Machine* (Cambridge: The MIT Press, 1999 [1948]), p. xii. At the same time, Wiener cautioned against looking for any direct "social efficacy" in the application of his theories because they retain much of the isolation of phenomenon from observer that is characteristic of scientific practices, p. 162.

3   Evelyn Fox Keller, *Secrets of Life, Secrets of Death: Essays on Language, Gender and Science* (New York: Routledge, 1992), p. 113.

4   Ibid., p. 125.

5   From a talk by Sean Cubitt in conjunction with the Images Festival of Independent Film and Video, Toronto, Spring 2000, in which he linked webcam and other computer-dependent video transmission with creative subversions of surveillance cameras and other forms of pervasive public data-gathering.

Embodiment and the Politics of Healing: Interview with Reiki Master Kate Daher

Maria Fernandez

F eminist critiques of electronic media theory tend to focus upon its rhetoric of disembodiment. Early cyberfeminists such as VNS Matrix and Sandy Stone inserted images of bodies and discussions of pleasure at the very heart of machine culture. Some recent work focuses on pain, especially the pain specific women have experienced in disease, therapy and disabling accidents.[1] In a way this makes sense. In critical theory, pain has long been established as a way of communication that precedes and overrides language. Thus, it is accorded more authority than language. Because this primal form of communication is located in the body, it validates the body. It is puzzling however, that in electronic media culture, it is primarily women who offer their own pain as a response to theories of disembodiment. Most white male electronic media theorists speak little about their own bodies, and even less about their pain.

At first sight, the emphasis on women's pain in cyber culture seems regressive. Is it not the pain of childbirth and other kinds of suffering that presumably validates women in traditional societies? It is worth noting that women accorded celebrity status in the West today include the Virgin Mary, Princess Diana, Mother Theresa, Marilyn Monroe and Frida Kahlo, all icons of suffering. The privileging of female suffering over other aspects of embodiment suggests a pervasive conservatism at the heart of electronic media theory, a position manifested in other theoretical responses related to embodiment/disembodiment.

To be sure, various female theorists invoke their experiences of pain and the technological interventions employed to alleviate it, to argue for the pervasiveness and even for the desirability of cyborgian conditions. This position foregrounds agencies and pleasures that prosthetics bring to human existence and sometimes even playfully casts prosthetic devices as elements of "fashion."[2]

In her book *How We Became Post Human*, Katherine Hayles makes an eloquent case for the elaboration of an embodied posthumanism, a philosophy and a manner of living integrating human bodies and intelligent machines. Despite her brilliant analysis and incisive critiques, she does not question the supposition that our "partnership" with intelligent machines must be the inevitable next stage of human evolution. While I accept the necessity of working with machines, intelligent or not, I refuse to view this as the only possible form of evolution. Theorists such as Manuel de Landa have argued for the evolution of machines independent of human will, yet individuals and institutions, commercial and military, have played an active role in shaping the symbiosis of humans and machines, currently accepted as the natural product of "evolution."[3]

Native American, African and Eastern philosophers, among others, have posited different kinds of human development. Some of the techniques prescribed to achieve the goals of these traditions (i.e., meditation in Eastern religions) are now accepted in some Western scientific and medical institutions. Yet discussions of forms of "evolution" alternative to the technophilic visions of the West, are anathema to critical writing. To choose only one example, critiques of the militaristic procedures of Western medicine abound in critical theory, yet few respectable theorists would delve into the territory of alternative healing practices. This area is powerfully repressed despite the engagement of numerous artists, critics, and academics in alternative healing traditions as healers or as clients. Discussions of these practices inevitably suggest different forms of embodiment, different utopian futures, and different social and economic priorities.

To the extent that states, institutions, and individuals have a vested interest, for political, military, or other reasons, in Western technological practices, non-

Western and non-technological practices are subject to suppression, suspicion, or derision—not to mention that the modes of being around which these practices are formed are antithetical to capitalist productivist/consumerist instrumentality. Perhaps this is why few theorists discuss the health costs of human "integration" with machines. As the increasing incidence of repetitive stress injury (RSI) and other muscular, psychological and immunological disorders linked to the use of recent technologies demonstrates, pain is an endemic condition of postindustrial societies. The predominance of women's voices in discussions of this phenomenon could be interpreted simultaneously as individual acts of resistance and as yet another version of the traditional role of women as enactors of collective suffering.

This is not to deny that the pursuit of pain is an established part of pleasure rituals in diverse social strata. Recently, however, various theorists have interpreted pain practices in various subcultures as testimonies to the alienation of feelings and lack of a "spiritual sense of organic connection" in postmodern society. In pain, the body reaffirms itself and refuses to disappear.[4]

If the reality of embodiment is undeniable in pain healing, the potential of the body speaks volumes. Why not examine healing as an avenue for empowerment? In this anthology, we can only begin to scratch the surface of this topic. To do it justice would necessitate several volumes on pain, practices of healing, and theories of embodiment. We have chosen Reiki for this interview, not because we desire to privilege it over other healing traditions, but because we are fortunate to know a practitioner in our community, Kate Daher, who is a teacher, healer, and activist and whose objectives align with the purpose of this book.

MF: What is the best way to describe Reiki?

KD: Reiki is an ancient healing art whose origins are a mystery.

The word *reiki* comes from Japanese: *rei* meaning "the wisdom of a higher power" and *ki* meaning life-force energy. The Reiki method of healing is performed when the 'life force energy' is passed through the hands into the human energy system. This is done in one of two ways: either by laying the hands directly on another person, or self, or by bringing the receiver's energy field into the practitioner's hands and working on the person from a distance. As a Reiki healer I may send the life force energy to anyone, anywhere on the planet. I can take someone into my hands, so to speak, ease the areas of their distress and send energy that can help them heal. I need only ask their permission, and they don't have to be present in the flesh to do that!

MF: How would you explain the process of healing in Reiki?

KD: With little or no effort, the healer's hands heat up and produce a warm, flowing energy. The energy travels through one person into the other and creates a deep state of relaxation. Reiki is holistic; it works on the entire self—spirit, mind and emotions. Fundamentally, its nature is gentle and loving. It is kind. It cannot harm. It has its own intelligence, seeking out areas of dis-ease, mental and emotional fatigue, and depression and it travels freely to those areas. Whether or not I can consciously pinpoint a person's area of distress, Reiki knows where to go. I've worked on people with back problems and found the exact source of their discomfort. I recently worked on someone who was having severe headaches. He was in terrible pain and had gone to the emergency room a few times in the middle of the night. They scheduled an MRI and gave him high doses of painkillers. The doctors couldn't figure it out. When I started working on him, I could feel the pain in his head through my hands, but at the same time, the Reiki seemed to know that the source of his troubles was in his neck. My hands turned to fire on the right side of his neck and shoulder. I was quite certain that he had suffered some injury there, and that if he could correct the problem with his neck, his headaches would go away. At first he argued with me about my findings but then after thinking about it, he considered the fact that he recently started rowing and it was possibly the root of his pain. He began seeing a chiropractor and the doctor confirmed my thinking on this. Which brings me to another point: Reiki works well with other branches of medicine.

MF: In Western medicine, the diagnosis of disease relies on the opinions of experts and the use of sophisticated technologies. Healing depends on the patient's consumption of prescribed pharmaceuticals and the application of various technologies to the body. The human body is viewed primarily as an object to act upon. Some alternative healing practices maintain there is knowledge in the body that allows the body to heal itself. What is your position on these issues?

KD: Without a doubt there is a place in the world of alternative medicine for Western medicine but the relationship is not often reciprocal. Recently a medical doctor who earned his M.D. from Stanford University was driven from the directorship of an alternative medical center of a local hospital for his controversial practices. In an attempt to discredit his work, the local press referred to him as the "Sweat Lodge Doctor." This doctor, who was also a Native American, was extremely well received by his patients and highly regarded by the professional staff alike, but, by all accounts, the hierarchy was not as tolerant of his views on alternative medicine. In a sense, what's changed? Millions of women were tortured and murdered between the 1400s and 1600s for healing methods not approved of by the physicians and Christian churches. Still, the interest in alternative medicine is exploding: Tai Chi is used to cure back problems; meditation is replacing painkillers, natural herbal remedies are replacing pharmaceuticals. Much of what people are turning to comes from Asian or Native cultures of the Americas—acupuncture, Reiki, herbal medicine, Chi Gong, sweat lodges. Millions are beginning to figure out that they play an important role in their own recovery and health. This is certainly true with Reiki. Anyone can practice it. Anyone can use it for self-healing and meditation.

About two years ago my gynecologist found a small lump on my breast and she was concerned, especially since my mother died of breast cancer. She insisted I be scheduled for a mammogram immediately. Meanwhile, I spent the next week Reiki-ing my breast. I could see through my "third eye" or "higher self" that there was a small mass, but after several days it disappeared. When I went for the mammogram it was gone. The radiologists couldn't make heads or tails out of the doctor's description of what they were supposed to find. It was almost comical to see how desperately they tried to find something. While I insisted they wouldn't, they insisted they must! We went round and round until they finally conceded that while they saw some sort of "shadow" on the x-ray, actually no mass or lump existed. They shrugged their shoulders at this mystery and it was beyond me to explain the truth of what had happened. I can't imagine they would have believed me, can you?

Reiki allows you to heal yourself—to heal depression, anxiety and physical ailments, but it can also give the power to heal others. My father who lives 300 miles away from me had a bad knee that interfered with his walking and most certainly interfered with his golf game! He was miserable! Again by using Reiki II - distance healing, I could see the imbalance in the knee and I proceeded to send healing energy over a matter of a few weeks. Since then, his knee no longer bothers him. He is now a Reiki healer and in many ways, a different person. He is more reflective and centered. This combination of Reiki and working on the self is what benefited him.

MF: I understand that you were an activist prior to becoming a healer. Are there political aspects to the practice of Reiki?

KD: In the sense that Reiki is empowering and that it teaches us that we can heal ourselves it is very political. It also, by its nature, challenges Western medicine and the notion that someone or some technology has all the answers for our well being. Reiki does come from a higher power but that power is also internal. When used, Reiki creates a sense of wholeness and health. In this way it challenges the notion that we are dependent on commodities, on government or some outside force for happiness. Mental and emotional well-being results from practicing Reiki and in this society that is very political.

I don't know that my activism led me to Reiki. Maybe so. I've been active in social movements for over 20 years—in the women's movement, in solidarity with the peoples of Latin America, the movement to end apartheid in South Africa. I've also been a member of several trade union organizations. So I guess in a broader sense I've been active in movements that attempted to heal the planet, to eliminate racism and sexism, or to struggle against oppression whether it's in a factory in Georgia or a barrio in Nicaragua. I became interested in Reiki when I met nurses who practiced therapeutic touch healing. I started researching alternative healing methods and found my way to Reiki. Or maybe it found me, I'm not sure. At any rate, after receiving the attunements I remember thinking that, "I've finally come home." That's the best I can explain it. It was something I was quite familiar with, something that I had known a long time ago and far away from here and it was back. We reconnected. It seems to me that the ability to heal oneself or others on an individual level is an integral part of healing the planet on a global level. It is the dance of unity. The self and the whole, one connected to the other and vice versa. The whole is the sum of its parts and the parts are the sum of the whole. I don't think it's enough to just work on oneself, though. I think through giving of oneself, say, to the struggle for social change, one can also heal. I think this very ill, very sorry planet is demanding it of us.

MF: How do you view social change at this point in history?

KD: As an absolutely necessary and inevitable phenomenon. One way or another, there will be social change. Of course we can't predict in what form, or whether it will be progressive or reactionary, but it will happen. If enough people, healers and activists alike, work for progress—real progress then we have a shot at ending the tremendous oppression and exploitation the majority in the world face on a daily basis. *The New York Times* just reported that slavery is on the rise in the United States. Slavery, imagine that! We abolished human bondage in 1865 with a Constitutional amendment and now it is being discussed in the press, almost as if it is business as usual. How can this be? The *Times* article was based on a CIA report: "International Trafficking in Women to the United States: A Contemporary Manifestation of Slavery." The report asserts that more than 50,000 women and children are brought to the United States each year as slaves or indentured servants and argues that there is virtually nothing that can be done to stop it because the cases are difficult to investigate and prosecute. To me that sounds like business as usual, that is, that the capitalists deal in commodity trade, profiteering, and consumption—whatever the market dictates! This is but the tip of the iceberg of social problems that the world's poor and exploited face. Dozens of countries can barely pay the interest on their debt to the World Bank and other profit-making institutions and governments. What's the solution? Cancel the Third World debt; reorganize the wealth for more equitable distribution; take the profit out of production and apply it to human needs. Social change and social organization are necessary for a more balanced world. But I think we need a radical break from the institutions and governments that support a profit-making economic system.

MF: Our educational system trains us to view mind and body as separate entities and to favor mind over body. Further, it prepares us to treat our bodies as objects that are modifiable and even replaceable. This is unlikely to change unless there is intervention at early stages of education. It is well known that elementary and high school teachers have been instrumental in disseminating awareness about environmental issues. Do you have any suggestions for a pedagogy of embodiment?

KD: I agree that the educational system trains us to view mind and body as separate entities but it depends on what class one belongs to as to whether or not the mind is favored over the body or vice versa. I teach in an inner-city high school, mainly working-class kids that are tracked in what is called "mainstream" classes; these are the "tough" kids, the "bad" kids, the ones who are expected to "get by or get out" and it is a struggle to get them to realize that they have a mind that they can use, and with that mind combined with critical thinking comes empowerment. They use their bodies to labor. Most of them work in the evenings—school to work with very little studying, thinking, and reflecting. I am challenged by and challenge this every day. Teachers compete with MTV, commodity consumption, racism, and sexism and, like salmon running upstream, progressive teachers combat the constant barrage of propaganda coming from the market system. On the other hand, while the middle class is taught to favor the mind over the body they are also expected to be consumers and producers as their primary function.

MF: Do you think it is possible to devise teaching methods that combine both the mind and the body?

KD: I do. But I don't think this exists so much in the United States, certainly not in the public schools where I teach. I am traveling to China this summer and will be able to visit several schools. I'd like to know how they work with Tai Chi and Chi Gong in the schools, since millions there practice. I will ask this question of those who use both the body and the mind.

MF: Finally, I have heard that most Reiki masters are women. In your view, what accounts for this?

KD: Well, I can't say that is the case. I know both women and men who practice Reiki in this country, and I believe that it is practiced worldwide by both men and women. A friend of mine traveling through India by rail found books at various stops that taught about Reiki. It is possible that the majority of Western practitioners are women since we tend to be more interested in alternative healing methods but as a worldwide practice, I don't have any statistics.

MF: What do you think makes women interested in alternative healing?

KD: I will speak from my knowledge and history as a woman in the United States. In the 1970s, out of the women's movement—the second wave of feminism—there was an explosion of interest in discovering our own bodies. Women demanded the right to choose abortions legally. We organized self-help clinics, and began delivering our children at home. We started working with herbs and other forms of natural healing. This revolution in thinking and behavior, the idea that we could control our own bodies, empowered us. It gave us hope and self-confidence. It made us look at each other in a whole new light: as allies, as sisters. This was not limited to the middle-class communities, but poor women as well. Blacks, Latinas and Native American women also challenged the medical establishment and its contempt towards women. There were too many hysterectomies performed, forced sterilizations were common, especially in the poor neighborhoods in the United States and Puerto Rico, and there were very few medical doctors who were female. We had no voice. The women's movement opened our eyes and gave us the determination to begin caring for each other and ourselves. It awakened our interest in healing and self-healing and deepened our concern for the environment and the whole earth. I don't mean to speak in the past as if we accomplished our goals. There is still a long road to travel. ★

---

1 Linda Dement, "Typhoid Mary," Diane J. Gromala and Jacov Sharir, "Dancing with the Virtual Dervish: Virtual Bodies" in *Immersed in Technology: Art and Virtual Environments,* ed. Mary Anne Moser, and Douglas MacLeod (Cambridge, Mass.: The MIT Press, 1996). Phoebe Sengers, "Technological Prostheses: An Anecdote." ZKP-4 Net>*Criticism Reader,*" ed. Geert Lovink and Pit Schultz, 1997. Vivian Sobchack, "Beating the Meat/Surviving the Text: or How to Get out of this Century Alive" in

The Visible Woman, eds. Paula Treichler, Lisa Cartright, Constance Penley (New York: New York University Press, 1998); Victoria Vesna, Keynote address to the Digital Arts and Culture Symposium, Bergen, Norway, August 2000; Li Chiao Ping and Douglas Rosemberg, paper/performance at Performative Sites: Intersecting Art, Technology, and the Body, October 24–28, 2000.

2   Petra Kuppers, paper presented at Performative Sites: Intersecting Art, Technology, and the Body, October 24-28, 2000. Penn State University, USA.

3   Brian Winston, *Media Technology and Society: A History: From the Telegraph to the Internet* (New York: Routledge, 1998).

4   Celeste Olalquiaga, "Pain Practices and the Reconfiguration of Physical Experience" in *When Pain Strikes*, eds. Bill Burns, Cathy Bushby, and Kim Sawchuk (Minneapolis: University of Minnesota Press, 1999). See also Arthur Kroker and Michael A. Westein, *Data Trash: The Theory of the Virtual Class* (New York: St. Martin's Press, 1994).

consider a new career

Did you know that millions of yuppie couples—rich and educated first-world types of all sexual persuasions—have a deep desire for a child they are incapable of producing themselves? You can help a miracle happen for each and every one of them in the exciting new Flesh Marketplace of High-Tech Repro Careers.

Egg Donor ☐ A-6491
Got Eggs? Participate in a miracle while covering college tuition expenses. $5,000–$25,000/cycle, depending on university.

Egg/Surrogacy Broker ☐ A-6492
Be the grease that helps the supply and demand wheels turn! Commissions vary with market demand.

Repro Clinic Cleaning Staff ☐ A-6493
Cleanliness is next to Godliness. $12,000/yr or $5.76/hr.

Surrogate Mom ☐ A-6494
Fabulous supplemental income with comprehensive medical coverage. $10,000–25,000 per live birth.

Sperm Bank Administrator ☐ A-6495
Combine your business and family planning skills in the world of Repro Tech. $50,000/yr or $24/hr

Genetics Counselor ☐ A-6496
An exciting new career blending social engineering, health and psychology. $50,000/yr or $24/hr.

Sperm Handler/ Shipper ☐ A-6497
Requires dexterity, an eye for detail, and the ability to stand for long hours. $27,000/yr or $13/hr.

Medical Equipment Designer ☐ A-6498
Your ideas and industrial design skills are needed in this rapid-growth industry. $50,000/yr or $24/hr.

Medical Equipment Assembler ☐ A-6499
Your craftsmanship and assembly skills are needed for market deployment. $20,000/yr or $9.60/hr.

Child Care Worker ☐ A-6500
Do you love childen? Are you responsible and attentive? This is for you! $13,540/year or $6.50/hr.

Fertility Research Scientist ☐ A-6501
Are you good at reading and figuring things out? $200,000–1,000,000/year. ($76/hr to start)

Health Insurance Data Processor ☐ A-6502
Pay attention to detail and good with numbers? $18,000–25,000/year. ($8.65/hr to start)

No Delay! Check All That Apply!

in REPRODUCTIVE technology!

Rant of the Menopausal Cyborg

Faith Wilding

O ld women and men in America today are a class of liminal beings who daily commit public nuisances as they clutter up space and use up resources just by staying alive. On the one hand, they are often treated much like imprisoned criminals: Subjected to involuntary confinement (in nursing homes and hospitals), experimental medication, sedation, material dispossession, loss of the right to drive, physical abuse, sexual deprivation, surveillance, and the like. On the other hand, as the baby boom generation approaches age 55, they are also a growing consumer market and a politically powerful voting population. Still, the dominant representation of the old—and particularly of old women—is one of obsolescence, irrelevance, uselessness. They waft among us like wraiths, reminding us of our repressed fears of death and decay; they are a hindrance to the high-speed, youth-driven, novelty-propelled information culture. The old have no information anyone needs or wants to hear. Their minds and bodies belong to the past.

New flesh technologies, genetic engineering, and computer-driven medical technologies of the body have a perfect new subject and marketing target: The aging woman. Old(er) women are becoming compulsory menopausal cyborgs and involuntary experimental subjects for new medications and medical procedures which have little proven healing value. They are the paradigmatic patient for hormone and drug therapies, for diet and fitness marketeers, for experimenting with the boundaries of new fertility technologies, for aesthetic and reconstructive surgery, and for somatic cell genetic engineering; they are also apt subjects for gerontology studies and experiments, given that the majority of nursing home residents are women. It is worth noting that the definition of what constitutes "old" has become more flexible, and is often determined by commercial or institutional interests. For example, many plastic surgeons now advise consumers to start with face lifts in their mid-thirties; fertility doctors are often reluctant to accept patients older than 40 (so as not to lower their success rates); pharmaceutical companies compete to entice the over-60 set to try new virility medications and youth-enhancing hormones and drugs; meanwhile the cosmetics industry produces new miracle anti-wrinkle and age-defying lotions every month for a spectrum of ages from 20 to 80. Class, race, and economic factors also play important roles in determining the stages and experiences of aging: Looking (and acting) young beyond one's chronological age depends so much on access to a wide array of technologies and services, as well as on the economic resources and time to take care of oneself.

Old bodies are seen as abject. They walk among us as a living testimony to death and decay. They walk among us deformed yet still desiring, still consuming, still lusting, still covetous, still angry, still proud. The old are infertile; they produce only excrement and effluvia. They commit the supreme crime of biological uselessness, which ironically could be their strongest point of autonomy. The ironic utopian Cartesian slogan, "The body [meat] is obsolete" (often repeated by the [mostly] young, male, and wired), takes on a very different meaning for old people who are not "wired," and creates an ever more painful generational separation and alienation in the menopausal cyborg population. In the pre-biotech age, female bodily obsolescence meant the cessation of ovulation and menstruation (menopause), and the concomitant loss of fertility and reproductive powers. However, older women could still be valued by the culture as carriers of collective memory, and for their knowledge of life processes; as teachers and mentors for younger women and children; and—more metaphorically—their aging bodies functioned as signs of mortality and gateways for experiencing the mystery of death. While old female bodies were often feared, loathed, and avoided, they were also understood to be fundamentally instructive and cautionary—a necessary part of the life cycle. Yet who in the American youth-worshipping culture wants to represent death to others? Strangely, while the bodies of older women function for others as strong cultural signs of nonrational fears and desires about the ultimate experience of death and dissolution, they themselves can experience this life stage as a powerfully autonomous moment when body and subjectivity are released from (re)productive and utilitarian necessities.

Ironically, in the age of biotechnological nature, older women can now take advantage of the very virtuality that isolates them and renders their "real" bodies invisible, by masquerading as whatever they want to be online, and by using new flesh, drug, genetic, and aesthetic surgery technologies. And who can judge anyone for wanting to take this advantage? The desire for transcendence and immortality, for ideal beauty and eternal youthfulness, has sparked philosophers, artists, scientists and poets since before recorded history. These desires are as strong as ever today; current scientific literature promises that the new genetic and biotechnologies are bringing us to the brink of actualizing these desires now and here in the "real" flesh. While the actuality of a genetically re-engineered body that will not express visible signs of aging is still very far off, the *possibility* of this scientifically re-engineered biologically ageless body acts as a disturbing cultural probe, setting off a complex set of responses.

Obsolescence is a state of unproductiveness and uselessness. Built-in obsolescence is a fundamental tenet of American material production and fuels much of the market economy. Obsolescence also fuels much of the computer and electronics economy: Both software and hardware change almost monthly and have to be retooled and relearned; computer programmers, tech workers, web designers, data entry workers, and others have to upgrade their skills constantly; workers in the tech industries are often considered redundant by their mid-thirties. Gerontologists and geneticists are beginning to discover that obsolescence is also built into our cells and our genes. The consumer market demands that that which is obsolete be discarded and made invisible. So too must it be with human obsolescence—it must be hidden, discarded, or transcended by re-engineering. Fears of death, decay, and obsolescence underlie the frantic rush to re-engineer the physical human body through the new bio-, medical-, and genetic technologies. Much of this research is directed towards treatments which will mitigate, delay, and conceal the appearance—and actuality—of aging. Providers of hormone therapies, potency and fertility drugs, genetic implants, organ and tissue replacement, microsurgery, aesthetic surgery, and enhancement and rejuvenation therapies do a roaring business among middle-aged and older male and female consumers. Showing signs of aging is taken as evidence that one doesn't care anymore, that one has given up on oneself. From the point of view of biotech medicine, death itself is seen as a kind of failure. Increasingly, people feel the compulsion—which is usually expressed as "choice"—to avail themselves of all treatments and technologies that can help them stave off aging, decay, and bodily ugliness or deviation from the "healthy" norm. This compulsion sets ever higher standards for "good looks" among the population as a whole which are ever more impossible to attain through simple bodily maintenance and self-care. Ironically, if signs of obsolescence are hidden, and there are fewer "real" older looking people around, younger and younger people will be designated as not youthful anymore in comparison with adolescents. Many of my 20-year-old students, for example, complain that they feel old.

As an increasing population of computer and Internet users log on to the virtual sex spectacle of pornographic female images and cyber-babes on the Net, the actual bodies and sexualities of aging women are rendered ever more monstrous and un-representable by comparison. Compulsory youthfulness, fitness, and mainstream ideals of beauty have become the norm for all who can afford them, and are valued far above wisdom and experience. The race and class discrimination that underlies this norm is silenced. Ironically, "positive" liberal views of aging expressed in euphemisms like "ripening" and "you're not getting older, you're getting better," and "you don't look your age" contribute to the demonization of aging and of not looking "good." Increasingly the culture applauds older celebrities (like Cher) who have undergone much plastic surgery and who are deployed as models for all other aging folks. Self-imposed (disciplinary) cyborgification is increasingly becoming the response to these conditions.

While it can offer certain kinds of access to the world for people who are housebound or unable to negotiate "real" space, virtual connectedness often actually increases embodied social conditions of isolation, alienation, and loneliness—problems that already assail older people whose children have grown up and moved away, and whose spouses and friends are aging and dying. Widowed and single older women, and especially women of color, are a particularly vulnerable population since they tend to live longer than men, tend to be much poorer, and are less likely to be active in the world. Due to poverty and cultural discrimination, older women of color are also statistically the least likely population to be "wired," and there is very little (if any) mention of this group in discussions of women's use of new technologies. For the middle class there's a proliferation of electronic gadgets for staying "in touch" with the grandparent population—email, baby web pages, framed photos with audio messages, web cams that transmit the family's day-to-day life, a nursebot developed at Carnegie Mellon to be a companion to the aged—and the like. But I suspect that these screenal and machinic incarnations cannot make up for the actual touch, sight, and smell of the bodies of loved ones—isn't it pheromones after all which trigger so much of the limbic brain? When I recently visited my hospitalized, fragile mother, I was riveted by the feel, smell, and sight of her delicate, withering old body, by the constant nuanced changes in her face, her gait, her eyes, her speech and memory patterns. I talk to her on the phone often, but I never really know how she is in the same way as I do when sitting next to her chair, trimming her hair, or taking her arm for a walk around the garden. The complex organism of the body needs to avail itself of so many different means to express its full life.

Cyber-colonialism is rearing its ugly head everywhere under the sign of a new global culture. The obsolescence and cultural irrelevance of the knowledge and life experience of older women has become especially acute in rural and traditional cultures and societies that are rapidly being forced to assimilate the global consumer commodities and adapt to new labor markets. A new generation of (mostly third-world and poor) young women are now the most desired labor pool in the global economy, through which they are also being seduced into a global consumer market and concomitant new social relations, which are centuries removed from the embodied experience of their mothers and grand-mothers. Without quite realizing the full effects of the magnitude and speed of these cultural changes, much "traditional wisdom" has already been consigned to the historical dung heap and replaced by a survival-driven, first-world rever-ence for "smart" technologies; these are proving profoundly disruptive for many populations of different economic, racial, and cultural backgrounds. "Smart" technologies are preprogrammed "reactive" (cybernetic feedback loop) technologies designed to react to changing conditions (such as toasters which "sense" the moistness and thickness of the bread to be toasted and adjust themselves accordingly). The problem with smart technologies is that they circum-vent the experience, knowledge, and decision-making power of the user, by sub-stituting preprogrammed "responses" to a set of conditions (examples from the mundane to the crucial include those new smart toasters, and fetal heart mon-itors which now often determine the course of childbirth). It is easy to see that while smart technologies may be very useful in many daily tasks of all kinds—such as toasting—surely they could never replace the emotional, psychological and experiential wisdom and responses of a complex human being engaged in a major activity such childbirth.

Now that your body and subjectivity are not useful for reproduction and production, use them as autonomous sites for your own resistant research into uselessness, obsolescence and pleasure, be it physical, social, political, emo-tional, or spiritual. Refuse to shut up and hide; remain visible, remain vocal. Refuse to be ghettoized in resort or senior "communities." Commit all seven deadly sins over and over, and pretend to be forgetful or nuts if you're caught. Cling to loved memories and cherished customs: Demand the foods and prod-ucts of your youth. Slow everyone else down: Refuse to be hurried; clog up the aisles at the supermarket and the space at the post office; always go to the front of the line; demand the best tables at restaurants; drive 40 miles an hour in the middle lane with all your lights on. Park anywhere you like. Demonstrate the futility of fashion: Wear your nightgowns and slippers on the street; flaunt your wrinkles, decay, and death. Dance if you want to, but don't bother working out if you don't want to. Don't be decorous and self-effacing: Be opinionated and demanding, be angry and funny. If you desire sex, pool your sexual resources with others. Revel in your uselessness; don't work; demand full service. Resist the imperative to retool or retrain. Refuse the compulsion to be wired, but get online and mouth off if you want; refuse to be smart, new, and improved. Make coalitions with younger people to help you take over the nursing homes and convert them into livable homes and residential collectives. Live as well as you can; share your wealth with others and don't give up conviviality, friendships, and parties; eat all you want; eat what you want; insist that Meals on Wheels hire a good chef. Don't let the churches have control of spirituality but figure out your own spiritual practices and share them with others. Practice inter-generational collaboration, friendship, love, sexuality, and intimacy. Share resources with those that have less, and hire good lawyers to help you exploit and navigate the system. Spend all you have, don't leave it for the kids. Demand recreational drugs and mind-altering substances to ease pain and loneliness. Check into the best hotels and make a row if they throw you out. Don't pay taxes; refuse to fill out forms. Do not pre-pay for your own burial and funeral. Stay alive if you wish, but use your right to a humane self-chosen assisted death if you want it. Refuse efficiency; be noise, in the codes of bureaucracy, au-thority, and utility. ★

REFUGIA

MANIFESTO FOR BECOMING AUTONOMOUS ZONES [BAZ]

REFUGIA: A place of relatively unaltered climate that is inhabited by plants and animals during a period of continental climate change (as a glaciation) and remains as a center of relict forms from which a new dispersion and speciation may take place after climatic readjustment. (WEBSTER'S NEW COLLEGIATE DICTIONARY, 1976)

REFUGIA: Sections of agricultural fields planted with non-transgenic crops, alternating with transgenic crops. This is thought to slow the rate of resistance mutation caused in susceptible insect and weed species by gene transfer from GM (Genetically Modified) mono-culture crops.

REFUGIA: A Becoming Autonomous Zone (BAZ) of desirous mixings and recombinations; splicing female sexual liberation and autonomy with cyberfeminist skills, theory, embodiment, and political activism.

REFUGIA: A critical space of liberated social becoming and intellectual life; a space liberated from capitalist Taylorized production; a space of unregulated, unmanaged time for creative exchange and play; experimental action and learning; desiring production, cooking, eating, and skill sharing.

REFUGIA: A reproducible concept that can be adapted to various climates, economies, and geographical regions worldwide. Any useless space can be claimed as a refugium: Suburban lawns, vacant urban

lots, rooftops, the edges of agricultural lands, clear-cut zones in forests, appropriated sections of monoculture fields, fallow land, weed lots, transitional land, battlefields, office buildings, squats, etc. Also currently existing Refugia such as multi-cultivar rice paddies, companion planted fields, organic farms, home vegetable gardens, etc.

REFUGIA: A postmodern commons; a resistant biotech victory garden; a space of convivial tinkering; a commonwealth in which common law rules. Not a retreat, but a space resistant to monoculture in all its social, environmental, libidinal, political, and genetic forms.

REFUGIA: A habitat for new AMOs (Autonomously Modified Organism) and agit-crops; for example, "ProActiva," an herb that is a grafting of witch-root, mandrake, and all-heal.

REFUGIA: A place of asylum for the recuperation, regeneration and re-engineering of essential crops that have been corrupted by capitalist viruses and agribusiness greed.

REFUGIA: A space of imaginative inertia that slows down the engines of corporate agro/biotech and allows time to assess its risks and benefits through long-term testing.

REFUGIA: Neither a utopia nor a dystopia, but a haunted space for reverse engineering, monstrous graftings, spontaneous generation, recombination, difference, poly-versity hybridization, wildlings, mutations, mongrelizing, crop circles, anomalies, useless beauty, coalitions, agit-crops, and unseemly sproutings. Biotech and transgenic work in Refugia will be based on desire, consensual public risk assessment, informed amateur experimentation, contestational politics, nourishment and taste value, non-proprietary expertise, convivial delight, and healing.

REFUGIA: subRosa's on-going cyberfeminist hothouse of strategies and tactical actions.

Appendices

Contributor Biographies:

Irina Aristarkhova teaches a studio-based Cyberarts course, and heads the Cyberarts Initiative at the University Scholars Programme, National University of Singapore. She was formerly Senior Lecturer at the LaSalle-SIA College of the Arts. She holds an MA from the University of Warwick, UK, and Ph.D. from the Russian Academy of Sciences. Her other interests include issues of ethnicity and gender in cyberspace; theories of power; Russian nationalism; constructions of sexuality; cyberethics and cyberaesthetics.

Emily de Araujo received her MFA from Carnegie Mellon in 2001. She is an artist currently living and teaching in Ohio.

Maria Fernandez is an art historian whose interests center on postcolonial studies, electronic media theory, Latin American colonial and modern art and the intersections of these fields. She received her Ph.D. from Columbia University, New York, in 1993. Since then she has taught at various institutions including the University of Pittsburgh, Carnegie Mellon, the University of Connecticut, and Vermont College of Norwich University.

Radhika Gajjala is Assistant Professor of Interpersonal Communication/Communication Studies. She teaches courses on Cyberculture. Her publications have appeared in journals such as *Gender and Development* and *Works and Days,* and in books such as *Technospaces: Inside the New Media.*

Pattie Belle Hastings is an artist, designer, educator and author living in New Haven, Connecticut. She is an Assistant Professor of Interactive Digital Design in the Computer Science department at Quinnipiac University. Cyborg Mommy continues to replicate at <http://www.icehousedesign.com/cyborg_mommy/home.html>. She can be contacted via cyborgmommy@hotmail.com.

Christina Hung, recipient of a 1999 Pennsylvania Council on the Arts Media

Arts Fellowship, received her MFA from Carnegie Mellon in 1997. Her recent work includes the co-development of web sites, video, performances and sculpture with subRosa. Her first written piece was published in *Tilting the Continent*, an anthology of South East Asian American writing, by New Rivers Press in August 2000. Currently, Hung is teaching at UMBC in Baltimore, Maryland.

Amelia Jones is Professor of Art History at the University of California, Riverside. She has written books and articles on contemporary art, postmodernism, and feminism and has organized exhibitions. She is currently working on a book on New York Dada and a book entitled *Self/Image* on technologies of representation, the body, and subjectivity. JonesSher@aol.com.

Terri Kapsalis is a health educator, performer, and the author of *Public Privates: Performing Gynecology from Both Ends of the Speculum* (Duke University Press, 1997). She teaches at the School of the Art Institute of Chicago.

Tania Kupczak recently gave up a financially solvent life in molecular biology to pursue her MFA in studio art. She is conducting rigorous scientific experiments on women's underwear in search for markers of identity. Visit her cyberhome at: <http://www.home.earthlink.net/~tania232>.

Annapurna Mamidipudi is a field worker and trustee for *dastkar andhra*, an NGO that has been working with artisans, specifically cotton handloom weavers in Andhra Pradesh, India, for the last ten years. She co-ordinates the financial section and the technical programs in natural dyes, and is part of the marketing and development team for the organisation. email: annapurna@cyberdiva.org.

Lisa Nakamura is Assistant Professor of English at Sonoma State University, where she teaches postcolonial literature and theory. She is the author of *Cybertypes: Race, Ethnicity, and Identity on the Internet* (Routledge, forthcoming, Spring 2002) and the co-editor of *Race in Cyberspace* (Routledge, 2000).

Susanna Paasonen, researcher, department for Media Studies, University of Turku (Finland), is finishing her PhD on the popularization of the Net, and has a special passion for feminist theory old and new. suspaa@utu.fi.

Claire Pentecost is a writer, an artist and a New Yorker. She lives and teaches in Chicago.

Lucia Sommer is a multidisciplinary artist, writer, activist, and art educator whose work investigates knowledge systems and their hauntings. She has taught art to children of all ages in various settings, from public schools to museums. She is currently studying Film, Video, & New Media and critical theory at the School of the Art Institute of Chicago.

Nell Tenhaaf, electronic media artist and writer, has exhibited extensively in North America and in Europe. Her work focuses on links between art practice and the bio-sciences. She is an Associate Professor of New Media at York University in Toronto.

Faith Wilding is an/Other genre artist, writer, and teacher whose work addresses aspects of the somatic, psychic, and socio-political history of the body. She is a founding member of the cyberfeminist collective subRosa, and a Fellow at the STUDIO for Creative Inquiry, Carnegie Mellon. Wilding teaches performance at the School of the Art Institute of Chicago. fwild@ artic.edu.

Hyla Willis is a multidisciplinary artist and designer, whose work crosses boundaries between music, graphic design, sculpture and performance. She is a founding member of subRosa and a senior designer at EDGE studio in Pittsburgh, Pennsylvania. She was recipient of a 2002 Pennsylvania Council on the Arts fellowship for her work with subRosa.

Michelle M. Wright received her Ph.D. in Comparative Literature from the University of Michigan in 1997. From 1997 to 2000, she held the Loomis McCandless Junior Faculty Research chair at Carnegie Mellon. She is now an Assistant Professor of English at Macalester College, where she teaches literature and theory from the African Diaspora. Her book, *Missing Persons: The Search for Postcolonial Subjects in the African Diaspora*, is under contract to Duke University Press.

subRosa's Selected Bibliography

NEW REPRODUCTIVE TECHNOLOGIES:

Baker, Robin. *Sperm Wars: The Science of Sex*. New York: Basic Books, 1996.

Casper, Monica. *The Making of the Unborn Patient: Medical Work and the Politics of Reproduction in Experimental Fetal Surgery 1963–1993*. Unpublished Ph.D. Dissertation, University of California, Berkeley.

Corea, Gena, et al. *Man-Made Women: How New Reproductive Technologies Affect Women*. London: Hutchinson, 1985.

Critical Art Ensemble. *Flesh Machine: Cyborgs, Designer Babies, and New Eugenic Consciousness*. New York: Autonomedia, 1998.

Davis-Floyd, Robbie, and Joseph Dumit, Eds. *Cyborg Babies: From Techno-Sex to Techno-Tots*. New York: Routledge, 1998.

Duster, Troy. *Backdoor to Eugenics*. Boston: Routledge and Kegan Paul, 1990.

Hartmann, Betsy. *Reproductive Rights and Wrongs: The Global Politics of Population Control*. Boston: South End Press, 1995.

Hartouni, Valerie. *Cultural Conceptions: On Reproductive Technologies + The Remaking of Life*. Minneapolis: University of Minnesota Press, 1997.

Lublin, Nancy. *Pandora's Box: Feminism Confronts Reproductive Technology*. Lanham: Rowman & Littlefield Publishers, Inc., 1998.

Marrs, Bloch, and Silverman. *Dr. Richard Marrs' Fertility Book*. New York: Dell Publishers, 1997

Moraga, Cherrie. *Waiting in the Wings: Portrait of a Queer Motherhood*. Ithaca: Firebrand, 1997.

Raymond, Janice G. *Women as Wombs: Reproductive Technologies and the Battle over Women's Freedom*. New York: HarperCollins, 1993.

Robertson, John A. *Children of Choice: Freedom and the New Reproductive Technologies*. New Jersey: Princeton University Press, 1994.

Sen, Gita, and Rachel Snow, Eds. *Power and Decision: The Social Control of Reproduction*. Boston: Harvard University Press, 1994.

Silber, Sherman J. *How to Get Pregnant with the New Technology: A World-renowned Fertility Expert tells you What really Works, What doesn't, and Why*. New York: Warner Books, 1991.

Silver, Lee M. *Remaking Eden: Cloning and Beyond in a Brave New World*. New York: Avon Books, 1997.

Squier, Susan Merrill. *Babies in Bottles: Twentieth-Century Visions of Reproductive Technology*. New Brunswick: Rutgers University Press, 1994.
Stanworth, Michelle, Ed. *Reproductive Technologies: Gender, Motherhood, and Medicine*. Cambridge: Polity Press, 1987.

SEX/GENDER/BODY/TECHNOLOGY:

Balsamo, Anne. *Technologies of the Gendered Body: Reading Cyborg Women*. Durham: Duke University Press, 1997.
Bynum, Carol Walker. *Holy Feast and Holy Fast: The Religious Significance of Food to Medieval Women*. Berkeley: University of California Press, 1987.
Pinto-Correia, Clara. *The Ovary of Eve: Egg and Sperm and Preformation*. Chicago and London: The University of Chicago Press, 1997.
Springer, Claudia. *Electronic Eros: Bodies and Desire in the Postindustrial Age*. Austin: University of Texas Press, 1996.

MEDICALIZATION/MEDICALIZED REPRESENTATION OF SEX AND GENDER:

Blumenfeld-Kosinski. *Not of Woman Born: Representations of Caesarean Birth in Medieval and Renaissance Culture*. Ithaca: Cornell University Press, 1990.
Gilman, Sander L. *Sexuality: An Illustrated History. Representing the Sexual in Medicine and Culture from the Middle Ages to the Age of AIDS*. New York: John Wiley and Sons, Inc., 1989.
Kitzinger, Sheila. *Freedom and Choice in Childbirth*. London: Penguin, 1987.
Treichler, Paula A., Lisa Cartwright, and Constance Penley, Eds. *The Visible Woman: Imaging Technologies, Gender, and Science*. New York: New York University Press, 1998.

QUEER THEORY; FEMINIST THEORY; POSTCOLONIAL THEORY:

Butler, Judith. *Gender Trouble: Feminism and the Subversion of Identity*. New York: Routledge, 1990.
Cornell, Drucilla. *The Imaginary Domain*. New York: Routledge, 1995.
Grosz, Elizabeth. *Volatile Bodies: Toward a Corporeal Feminism*. Bloomington: Indiana University Press, 1994.
hooks, bell. *Feminist Theory: From Margin to Center*. Boston: South End Press, 1984.
Kroker, Arthur and Marilouise, Eds. *The Hysterical Male: New Feminist Theory*. New York: St. Martin's Press. New World Perspectives, CultureText Series, 1991.
Kroker, Arthur and Marilouise, Eds. *The Last Sex: Feminism and Outlaw Bodies*. New York: St. Martin's Press. New World Perspectives, 1993.
Laqueur, Thomas. *Making Sex: Body and Gender from the Greeks to Freud*. Cambridge: Harvard University Press, 1990.
Weston, Kath. *Families We Choose: Lesbians, Gays, Kinship*. New York: Columbia University Press, 1991.

Cyberfeminism/Science/Gender/Technology:

Collier, J.F. and S.J. Yanagisako, Eds. *Gender and Kinship: Essays toward a unified analysis*. Stanford: Stanford University Press, 1987.

Fox Keller, Evelyn. *Refiguring Life: Metaphors of Twentieth-Century Biology*. New York: Columbia University Press, 1995.

_____*Reflections on Gender and Science*. New Haven: Yale University Press, 1985.

Kirkup, Gill, and Laurie Smith Keller, Eds. *Inventing Women: Science, Technology, and Gender*. Cambridge: Polity, 1998.

Haraway, Donna J. *Modest_Witness@Second_Millenium.FemaleMan_ Meets_OncoMouse TM: Feminism and Technoscience*. New York, London: Routledge, 1997.

_____*Simians, Cyborgs and Women: The Reinvention of Nature*. New York: Routledge, 1991.

Harding, Sandra. *Whose Science? Whose Knowledge? Thinking from Women's Lives*. Ithaca: Cornell University Press, 1991.

Jones, Amelia. *Body Art/Performing the Subject*. Minneapolis: University of Minnesota Press, 1998.

Kaufman-Osborn, Timothy V. *Creatures of Prometheus: Gender and the Politics of Technology*. Lanham: Rowman & Littlefield Publishers, Inc., 1997.

Lauretis, Teresa de. *Technologies of Gender: Essays on Theory, Film, and Fiction*. London: Macmillan, 1989.

Carolyn Marvin, *When Old Technologies Were New*. New York: Oxford University Press, 1988.

Nader, Laura, Ed. *Naked Science*. New York: Routledge, 1996.

Nelkin, Dorothy, and Susan Lindee. *The DNA Mystique: The Gene as Cultural Icon*. New York: Freeman Books, 1995.

Plant, Sadie. *Zeros + Ones: Digital Women + The New Technoculture*. New York: Doubleday, 1997.

Rifkin, Jeremy. *The Biotech Century: Harnessing the Gene and Remaking the World*. New York: Jeremy P. Tarcher, 1998.

Robertson, George, Melinda Mash, Lisa Tickner, et al., eds. *Future Natural: Nature/Science/Culture*. London: Routledge, 1996.

Stabile, Carol. *Feminism and the Technological Fix*. Manchester: Manchester University Press, 1994.

Wacjman, Judy. *Feminism Confronts Technology*. Cambridge: Polity Press, 1991.

Welton, Donn, Ed. *Body and Flesh: A Philosophical Reader*. Oxford: Blackwell Publishers, Ltd. 1998.

More Books from Autonomedia

Visit our web site for online ordering,
topical discussion, events listings,
book specials, and more.
www.autonomedia.org

Autonomedia • PO Box 568
Williamsburgh Station
Brooklyn, NY 11211-0568
T/F 718-963-2603
info@autonomedia.org